SINGLE-FAMILY HOUSES IN SWITZERLAND & AUSTRIA

ARCHITEKTENHÄUSER IN DER SCHWEIZ & ÖSTERREICH

Chris van Uffelen

SINGLE-FAMILY HOUSES IN SWITZERLAND & AUSTRIA

ARCHITEKTENHÄUSER IN DER SCHWEIZ & ÖSTERREICH

BRAUN

CONTENT INHALT

CONTENT INHALT

SINGLE-FAMILY HOUSES IN SWITZERLAND & AUSTRIA
ARCHITEKTENHÄUSER IN DER SCHWEIZ & ÖSTERREICH

AN INTRODUCTION
EINE EINLEITUNG

After "Single-Family Houses – Contemporary Homes in Germany" (ISBN 978-3-03768-253-1), the topic of "ordinary living" – neither palace nor hermit's hut – is addressed again in this volume for Austria and Switzerland. The two countries, in which building in the mountains plays an above-average role, are complemented by South Tyrol in Italy, which has much in common with them. In the west it is bordered by the Grisons in Switzerland, in the north by Vorarlberg in Austria, and together with these two regions South Tyrol formed the triumvirate of an Alpine modernity at the end of the 20th century, which dealt with contemporary building on the one hand, and tradition-conscious regionalism on the other. From this center, the geographical focus of this volume extends to the Jura and Lake Geneva in the east and to Burgenland in the west. At both poles the high mountains have been left behind. So there are not only alpine single-family homes – the Swiss midlands between Geneva and Zurich and Lower Austria east of Vienna are rather hilly.

The buildings of this volume grow out of very different influences and are part of very differentiated, regional traditions, although similarities are unmistakable. The widespread use of wood is striking as well as the frequent reference to regional rural building traditions. Often, the local building culture is specifically addressed, whether in a tradition-conscious continuation, modern reinterpretation or a clear separation from the traditional. Thus roof forms and roof overhangs play an important role again and again. The examination of views and their integration into the topography are also recurring themes, so that the reader is offered not only a survey of contemporary single-family homes, but also a collection of how architecture deals with landscape and cultural spaces.

Nach „EFH_D – Architektenhäuser in Deutschland" (ISBN 978-3-03768-252-4) wird das Thema des „normalen Wohnens" – weder Palast noch Einsiedlerhütte – in diesem Band mit Häusern aus Österreich und der Schweiz erneut aufgegriffen. Die zwei Länder, in denen das Bauen im Gebirge eine überdurchschnittliche Rolle spielt, werden um Südtirol in Italien ergänzt. Diese Region hat vieles mit ihnen gemein. Im Westen stößt sie an Graubünden in der Schweiz, im Norden an Vorarlberg in Österreich und zusammen mit diesen beiden Gebieten bildete Südtirol im ausgehenden 20. Jahrhundert das Dreigestirn einer alpinen Moderne, die sich mit zeitgenössischem Bauen einerseits, traditionsbewusstem Regionalismus andererseits auseinandersetzte. Aus diesem Zentrum erstreckt sich der Betrachtungsraum dieses Bands bis an das Jura und den Genfersee im Osten und bis ins Burgenland im Westen. An beiden Polen hat man das Hochgebirge verlassen. Es sind also nicht nur alpine Einfamilienhäuser – das Schweizer Mittelland zwischen Genf und Zürich sowie Niederösterreich östlich Wiens sind eher hügelig.

Die Bauten entwachsen also ganz unterschiedlichen Einflüssen und stehen in sehr differenzierten regionalen Traditionen, während Gemeinsamkeiten unverkennbar sind. Augenfällig ist der große Anteil hölzerner Bauten und der häufige Bezug auf jeweils regionale ländliche Bautraditionen. Oft wird gezielt auf den Bestand eingegangen, sei es in traditionsbewusster Fortsetzung, moderner Umdeutung oder klarer Abnabelung von Überliefertem. So spielen Dachformen und Dachüberstände immer wieder eine große Rolle. Auch die Auseinandersetzung mit Ausblicken und die Einbettung in die topografische Situation sind wiederkehrende Themen, sodass dem Leser hier nicht nur eine Bestandsaufnahme des zeitgenössischen Einfamilienhauses geboten wird, sondern auch eine Sammlung des Umgangs von Architektur mit Landschafts- und Kulturräumen.

SCHWEIZER HAUS XXII

The project site lies north of the historical center of the village of Preonzo, Switzerland. This site is dotted with traditional stone volumes, where animals once lived on the ground floor and the families above and thereby bears witness to the former farming community. The original building was one of these vernacular volumes. Recognizing the significance of preserving the historical memory, the design retains this original volume – now the full-height living room of Swiss House XXII. The client's need for a larger habitable space resulted in the addition of two new volumes that work in dialogue with the existing in terms of their character and scale, creating a new equilibrium caused by the historical context but interpreted with a contemporary language. The materials used for the construction emphasize this relationship. The old buildings were built completely in stone and appear as compact volumes. The new buildings mirror this compactness by an homogeneous finish on the exterior and interior surfaces. The openings on the east of the house are the reflection of the flower beds laid out on the ground below. The spaces generated by the three volumes create a positive-negative effect on the façade; one projected, one carved out, with the sky as roof.

1, 2

Architects: Davide Macullo Architects
Completion: 2015
Location: Preonzo, Switzerland
Gross floor area: 206 m^2
Number of bedrooms: 2
Main materials / building construction: reinforced concrete / plastered reinforced concrete construction
Ecological aspects: thermal insulation

10

Architekten: Davide Macullo Architects
Fertigstellung: 2015
Ort: Preonzo, Schweiz
Bruttogeschossfläche: 206 m^2
Anzahl der Schlafzimmer: 2
Hauptmaterialien / Konstruktionsweise: Stahlbeton / verputzte Stahlbetonkonstruktion
Ökologische Aspekte: Wärmedämmung

Das Projekt liegt nördlich des historischen Zentrums des Schweizer Dorfes Preonzo. In der ehemaligen Bauerngemeinschaft finden sich traditionelle Steinbauten, in denen einst Tiere im Erdgeschoss und die Familien darüber lebten. Das historische Erbe wahrend, integriert das Schweizer Haus XXII solch einen traditionellen Bau. Er bildet nun das raumhohe Wohnzimmer. Da der Bauherr mehr Wohnraum benötigte, wurde seine Substanz mit zwei adäquaten Gebäudeteilen ergänzt, die in Charakter und Umfang mit dem Bestehenden im Dialog stehen und ein neues Gleichgewicht schaffen. Die verwendeten Materialien unterstreichen diese Beziehung. Die alten Gebäude bestehen komplett aus Stein und erscheinen als kompakte Volumen. Die neuen Gebäudeteile des Schweizer Haus XXII greifen die Kompaktheit durch eine homogene Oberflächenbeschaffenheit der Außen- und Innenflächen auf. Die Öffnungen auf der Ostseite spiegeln die davor angelegten Blumenbeete. Die Räume der drei Volumen erzeugen einen Positiv-Negativ-Effekt auf der Fassade; einer projiziert, der andere ausgeschnitten, mit dem Himmel als Dach.

3

4

1 Exterior view from east
2 Exterior view of the Swiss House XXII and an old building
3 Exterior view from southwest
4 Exterior view in evening mood

1 Außenansicht von Osten
2 Außenansicht von Schweizer Haus XXII und einem traditionellen Steinhaus
3 Außenansicht von Südwesten
4 Außenansicht in Abendstimmung

1

2

1 Living area with view outside
2 Living area
3 First floor plan
4 Ground floor plan
5 Section

1 Wohnraum mit Blick nach draußen
2 Wohnraum
3 Grundriss OG
4 Grundriss EG
5 Schnitt

3

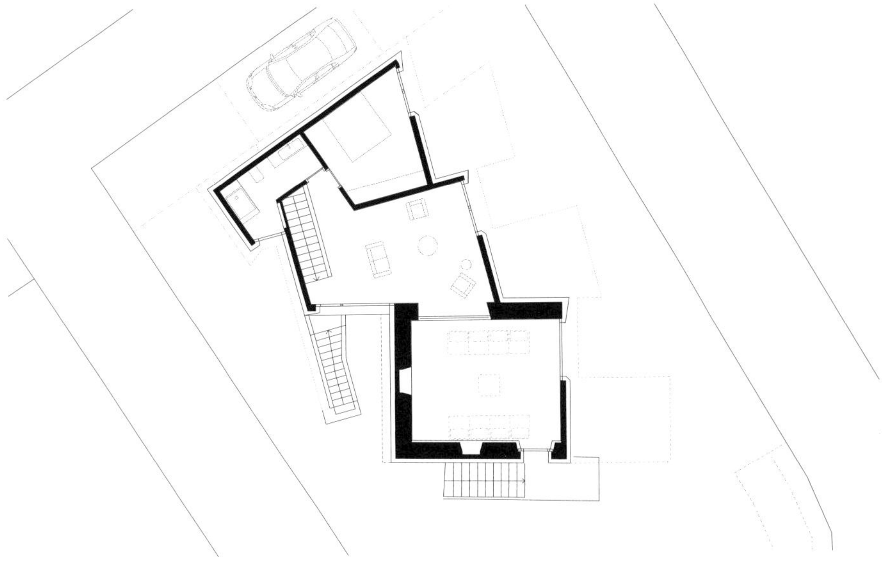

4

5

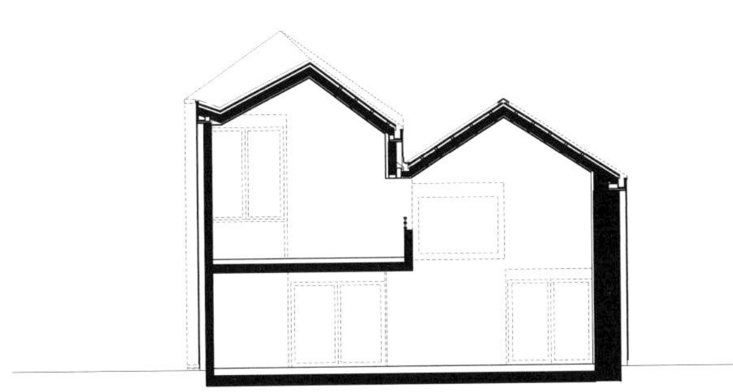

1

HAUS AM BACH

1 Front door
2 Exterior view from north
3 Exterior view with the brook
4 View through ground floor

1 Eingangstür
2 Außenansicht von Norden
3 Außenansicht mit Bach
4 Durchsicht Erdgeschoss

2

Architects: Lukas Mayr Architekt
Completion: 2015
Location: Percha, South Tyrol
Gross floor area: 180 m²
Number of bedrooms: 3
Main materials / building construction: larch wood, concrete / basement and ground floor in concrete construction, living floor in timber frame construction
Ecological aspects: wood-clay blow-in insulation

Architekten: Lukas Mayr Architekt
Fertigstellung: 2015
Ort: Percha, Südtirol
Bruttogeschossfläche: 180 m²
Anzahl der Schlafzimmer: 3
Hauptmaterialien / Konstruktionsweise: Lärchenholz, Beton / Kellergeschoss und Erdgeschoss in Betonbauweise, Wohngeschoss in Holzrahmenbauweise
Ökologische Aspekte: Holz-Lehm-Einblasdämmung

The house is situated like a block of wood on a concrete table next to a small stream in the east and a little frequented village road in the west. The aim was to design the living areas to be extraordinarily light-flooded. The attic with the living area is sunny almost the whole day. The large openings in the west are directed towards a corridor between the neighboring buildings, so that a wide view is possible.

The building is accessed via a compact staircase. Except for Brahmasthan, a central room provided for in Ayurvedic architecture, the development areas are rationally dimensioned. The living area is located on the top floor, the sleeping areas on the upper floor and the bathroom in the basement. The ground floor offers an open space, the entrance and the bonsai room. The new residential building is intended to be an atmospherically pleasant place and was built according to biological building principles. The two upper floors are designed as a timber frame construction, the interior is planked with larch wood and the exterior is a new interpretation of the log house. The ceilings are plastered smooth with clay. The glazings are executed by means of highly heat-insulating glazing and all are equipped with a vertical awning as sun protection.

Das Haus liegt wie ein Holzblock auf einem Betontisch an einem kleinen Bach im Osten und an einer wenig befahrenen Dorfstraße im Westen. Ziel war es, die Wohnbereiche außergewöhnlich lichtdurchflutet zu gestalten. Das Dachgeschoss mit dem Wohnbereich wird nahezu den ganzen Tag besonnt. Die großen Öffnungen im Westen richten sich in Richtung einer Schneise zwischen den Nachbargebäuden, sodass ein weiter Blick möglich ist.

Das Gebäude wird über ein kompaktes Treppenhaus erschlossen. Die Erschließungsflächen sind, bis auf den Brahmasthan, einem in der ayurvedischen Architektur vorgesehenen Zentrumsraum, rational bemessen. Der Wohnbereich befindet sich im Dachgeschoss, die Schlafbereiche im Obergeschoss und das Bad im Untergeschoss. Das Erdgeschoss bietet eine offene Freifläche, das Entree und einen Bonsairaum. Das neue Wohnhaus soll ein atmosphärisch angenehmer Ort sein und wurde nach baubiologischen Gesichtspunkten errichtet. Die beiden oberen Geschosse sind als Holzrahmenbau ausgeführt, im Inneren mit Lärchenholz beplankt und im Außenbereich als Neuinterpretation des Blockhauses ausgeführt. Die Decken sind mit Lehm glatt verputzt. Die Verglasungen sind mittels hochwärmedämmender Isolierverglasungen ausgeführt und alle mit einer Vertikalmarkise als Sonnenschutz ausgestattet.

3, 4

1

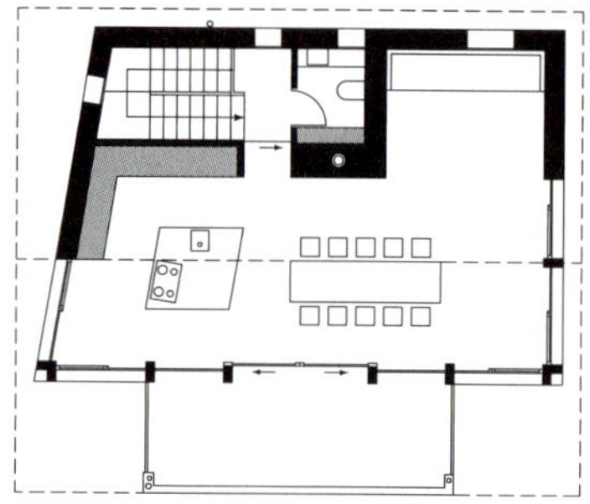

2

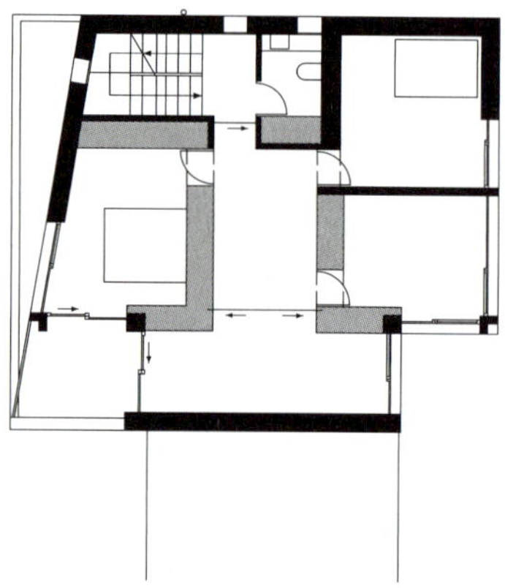

3

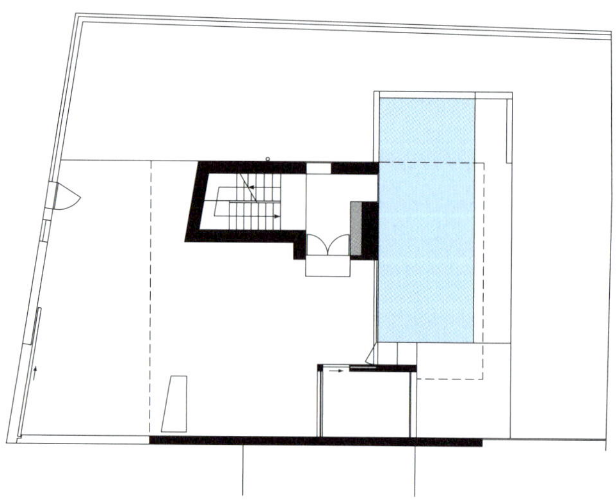

4

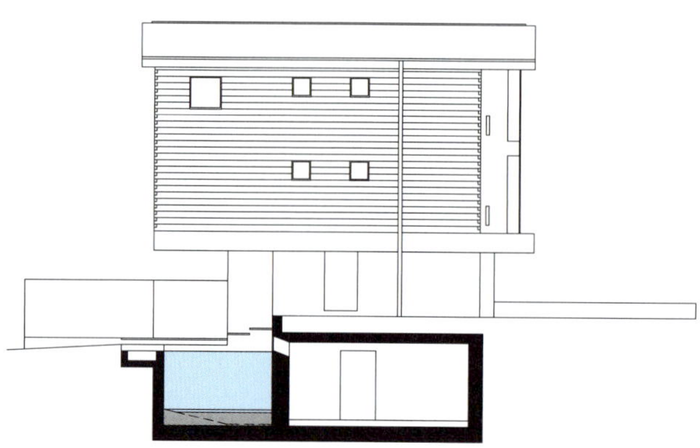

5

6

7

8

1 Top floor plan with living, cooking and dining area
2 First floor plan
3 Ground floor plan with load-bearing stair core
4 North elevation
5 Dining and cooking area
6 Dining and cooking area at night
7 Brahmasthan, the vedic center of the building
8 Exterior view from the street

1 Grundriss DG mit Wohn-, Koch- und Essbereich
2 Grundriss OG
3 Grundriss EG mit tragendem Treppenkern
4 Aufriss Nordseite
5 Ess- und Kochbereich bei Tag
6 Ess- und Kochbereich bei Nacht
7 Brahmasthan, das vedische Zentrum des Baus
8 Außenansicht von der Straße

EFH GROTH

1

A spatial flow running along the slope and a floor plan openly organized on three levels form the basis of this family home. Covered loggias extend the living levels both uphill and downhill and form the interfaces to the surroundings. The room allocation concept is manageable: a living room, cooking and eating integrated, sleeping area and guest room, each with the necessary bathrooms, and a covered outdoor space. A carport and practical storage spaces round off the space allocation plan. Each level is differentiated in its formulation despite the coherent space. The exterior black colored wood construction confidently asserts its place in the surroundings. The interior, light, bright and warm, on the other hand, is intended to offer the residents a pleasant environment in which they can draw new strength.

Architects: LP architektur
Completion: 2014
Location: Lofer, Austria
Gross floor area: 132.44 m²
Number of bedrooms: 2
Main materials / building construction: wood / hybrid construction, reinforced concrete base, structure timber frame construction
Ecological aspects: infrared heating with underfloor heating

2

3

Architekten: LP architektur
Fertigstellung: 2014
Ort: Lofer, Österreich
Bruttogeschossfläche: 132,44 m^2
Anzahl der Schlafzimmer: 2
Hauptmaterialien / Konstruktionsweise: Holz / Hybridbau, Stahlbetonsockel, Aufbau Holzrahmenbauweise
Ökologische Aspekte: Infrarotheizung mit Fußbodenheizung

Ein am Hang verlaufender Raumfluss und ein in drei Ebenen offen organisierter Grundriss bilden die Basis dieses Wohnhauses. Gedeckte Loggien erweitern sowohl hangauf- als auch hangabwärts die Wohnebenen und bilden die Schnittstellen zur Umgebung. Das Raumprogramm ist überschaubar: ein Wohnraum, Kochen und Essen integriert, Schlafbereich und Gästezimmer jeweils mit den notwendigen Bädern und ein gedeckter Außenraum. Ein Carport und praktische Stauräume runden das Raumprogramm ab. Jede Ebene ist trotz des zusammenhängenden Raums differenziert in ihrer Formulierung. Der außen schwarz gefärbte Holzbau behauptet selbstbewusst seinen Platz im Umfeld. Der Innenraum, leicht, hell und warm, bietet den Bewohnern hingegen ein angenehmes Ambiente, in dem man neue Kraft schöpfen kann.

4

5

6

1 Exterior view from southwest in the evening
2 Exterior view from southeast with view towards the valley
3 Exterior view from southwest
4 External staircase
5 View from balcony
6 Interior view

1 Außenansicht von Südwesten am Abend
2 Außenansicht von Südosten mit Blick Richtung Tal
3 Außenansicht von Südwesten
4 Außenaufgang
5 Ausblick vom Balkon
6 Innenansicht

1

2

1 View inside
2 Interior view with the three levels
3 Site plan
4 First floor plan
5 Ground floor plan
6 Section

1 Blick ins Innere
2 Innenansicht mit den drei Ebenen
3 Lageplan
4 Grundriss OG
5 Grundriss EG
6 Schnitt

3

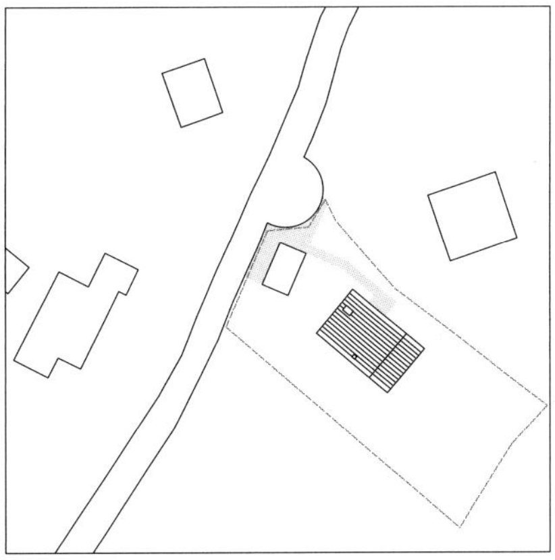

4

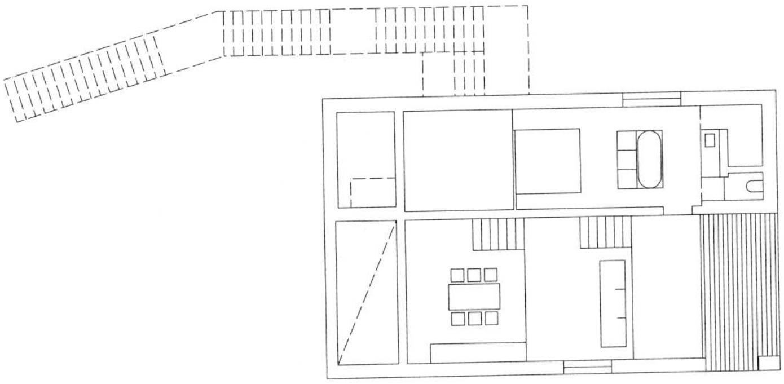

5

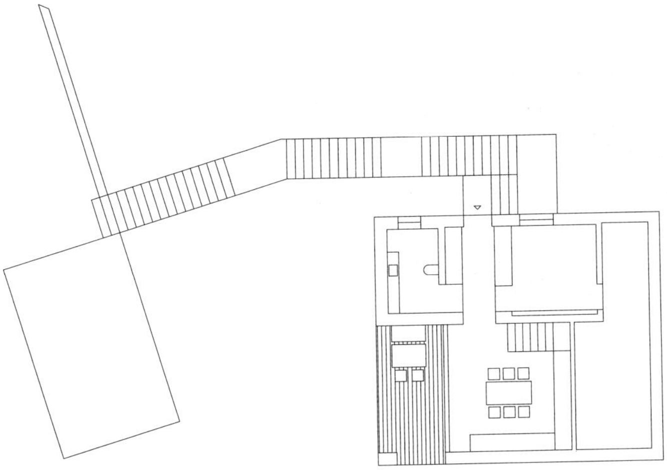

6

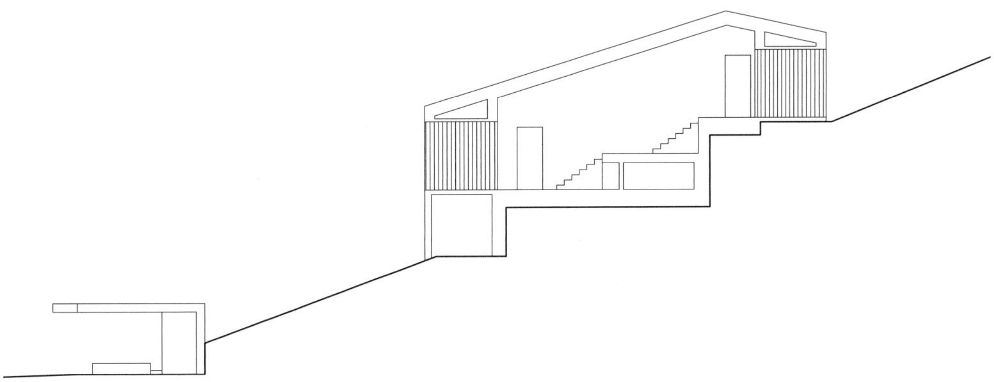

CASA FOREST

1

Architects: Daluz Gonzalez Architekten
Completion: 2016
Location: Basel-Country, Switzerland
Gross floor area: 360 m^2
Number of bedrooms: 4
Main materials / building construction: ceramic tiles, concrete / solid construction with curtain-type ventilated façade

The southward sloping, elongated plot is framed to the east and south by a magnificent deciduous forest. Breathtaking views of the dense, high green in summer and the leafless, light branch structure in winter, became the leitmotif of Casa Forest and materialized in the compact, crystalline form of the building. The differentiation of the bedrooms and open areas is made by tunnel-like stairs and landings. The high hall room is the center of the building and serves as a central connecting element of the entire living area. Walls and ceilings are made of fair-faced concrete and the simple furniture in oak appears elementarily reduced. The waxed raw gypsum walls of the private rooms are polished in such a way that the exterior space is reflected in them and interferes even more strongly with the interior. On the roof a large terrace is enthroned which, together with the earth-colored outer skin, is in constant dialogue with nature.

2

3

Die südwärts geneigte, längliche Parzelle wird gegen Osten und Süden von einem prächtigen Laubwald umrahmt. Atemberaubende Aussichten in das dichte, hohe Grün im Sommer und in die laublose, lichte Aststruktur im Winter wurden zum Leitmotiv für die Casa Forest und materialisieren sich in der kompakten, kristallinen Form des Gebäudes. Die Differenzierung der Schlafzimmer und offenen Bereiche wird durch tunnelartige Treppen und Podeste vorgenommen. Der hohe Hallenraum ist der Mittelpunkt des Gebäudes und dient als zentrales Bindeelement des gesamten Wohnbereichs. Wände und Decken sind aus Sichtbeton und die schlichten Möbel in Eiche wirken elementar reduziert. Die gewachsten rohen Gipswände der Privaträume sind so poliert, dass sich der Außenraum darin spiegelt und noch stärker in den Innenraum eingreift. Auf dem Dach thront eine große Terrasse, die zusammen mit der erdfarbenen Außenhaut in ständigem Dialog mit der Natur steht.

4

Architekten: Daluz Gonzalez Architekten
Fertigstellung: 2016
Ort: Basel-Landschaft, Schweiz
Bruttogeschossfläche: 360 m^2
Anzahl der Schlafzimmer: 4
Hauptmaterialien / Konstruktionsweise: Keramikplatten, Beton / Massivbau mit vorgehängter hinterlüfteter Fassade

1 Bird's-eye view
2 Exterior view from northeast
3 Exterior view from southeast
4 Garage
5 Staircase with skylight
6 Dining room

1 Vogelperspektive
2 Außenansicht von Nordosten
3 Außenansicht von Südosten
4 Garage
5 Treppe mit Oberlicht
6 Esszimmer

5, 6

1

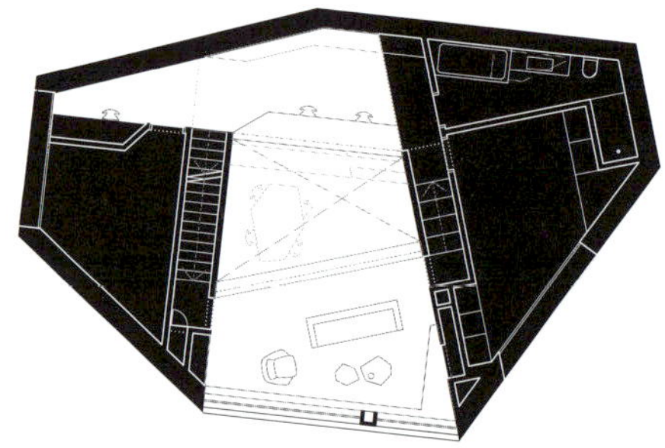

2

3

4

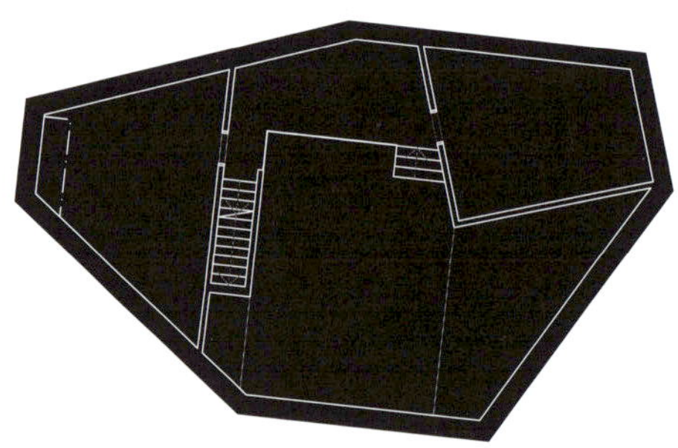

1 First floor plan
2 Ground floor plan
3 Section
4 Basement floor plan
5 Exterior view from west
6 Office and living room

1 Grundriss OG
2 Grundriss EG
3 Gebäudeschnitt
4 Grundriss UG
5 Außenansicht von Westen
6 Büro und Wohnzimmer

5

6

FLEXHOUSE

1

The single-family house Flexhouse occupies a small plot of land between the road and the railway in Meilen on the right bank of Lake Zurich. Flexhouse is an exceptional single-family house that sits easily and naturally on the site. The curves and sloping façades interlock the building with the landscape and thus allow a harmonious transition from building zone to recreational area. At the same time, they take up the movement of railway road, street and property. The Flexhouse consists of concrete ceilings, steel columns and timber prefabricated arches. Because of this, it was possible to construct the interior ceilings and arches with a constant size, which enables the curved movement of the building perfectly legible. The interior concept does not maximize the surface area, but rather the visual connections and linking to the outside. Between the ground floor and the upper floor, the space runs openly in the vertical, allowing views into the two bedrooms.

Architects: Evolution Design
Completion: 2016
Location: Meilen, Switzerland
Gross floor area: 150 m^2
Number of bedrooms: 3
Main materials / building construction: reinforced concrete, wood, glass, aluminum / reinforced concrete with steel columns and timber element arches
Ecological aspects: Minergie certificate

2

3

26

Architekten: Evolution Design
Fertigstellung: 2016
Ort: Meilen, Schweiz
Bruttogeschossfläche: 150 m²
Anzahl der Schlafzimmer: 3
Hauptmaterialien / Konstruktionsweise: Stahlbeton, Holz, Glas, Aluminium / Stahlbeton mit Stahlstützen und Holzelementbögen
Ökologische Aspekte: Minergie-Zertifikat

Das Einfamilienhaus Flexhouse belegt eine kleine Parzelle zwischen Straße und Bahn in Meilen am rechten Ufer des Zürichsees. Flexhouse ist ein außergewöhnliches Einfamilienhaus, das sich ganz leicht und wie selbstverständlich auf das Gelände setzt. Die Rundungen und schräg gestellten Fassaden verzahnen das Gebäude mit der Landschaft und ermöglichen so einen harmonischen Übergang von Bauzone zu Naherholungszone. Gleichzeitig nehmen sie die Bewegung von Bahntrasse, Straße und Grundstück auf. Das Flexhouse besteht aus Betondecken, Stahlstützen und aus Holz vorfabrizierten Rundbögen. Dadurch wurde es möglich, die Konstruktion der Innendecken und Rundbögen mit einem gleichbleibenden Maß auszuführen, wodurch die geschwungene Bewegung des Gebäudes perfekt lesbar wird. Das Innenraumkonzept maximiert nicht die Fläche, sondern die visuellen Verbindungen und die Vernetzung mit dem Außen. Zwischen dem Erdgeschoss und dem Obergeschoss fließt der Raum offen in der Vertikale und stellt Blickbeziehungen zu den zwei Schlafzimmern her.

4

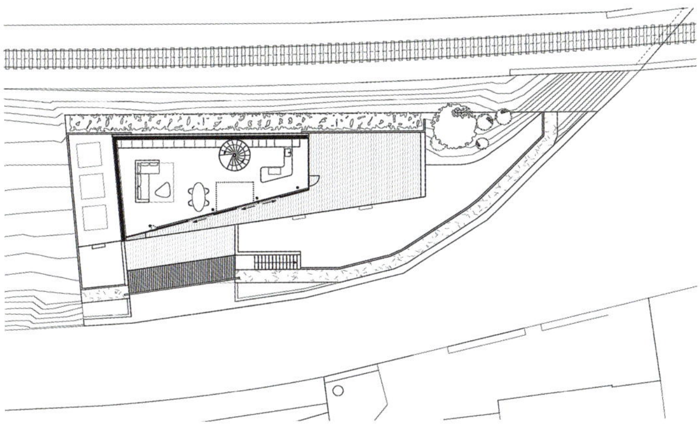

5

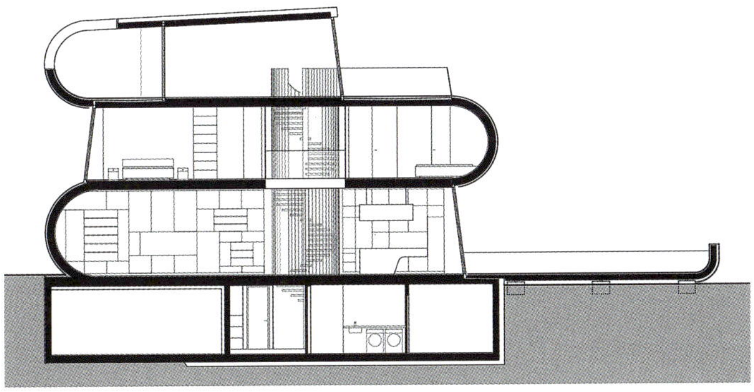

6

7

1 Exterior view from the garden
2 Exterior view from the street
3 Exterior view with surroundings
4 Ground floor plan with surroundings
5 Longitudinal section
6 Living area with view outside
7 Living and dining area with view towards the kitchen

1 Außenansicht vom Garten
2 Außenansicht von der Straße
3 Außenansicht mit Umgebung
4 Grundriss EG mit Umgebung
5 Längsschnitt
6 Wohnbereich mit Aussicht
7 Wohn- und Essbereich mit Blick Richtung Küche

WOHNHAUS KILCHBERG

Three ideas determine the concept of the house: Firstly, the ground floor consists of a nested, zoned spatial structure that connects the east and west gardens over three slightly offset levels. On the other hand, communal areas, with correspondingly modestly dimensioned individual rooms, are generously designed and partly usable as living space. This is most consistently implemented in the extra-wide central hall on the top floor, which can be combined with the adjoining terrace areas to form an S-shaped whole by means of concealable sliding glazing. This creates a great sense of spaciousness. Thirdly, finally, the stairs are staggered, creating a 40-meter-long promenade, which is characterized by versatile entrances, views and vistas as well as strongly varying room heights. A recurring element are L-shaped wall surfaces, which create ambiguities and, in conjunction with the carefully balanced lighting system with 20 windows, create a special room characteristic. The materiality and color of the external appearance refer to the neighboring houses from the 1970s.

1, 2

Architects: Frei + Saarinen Architekten
Completion: 2012
Location: Kilchberg, Zurich, Switzerland
Gross floor area: 450 m^2
Number of bedrooms: 5
Main materials / building construction: mineral exterior plaster, zinc plate, larch, wood-metal windows / mixed construction of concrete, masonry and wood
Ecological aspects: Minergie certified

Architekten: Frei + Saarinen Architekten
Fertigstellung: 2012
Ort: Kilchberg, Zürich, Schweiz
Bruttogeschossfläche: 450 m^2
Anzahl der Schlafzimmer: 5
Hauptmaterialien / Konstruktionsweise: mineralischer Außenputz, Zinkblech, Lärche, Holz-Metall-Fenster / Mischbauweise aus Beton, Mauerwerk und Holz
Ökologische Aspekte: Minergie zertifiziert

Drei Ideen bestimmen die Konzeption des Wohnhauses: Zum einen besteht das Erdgeschoss aus einem verschachtelten, zonierend wirkenden Raumgefüge, das Ost- und Westgarten über drei leicht versetzte Ebenen verbindet. Zum anderen sind gemeinschaftliche Bereiche, bei entsprechend bescheiden dimensionierten Individualräumen, großzügig und teilweise als Wohnfläche nutzbar gestaltet. Am konsequentesten ist dies bei der überbreiten zentralen Halle im Dachgeschoss umgesetzt, die sich durch kaschierbare Schiebeverglasungen mit den angrenzenden Terrassenbereichen zu einem S-förmigen Ganzen vereinen lässt. Hierdurch entsteht eine große Weitläufigkeit. Drittens schließlich sind die Treppen versetzt, wodurch eine 40 Meter lange Promenade entsteht, die durch vielseitige Ein-, Durch- und Ausblicke sowie stark variierende Raumhöhen geprägt ist. Wiederkehrendes Element sind L-förmige Wandflächen, die Mehrdeutigkeiten schaffen und in Verbindung mit der – mittels 20 Fenstern sorgfältig austarierten – Lichtführung eine besondere Raumcharakteristik erzeugen. Stofflichkeit und Farbe der äußeren Erscheinung nehmen Bezug zu den benachbarten Häusern aus den 1970er-Jahren.

3

4

1 Garden access and terrace
2 Exterior view with punch window façade and sheet metal roof
3 Bathroom
4 Fully concealable sliding doors

1 Gartenzugang und Terrasse
2 Außenansicht mit vielen Lochfenstern und Blechdach
3 Badezimmer
4 Vollständig kaschierbare Schiebetüren

1

2

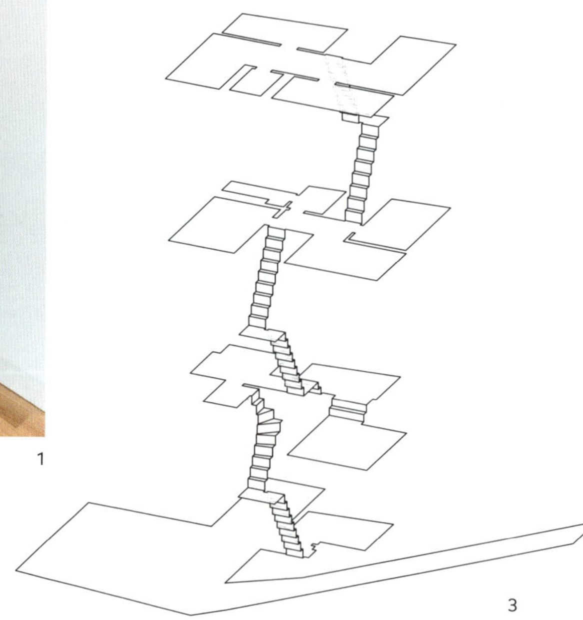

3

1 Interior with L-shaped walls
2 Seamless transition from shell to finishing
3 Promenade plan
4 Site plan
5 Top floor plan
6 First floor plan
7 Ground floor plan
8 Basement floor plan

1 Innenraum mit L-förmigen Wänden
2 Nahtloser Übergang von Roh- zu Ausbau
3 Plan Promenade
4 Lageplan
5 Grundriss DG
6 Grundriss OG
7 Grundriss EG
8 Grundriss UG

4

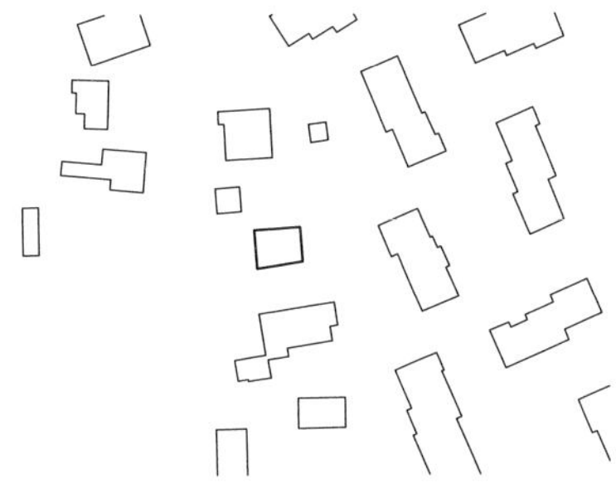

5

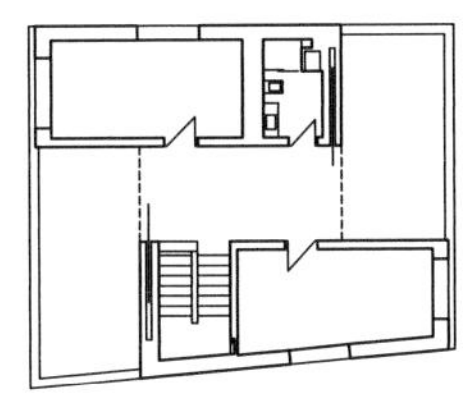

6

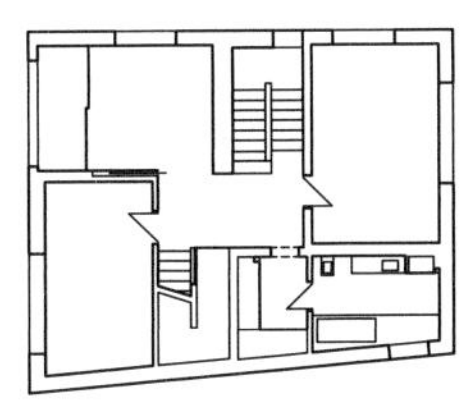

7

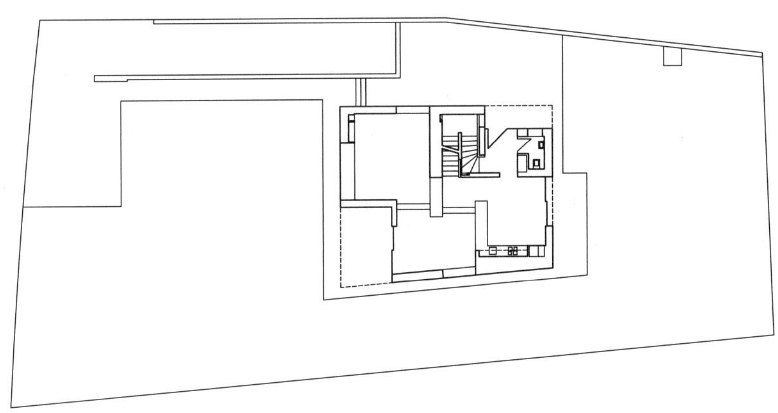

8

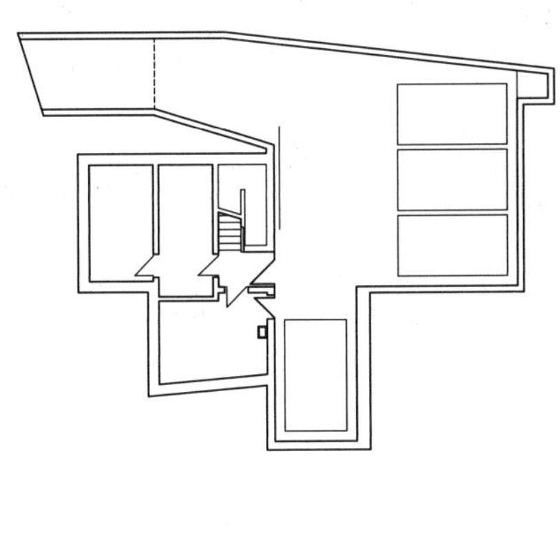

1

CASA CURVED

1 North façade and entrance
2 South façade and garden
3 Kitchen
4 Living room

1 Nordfassade und Eingang
2 Südfassade und Garten
3 Küche
4 Wohnzimmer

2

Architects: Daluz Gonzalez Architekten
Completion: 2016
Location: Basel-Country, Switzerland
Gross floor area: 280 m²
Number of bedrooms: 4
Main materials / building construction: maritime pine / timber construction

A 6.5-room house was built near Basel in a short construction period and on a tight budget. The Casa Curved had to adapt to the existing building on the parents' developed plot and the reduced dimensions of the location. A north-south orientation along the property was specified. The old building from the 1980s by architect Max Schnetz is characterized by a generous semi-circular extension. The architects took up these spatially concise curves as a formal language for the new building.

On the one hand, the so-called Schweizer-Box – the most economical form of construction – was taken up and, on the other hand, accentuated with the minimally curved deformations of the outer walls. The corners lend an unexpected expressiveness that characterizes and identifies the house.

The result is a wooden house which appears to be formally placed on a concrete base. The materiality of the project establishes a connection to the Swiss building tradition and underlines the duality between formal modernity and constructive tradition.

Architekten: Daluz Gonzalez Architekten
Fertigstellung: 2016
Ort: Basel-Landschaft, Schweiz
Bruttogeschossfläche: 280 m²
Anzahl der Schlafzimmer: 4
Hauptmaterialien / Konstruktionsweise: Seekiefer / Holzbau

In der Nähe von Basel entstand ein 6,5-Zimmer-Haus in kurzer Bauzeit und mit knappem Budget. Die Casa Curved musste sich auf der bebauten Parzelle der Eltern dem Bestand und den reduzierten Dimensionen des Ortes anpassen. Vorgegeben war eine Nord-Süd-Orientierung längs des Grundstücks. Der Altbau aus den 1980er-Jahren, vom Architekten Max Schnetz, wird von einer großzügigen halbkreisförmigen Ausdehnung geprägt. Diese räumlich prägnanten Rundungen griffen die Architekten als formale Sprache für den Neubau auf.

Einerseits wurde die sogenannte Schweizer-Box – die ökonomischste Bauform – aufgegriffen, andererseits wurde sie mit den minimal gekrümmten Verformungen der Außenwände akzentuiert. Die Ecken verleihen dem Haus eine unerwartete Ausdruckskraft, die es charakterisiert und identifiziert.

So entstand ein Holzhaus, welches formal auf einem Betonsockel abgestellt erscheint. Mit der Materialität des Projektes wird eine Verbindung zur Schweizer Bautradition hergestellt und Dualität zwischen formaler Moderne und konstruktiver Tradition unterstrichen.

3, 4

1

2

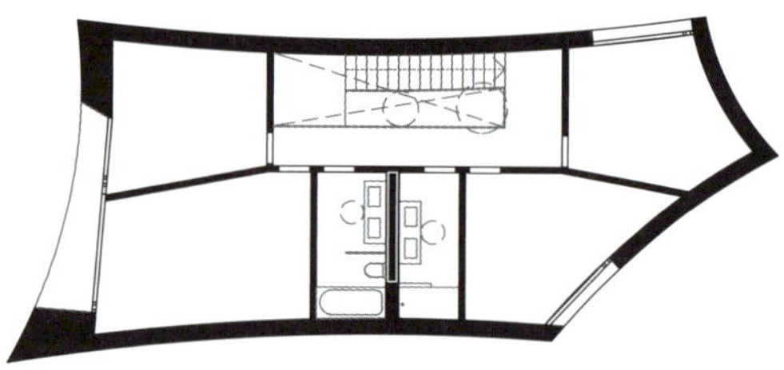

3

4

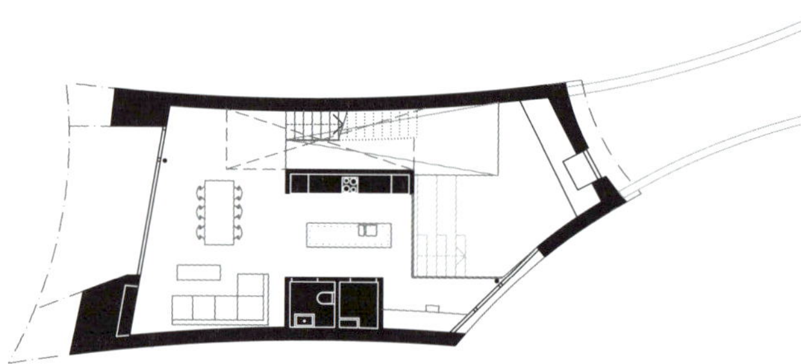

5

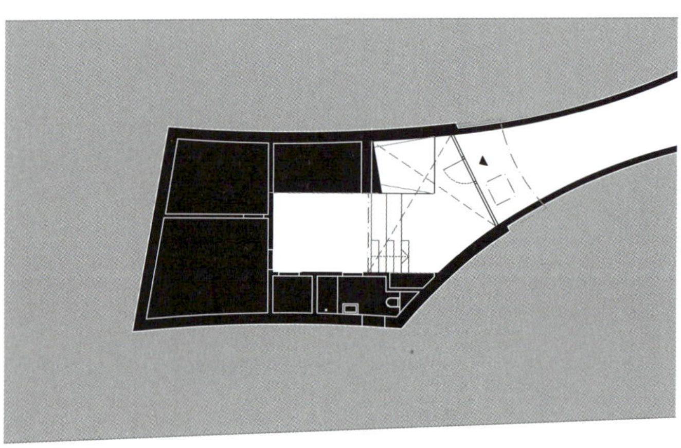

6

7

8

9

1 Section
2 First floor plan
3 Site plan in an environment dominated by detached houses
4 Ground floor plan
5 Basement floor plan
6 Connection stairs with ramp
7 Kitchen detail
8 Ramps and air space
9 Cinema room

1 Schnitt
2 Grundriss OG
3 Schwarzplan der von Einfamilienhäusern geprägten Umgebung
4 Grundriss EG
5 Grundriss Keller
6 Verbindung der Treppe mit Rampe
7 Detail Küche
8 Rampen und Luftraum
9 Kinoraum

FERIENHAUS BREITENBERG

1

Stefan Hitthaler renewed the bold modern form of the UFO holiday home, which the Innsbruck architect Josef Lackner had already placed in a clearing in 1972/73. It is a five-sided prism made of larch boards and glass lying on concrete pillars above Bruneck.

In the main room he was able to accommodate two bunks at each side and narrow twin-bed chambers at the back. By moving the toilet and shower to the new basement and large windows in the north façade, brighter and more comfortable bedrooms were created. The interior in spruce wood has been largely preserved and new spruce furniture has been added to the kitchen and bedrooms. A light wax cement covers the now heatable floor, the fireplace walls and the basement built into the slope with bathroom and technical room. A balcony of larch rods constructed much larger is supported by diagonal steel girders from the concrete pillars, and when the steel staircase disappears into the side wall, a UFO seems to float southwards from the sloping terrain.

Architects: Architekturbüro Stefan Hitthaler
Completion: 2017
Location: Breitenberg, Bruneck, South Tyrol
Gross floor area: 75 m^2
Number of bedrooms: 2
Main materials / building construction: larch and spruce wood, glass / stock in lightweight construction, extension in solid construction
Ecological aspects: new materials (concrete, steel, wax cement), geothermal heat pump (120 m deep drilling)

2

3

Architekten: Architekturbüro Stefan Hitthaler
Fertigstellung: 2017
Ort: Breitenberg, Bruneck, Südtirol
Bruttogeschossfläche: 75 m^2
Anzahl der Schlafzimmer: 2
Hauptmaterialien / Konstruktionsweise: Lärchen- und Fichtenholz, Glas / Bestand in Leichtbau, Zubau in Massivbau
Ökologische Aspekte: Wenige neu eingebrachte Materialien (Beton, Stahl, Wachszement), Erdwärmepumpe (120 m Tiefenbohrung)

Stefan Hitthaler erneuerte die kühn moderne Form des Ferienhauses UFO, die der Innsbrucker Architekt Josef Lackner schon 1972/73 in eine Waldlichtung gesetzt hatte. Es ist ein auf Betonpfeilern liegendes fünfseitiges Prisma aus Lärchenbrettern und Glas oberhalb von Bruneck.

Im Hauptraum konnte er seitlich je zwei Schlafkojen und hinten enge Zweibettkammern unterbringen. Mit der Verlegung von WC und Dusche ins neue Untergeschoss und großen Fenstern in der Nordfassade sind daraus helle, bequemere Schlafräume entstanden. Der Innenausbau in Fichtenholz ist weitgehend erhalten und wurde in Küche und Schlafräumen durch neue Fichtenmöbel ergänzt. Ein heller Wachszement verkleidet den jetzt heizbaren Boden, die Kaminwände und das in den Hang gebaute Untergeschoss mit Bad und Technikraum. Den aus Lärchenstäben deutlich größer konstruierten Balkon stützen diagonale Stahlträger von den Betonpfeilern her, und wenn die Stahltreppe in der Seitenwand verschwindet, scheint ein UFO aus dem abfallenden Gelände südwärts zu schweben.

4

5

6

1 Exterior view from south
2 Bird's-eye view
3 Worm's-eye view from south
4 Bird's-eye view in winter
5 Exterior view from southwest with opened stairs
6 Exterior view from north

1 Außenansicht von Süden
2 Vogelperspektive
3 Unteransicht von Süden
4 Vogelperspektive im Winter
5 Außenansicht von Südwesten mit aufgeklappter Treppe
6 Außenansicht von Norden

1

2

1 Exterior view from south at night
2 Interior view with living room and oven
3 Ground floor plan
4 Basement floor plan
5 Longitudinal section

1 Außenansicht von Süden bei Nacht
2 Innenansicht mit Wohnraum und Ofen
3 Grundriss EG
4 Grundriss UG
5 Längsschnitt

3

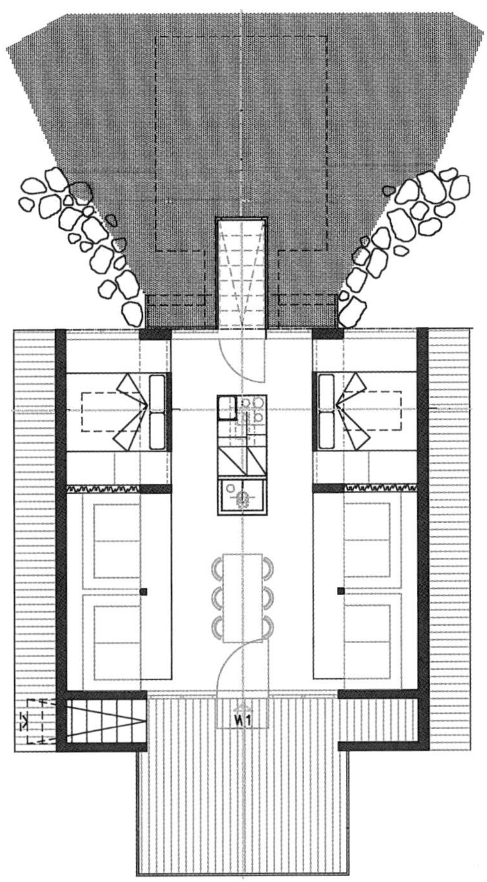

4

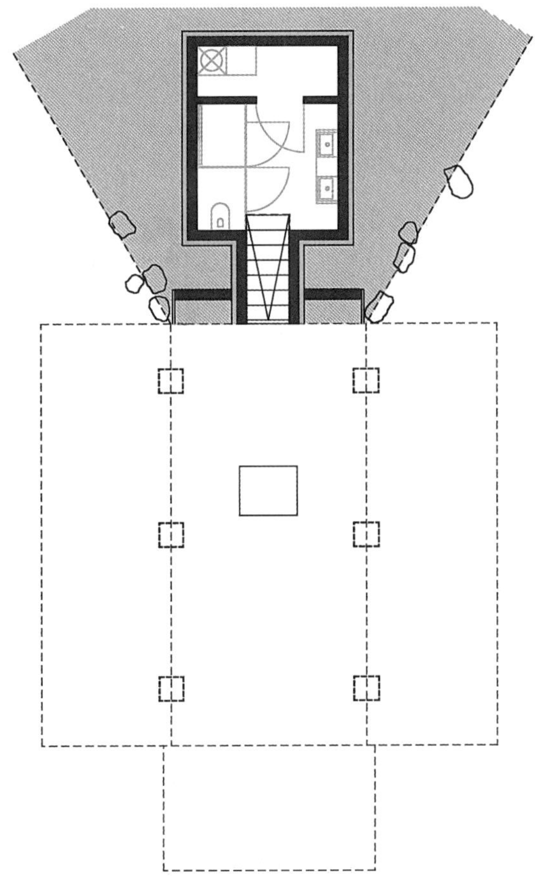

5

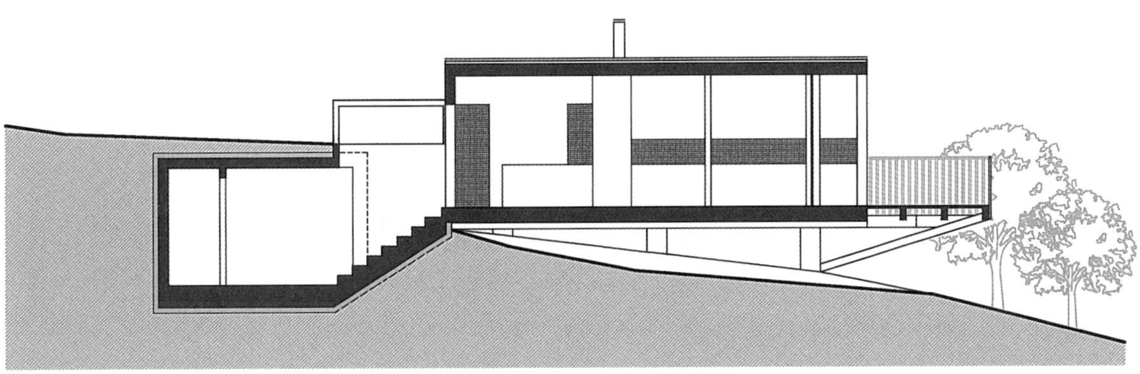

WOHNHAUS CARBONI BROT

1

In the beginning, the house should actually not be built from triangles. The architects tested different volumes and floor plans, which should fit the location in different ways, but no solution was found until they worked with triangles. That way they finally rethought space and form, proportion and movement.

Thus the parts of the house were graded in their heights and hierarchized. All the materials used were inexpensive and will be found as standards more often in the quarter. The drainage pipes break the symmetries, the plaster connects all building forms to a conglomerate. All in all, the impression of a randomly assembled house is created, which almost nestles up against the hill, almost like a simple garden house – but only almost.

Architects: Conradin Clavuot Architekt
Completion: 2014
Location: Rhäzüns, Switzerland
Gross floor area: 250 m^2
Number of bedrooms: 4
Main materials / building construction: brick, concrete, wood / partition walls natural wood, load-bearing inner shell bricked, outer insulation roughly plastered
Ecological aspects: passive house with two small pellet stoves, much storage mass, without comfort ventilation

2

Architekten: Conradin Clavuot Architekt
Fertigstellung: 2014
Ort: Rhäzüns, Schweiz
Bruttogeschossfläche: 250 m^2
Anzahl der Schlafzimmer: 4
Hauptmaterialien / Konstruktionsweise: Backstein, Beton, Holz / Trennwände Naturholz, tragende Innenschale gemauert, Außendämmung grob verputzt
Ökologische Aspekte: Passivhaus mit zwei kleinen Pelletöfen, viel Speichermasse, ohne Komfortlüftung

Zu Beginn sollte eigentlich gar kein Haus aus Dreiecken entstehen. Die Architekten testeten unterschiedliche Volumen und Grundrisse aus, die auf verschiedene Arten zum Ort passen sollten, aber kein Konzept überzeugte. Erst durch die Arbeit mit Dreiecken fand sich endlich eine Lösung. Raum und Form, Proportion und Bewegung konnten neu gedacht werden.

So wurden die Hausteile in ihren Höhen abgestuft und hierarchisiert. Alle verwendeten Materialien sind günstig und im Quartier standardmäßig wiederzufinden. Die Abflussrohre brechen die Symmetrien, der Verputz verbindet alle Bauformen zu einem Konglomerat. Insgesamt entsteht der Eindruck eines zufällig zusammengestellten Hauses, das sich fast wie ein einfaches Gartenhaus an den Hügel schmiegt – aber nur fast.

3

4

5

6

1 Exterior view with 60-degree corner
2 View into the triangular living room
3 Access yard
4 House on the edge of the hill
5 Children's room and place of work
6 Bedroom towards the hill

1 Außenansicht mit 60-Grad-Ecke
2 Blick in den dreieckigen Wohnraum
3 Zugangshof
4 Haus am Hügelrand
5 Kinderzimmer und Arbeitsort
6 Schlafzimmer in Richtung Hügel

1

2

1 Central staircase to the living room
2 Central staircase to the attic bedrooms
3 Sketches design process
4 Top floor plan
5 First floor plan
6 Ground floor plan

1 Zentraler Aufgang zum Wohnraum
2 Zentraler Aufgang zu den Dachschlafzimmern
3 Skizzen Entwurfsprozess
4 Grundriss DG
5 Grundriss OG
6 Grundriss EG

3

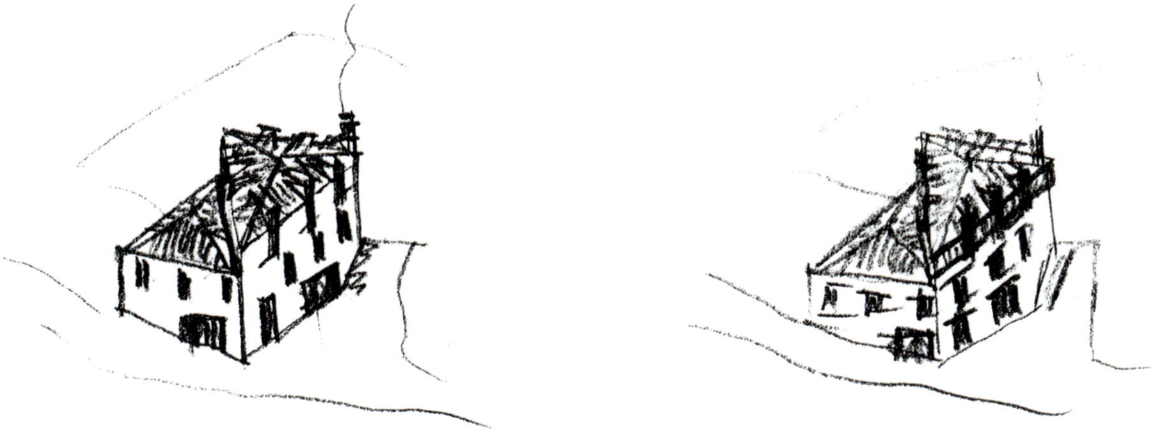

4

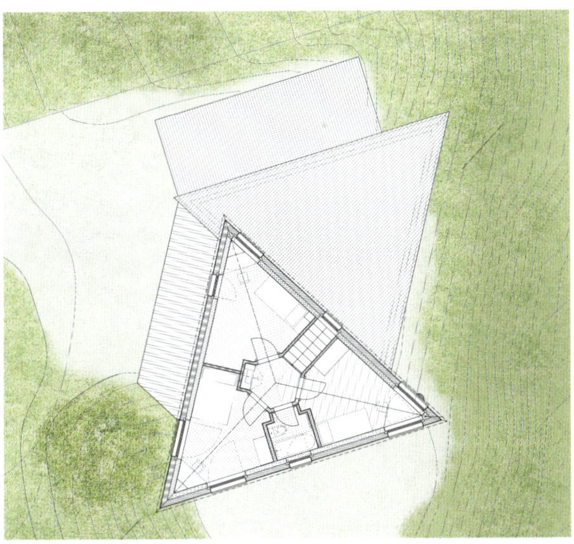

5

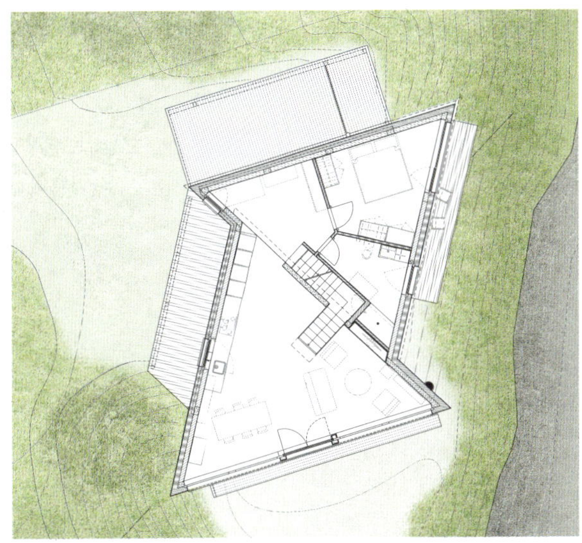

6

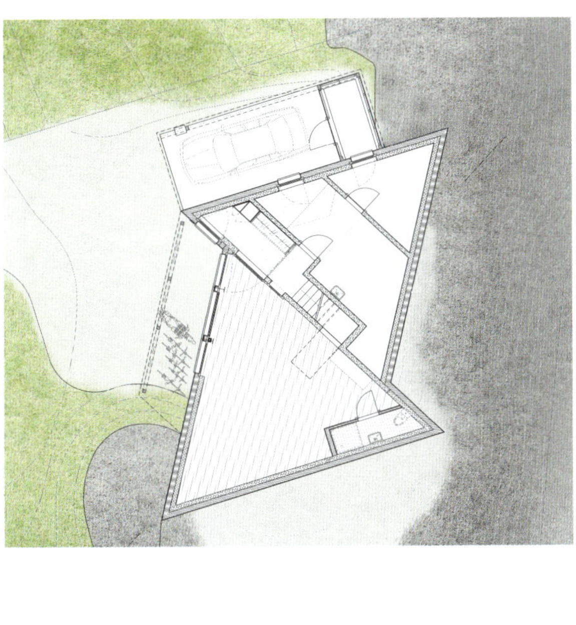

1

L-HAUS

1 Entrance
2 Terrace
3 Access patio

1 Eingang
2 Terrasse
3 Zugang Innenhof

2

Architects: Architects Collective
Completion: 2012
Location: Burgenland, Austria
Gross floor area: 450 m²
Number of bedrooms: 3
Main materials / building construction: fiber cement board / concrete and timber construction
Ecological aspects: nearly-zero energy building

Architekten: Architects Collective
Fertigstellung: 2012
Ort: Burgenland, Österreich
Bruttogeschossfläche: 450 m²
Anzahl der Schlafzimmer: 3
Hauptmaterialien / Konstruktionsweise: Faserzementplatten / Beton- und Holzkonstruktion
Ökologische Aspekte: Niedrigstenergie

The house blends harmoniously into the hilly landscape on the edge of a small settlement in southern Burgenland. The L-shape of the building has created a protected inner courtyard, which allows the division of living and sleeping area desired by the family. Generous glass surfaces optically extend the living area into the garden and provide it with plenty of natural light. The entrance area, which leads into a two-story foyer and the inner courtyard, is covered by the cantilevered L-shape. The upper level is divided into a sleeping area and the living room with kitchen. Between the two areas there is an open, flowing zone, the use of which is flexible and will change over the years through the residents.

Das Haus fügt sich, am Rande einer kleinen Siedlung im Südburgenland, harmonisch in die Hügellandschaft ein. Durch die L-Form des Gebäudes entstand ein geschützter Innenhof, der die von der Familie gewünschte Aufteilung von Wohn- und Schlafbereich ermöglicht. Großzügige Glasflächen erweitern den Wohnraum optisch in den Garten und versorgen ihn mit viel natürlichem Licht. Der Eingangsbereich, der in ein zweigeschossiges Foyer und den Innenhof führt, wird durch die Auskragung der L-Form überdacht. Die obere Ebene gliedert sich in ein Schlafareal und den Aufenthaltsraum mit Küche. Zwischen den beiden Bereichen befindet sich eine offene, fließende Zone, deren Nutzung flexibel ist und sich im Laufe der Jahre durch die Bewohner verändern wird.

3

1

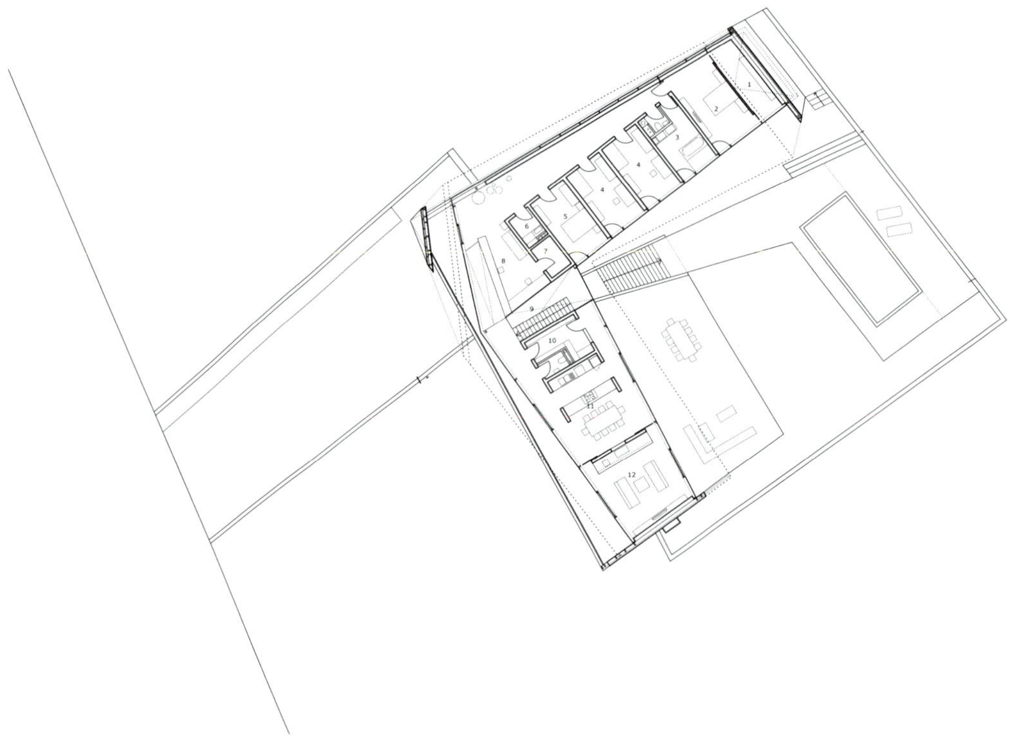

2

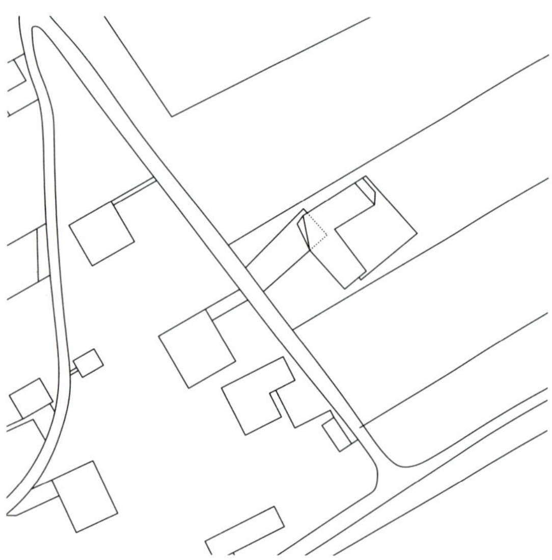

3

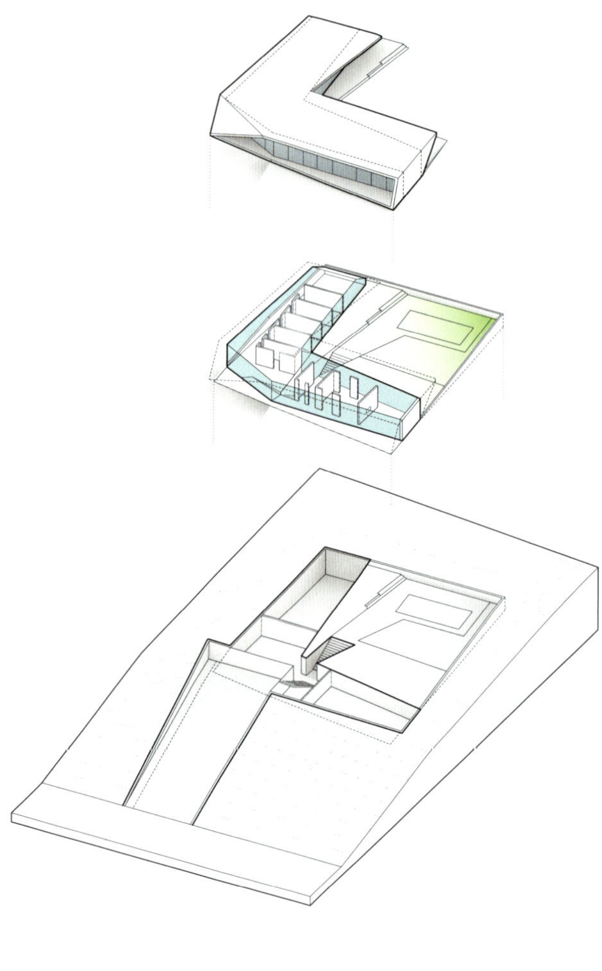

4

5

6

1 Floor plan
2 Site plan
3 Axonometry
4 Patio with swimming pool
5 Corridor
6 Patio

1 Grundriss
2 Lageplan
3 Axonometrie
4 Innenhof mit Swimmingpool
5 Hausflur
6 Innenhof

FELDERHOF

1

The old dwelling, covered with stone-weighted wooden shingles, and the barn with a thatched roof were two authentic witnesses of former life. This ensemble should not be disturbed by the extension. At the same time, the old living area and the extension were to become a functional unit. Due to the topography of the property, it made sense to arrange the new living areas partly underground. The new building was designed in such a way that it connects directly to the old residential floor below the course of the terrain, thus combining old and new into one unit. The new building extends from east to west, almost completely hidden in the mountain landscape on the slope side. To the south, however, it comes to light with a powerful gesture. Rooms with great heights contrast with the closed historical building fabric. The skylights additionally provide sunny and light-flooded rooms, the room geometry provides open spaces. The staircase represents the intersection between the historical and new building fabric.

Architects: Pavol Mikolajcak Architects
Completion: 2017
Location: Villanders, South Tyrol
Gross floor area: 380 m^2
Number of bedrooms: 2 (new part)
Main materials / building construction: exposed concrete / solid construction

2

3

Architekten: Pavol Mikolajcak Architects
Fertigstellung: 2017
Ort: Villanders, Südtirol
Bruttogeschossfläche: 380 m²
Anzahl der Schlafzimmer: 2 (Neubau)
Hauptmaterialien / Konstruktionsweise: Sichtbeton / Massivbau

Das alte Wohnhaus, eingedeckt mit steinbeschwerten Holzschindeln, und der Stadel mit Strohdach bildeten zwei authentische Zeugen früherer Kultur. Dieses Ensemble sollte durch den Anbau nicht gestört werden. Gleichzeitig musste aus dem alten Wohnbereich und dem Zubau eine funktionelle Einheit werden. Durch die Topografie des Grundstückes bot es sich an, die neuen Wohnbereiche teilweise unterirdisch anzuordnen. Im nach Westen ansteigenden Gelände wurde der Neubau so angelegt, dass er unterhalb des Geländeverlaufs direkt an das alte Wohngeschoss anschließt und so Alt und Neu zu einer Einheit verbindet. Der neue Baukörper erstreckt sich von Ost nach West, hangseitig fast vollständig in der Berglandschaft verborgen. Nach Süden dagegen tritt er mit einer kräftigen Geste auf. Räume mit großen Höhen stehen in Kontrast zur geschlossenen historischen Bausubstanz. Die Oberlichter sorgen zusätzlich für sonnige und lichtdurchflutete, die Raumgeometrie für offene Räume. Das Treppenhaus stellt den Schnittpunkt zwischen historischer und neuer Bausubstanz dar.

4

5

6

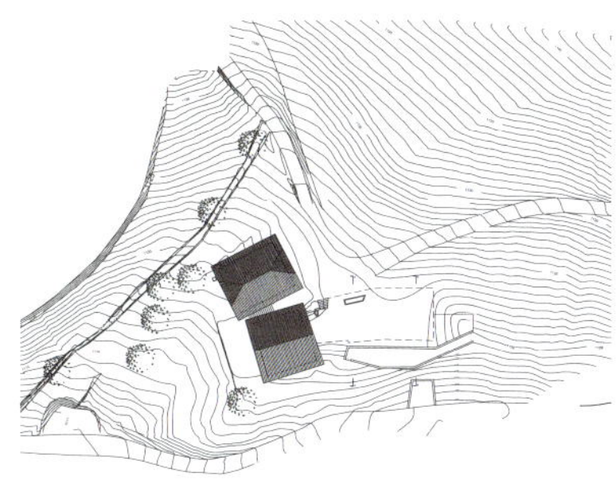

7

8

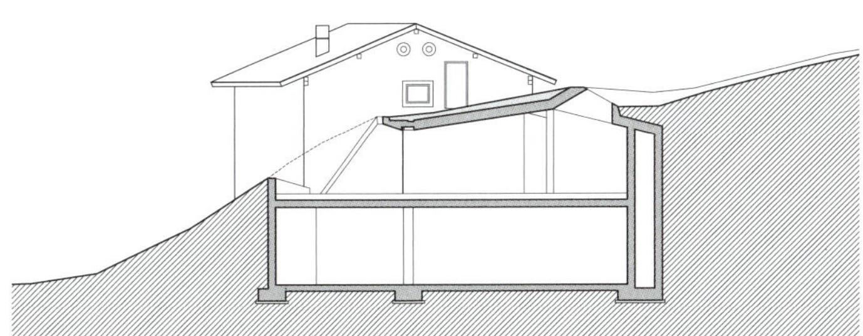

1 Old farm with new extension
2 New extension integrated into the landscape
3 Living and dining area
4 Living and dining area
5 Underground connection to existing building
6 Site plan
7 Sketch
8 Section

1 Alter Bauernhof mit neuem Anbau
2 In die Landschaft integrierter neuer Anbau
3 Wohn- und Essbereich
4 Wohn- und Essbereich
5 Unterirdische Verbindung zum bestehenden Gebäude
6 Lageplan
7 Skizze
8 Schnitt

ATRIUMHAUS

1

Architects: HSB Architekten
Completion: 2018
Location: Günsberg, Solothurn, Switzerland
Gross floor area: 160 m²
Number of bedrooms: 2
Main materials / building construction: heat-insulating single-layer masonry / solid construction, roof in timber construction

The building is located on the eastern edge of the municipality of Günsberg in the canton of Solothurn. The area is characterized by individual smaller detached houses. The house is classically divided into base, middle section and roof. The plinth was executed in fair-faced concrete and slides into the slightly sloping topography as a clearly set-off element, half of it cutting into the slope and the other half protruding from it. The homogeneous walls are executed in a massive and insulating single-layer masonry. The roof was erected in a conventional wooden construction. The roof covering consists of individual cement slate slabs, which differ in their dimensions per roof surface to ensure a continuous joint pattern. The centrally located atrium allows visual references within the house and at the same time allows for the lighting of the rooms in the attic. With its circumferential corridor, the building refers to the Roman atrium house.

2

3

Das Gebäude befindet sich am östlichen Rand der Gemeinde Günsberg im Kanton Solothurn. Das Gebiet ist geprägt von einzelnen kleineren Einfamilienhäusern. Das Haus gliedert sich klassisch in Sockel, Mittelteil und Dach. Der Sockel wurde in Sichtbeton ausgeführt und schiebt sich als klar zeichnendes Element in die leicht abfallende Topografie ein, zur Hälfte in den Hang einschneidend und zur anderen Hälfte aus dem Hang ragend. Die homogenen Wände sind in einem massiven und dämmenden Einsteinmauerwerk ausgeführt. Das Dach wurde in einer konventionellen Holzkonstruktion erstellt. Die Dacheindeckung besteht aus einzelnen Zementschieferplatten, die sich pro Dachfläche in ihrer Dimension unterscheiden, um ein umlaufendes Fugenbild zu gewährleisten. Durch das mittig liegende Atrium werden Sichtbezüge innerhalb des Hauses und zugleich die Belichtung der Räume im Dachgeschoss ermöglicht. Mit seinem umlaufenden Rundgang verweist das Gebäude auf das römische Atriumhaus.

4

Architekten: HSB Architekten
Fertigstellung: 2018
Ort: Günsberg, Solothurn, Schweiz
Bruttogeschossfläche: 160 m^2
Anzahl der Schlafzimmer: 2
Hauptmaterialien / Konstruktionsweise: wärmedämmendes Einsteinmauerwerk / Massivbau, Dach in Holzbauweise

1 Exterior view terrace
2 Exterior view from south
3 Exterior view from east
4 Exterior view from north
5 Atrium

1 Außenansicht Terrasse
2 Außenansicht von Süden
3 Außenansicht von Osten
4 Außenansicht von Norden
5 Atrium

5

1

2

1 Corridor
2 Atrium
3 Site plan
4 Cross section
5 Longitudinal section
6 Ground floor plan

1 Korridor
2 Atrium
3 Lageplan
4 Querschnitt
5 Längsschnitt
6 Grundriss EG

3

4

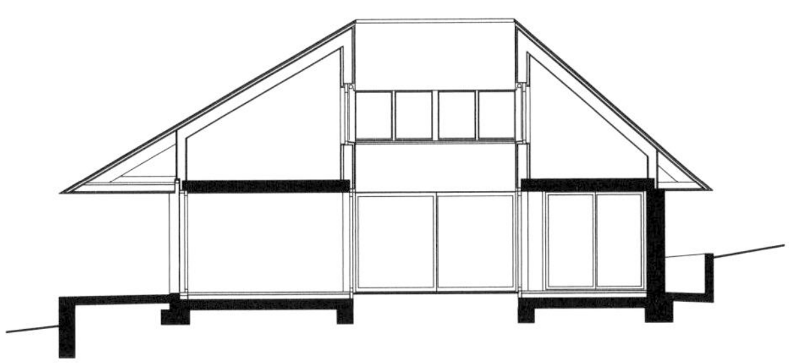

5

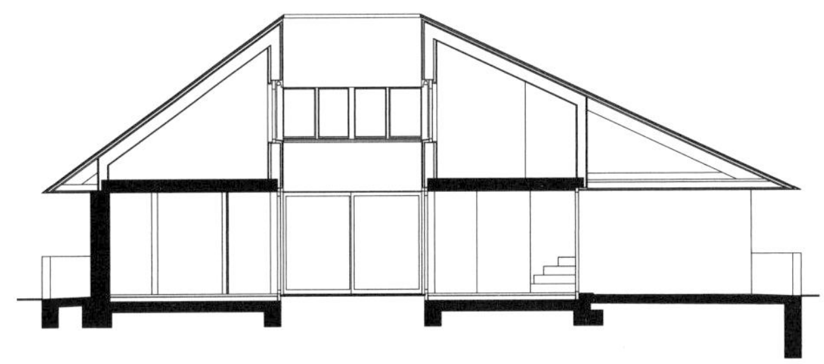

6

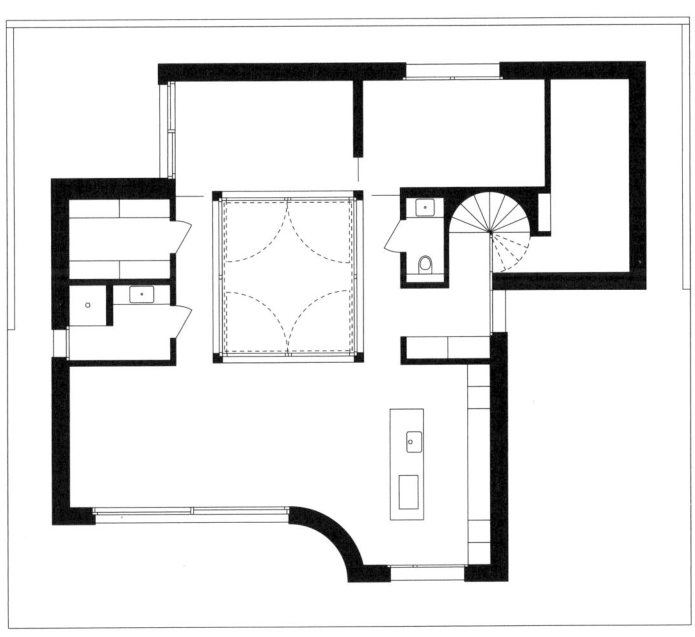

1

EFH HÖHTAL-STRASSE

1 Kitchen with light catcher and view of the outside terrace
2 Façade on the uphill side
3 Exterior view of the replacement building
4 Attic room with suspended ceiling

1 Küche mit Lichtfänger und Blick auf Außenterrasse
2 Bergseitige Fassade
3 Außenansicht des Ersatzneubaus
4 Dachzimmer mit abgehängter Decke

2

Architects: BEM Architekten AG, Baden
Completion: 2015
Location: Ennetbaden, Switzerland
Gross floor area: 160 m^2
Number of bedrooms: 4.5
Main materials / building construction: sandblasted concrete base, wooden shingle façade, copper roof; interior: parquet, white plaster / shell, prefabricated timber element construction on sandblasted concrete base
Ecological aspects: sustainable timber construction

Like a string of pearls, classic workers' houses from the late 1920s line the Höhtalstrasse on the northern slope of the Lägern. The replacement building is respectfully situated in this ensemble.

The contemporary architectural language interprets typical local building elements. The windows and roof openings are well-proportioned and precisely placed. They open up unusual interior moods and provide accurate defined views of the sunny landscape.

The precise lighting design allows plenty of zenithal light to flood into the centrally located interiors even in less sunny months. The sandblasted concrete base is carefully integrated into the topography. On the concrete base stands the timber element building, clad in a cedar shingle robe treated with mud paint and covered with a copper roof.

Architekten: BEM Architekten AG, Baden
Fertigstellung: 2015
Ort: Ennetbaden, Schweiz
Bruttogeschossfläche: 160 m^2
Anzahl der Schlafzimmer: 4,5
Hauptmaterialien / Konstruktionsweise: Betonsockel sandgestrahlt, Holzschindelfassade, Kupferdach; Innen: Parkett, Weißputz / Rohbau, vorgefertigter Holzelementbau auf sandgestrahltem Betonsockel
Ökologische Aspekte: nachhaltige Holzbauweise

Einer Perlenkette ähnlich reihen sich klassische Arbeiterhäuser der späten 1920er-Jahre an der Höhtalstrasse am Nordhang der Lägern. Der Ersatzneubau situiert sich respektvoll in dieses Ensemble ein.

Die zeitgemäße Architektursprache interpretiert ortstypische Bauelemente. Die Fenster und Dachöffnungen sind wohlproportioniert und präzise gesetzt. Sie erschließen innen ungewöhnliche Raumstimmungen und eröffnen genau definierte Ausblicke in die besonnte Landschaft.

Die exakte Lichtführung lässt auch in weniger sonnigen Monaten viel Zenitallicht in die zentral gelegenen Innenräume fluten. Der sandgestrahlte Betonsockel ist sorgfältig in die Topografie eingearbeitet. Auf dem Betonsockel steht der Holzelementbau, eingekleidet in ein mit Schlammfarbe behandeltes Zedernschindelgewand und eingedeckt mit einem Kupferdach.

3, 4

1

2

3

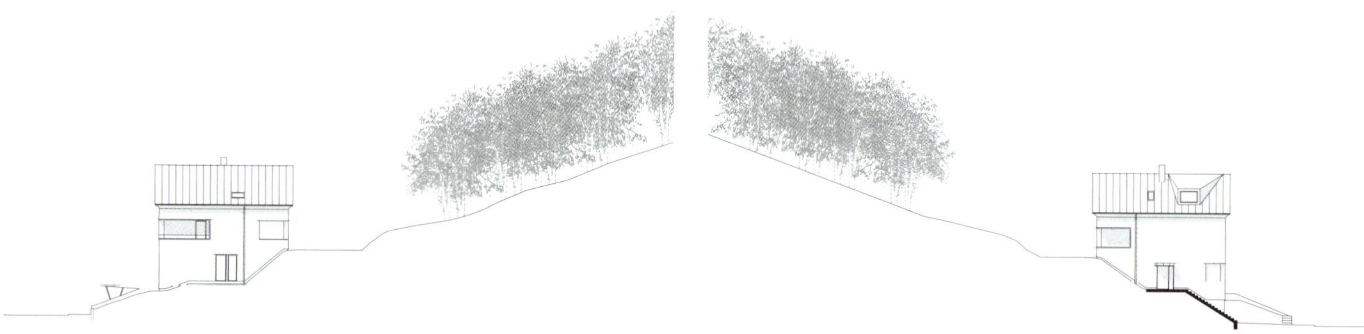

1 Attic room with open skylight
2 Living floor with view to the fireplace
3 Views with terrain
4 Cross section
5 Top floor plan
6 Entrance floor plan
7 Living floor plan
8 Street floor plan

1 Dachzimmer mit aufgestelltem Dachflächenfenster
2 Wohngeschoss mit Blick zum Cheminée
3 Ansichten mit Gelände
4 Querschnitt
5 Grundriss DG
6 Grundriss Eingangsgeschoss
7 Grundriss Wohngeschoss
8 Grundriss Straßengeschoss

4

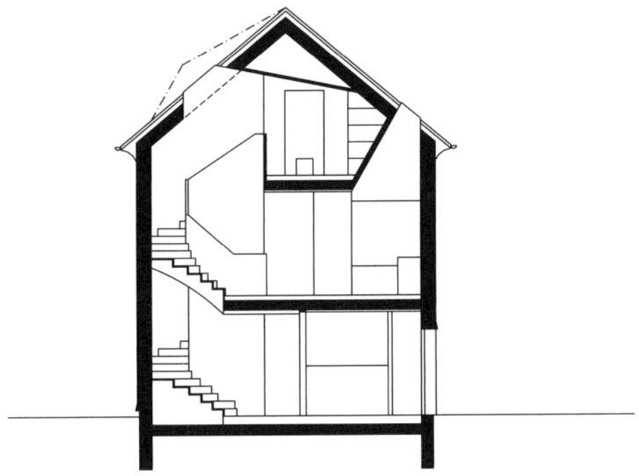

5

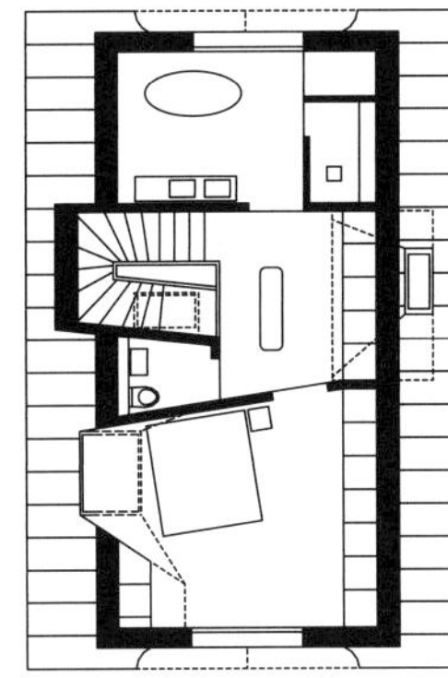

6

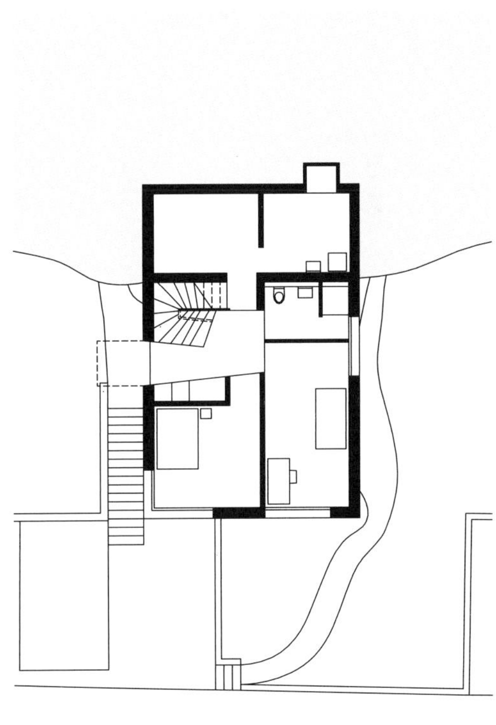

7

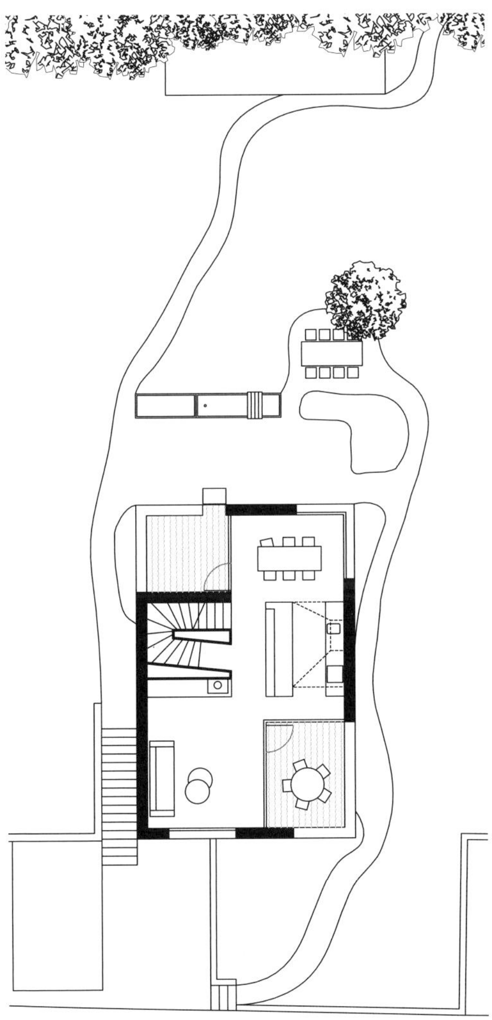

8

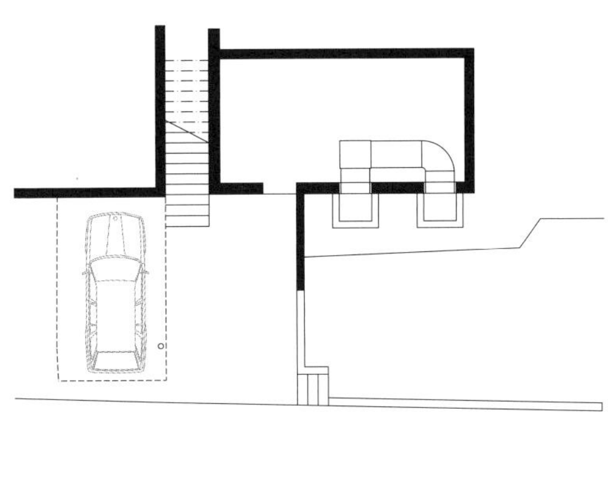

MUK

The house muk combines the requirements of a residential house and a practice for osteopathy in one building concept.

Two communicating volumes, consisting of the practice, which is located in the lower part of the building on the street side, and the two-story living area form the overall ensemble. Between the bodies there is a terrace and garden area, which takes on the function of a connecting element and at the same time serves as the roof area of the practice as well as the garden of the residential building. Thus the outdoor areas become an integral part of the individual living segments.

The floors are connected by air spaces and thus allow an open, bright flow of space. As a striking central connecting element a staircase was placed in the living room enhancing the free atmosphere of the rooms.

1, 2

Architects: mahore architekten
Completion: 2013
Location: Saalfelden, Austria
Gross floor area: 200 m^2
Number of bedrooms: 3
Main materials / building construction: wood, HPL boards, glass / reinforced concrete construction

Architekten: mahore architekten
Fertigstellung: 2013
Ort: Saalfelden, Österreich
Bruttogeschossfläche: 200 m²
Anzahl der Schlafzimmer: 3
Hauptmaterialien / Konstruktionsweise: Holz, HPL-Platten, Glas / Stahlbetonbauweise

Das Haus muk verbindet die Anforderungen eines Wohnhauses und einer Praxis für Osteopathie in einem Gebäudekonzept.

Zwei kommunizierende Volumen, bestehend aus dem Praxisteil, der im straßenseitig tiefer gelegenen Gebäudeabschnitt situiert ist, und dem zweigeschossigen Wohnbereich, bilden das Gesamtensemble. Zwischen den Körpern liegt eine Terrassen- und Gartenfläche, welche die Funktion eines verbindenden Elementes einnimmt. Sie ist zugleich Dachfläche der Praxis und dient als Garten des Wohnhauses. Somit werden die Außenbereiche zum integralen Bestandteil der einzelnen Wohnsegmente.

Die Etagen sind durch Lufträume verbunden und ermöglichen somit einen offenen, hellen Raumfluss. Eine Treppe als zentrales Verbindungselement wurde markant im Wohnzimmer platziert und verstärkt die freie Atmosphäre der Räume.

3

4

1 Living area
2 Garden view
3 Stairs
4 Street view

1 Wohnbereich
2 Gartenansicht
3 Treppe
4 Straßenansicht

1

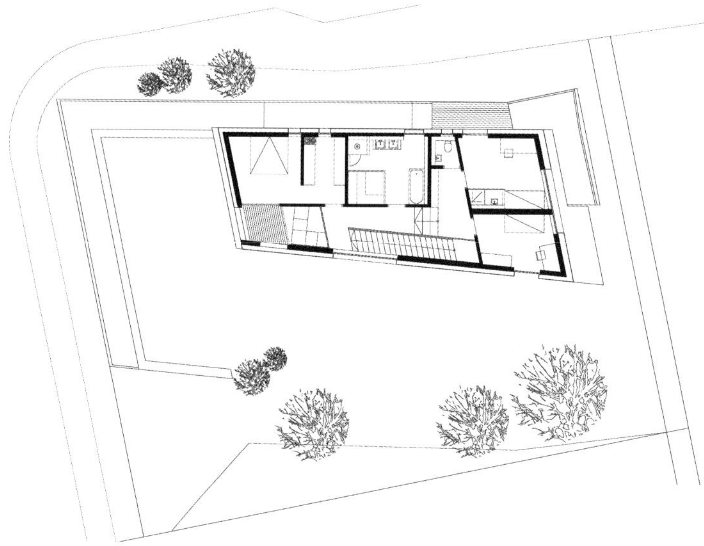

2

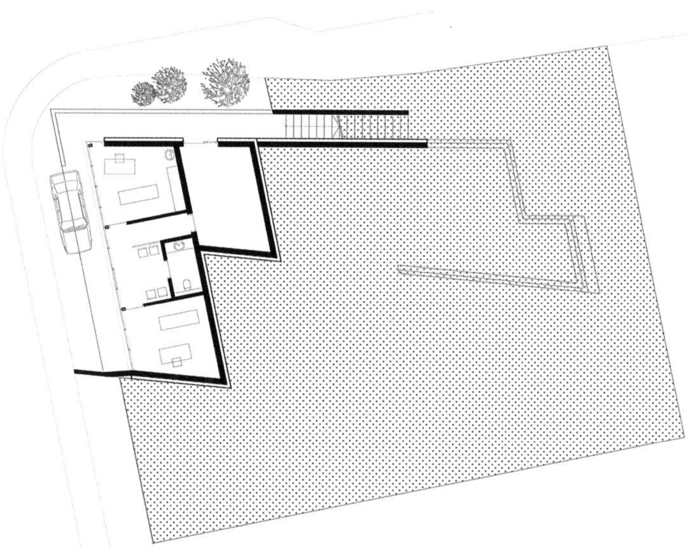

3

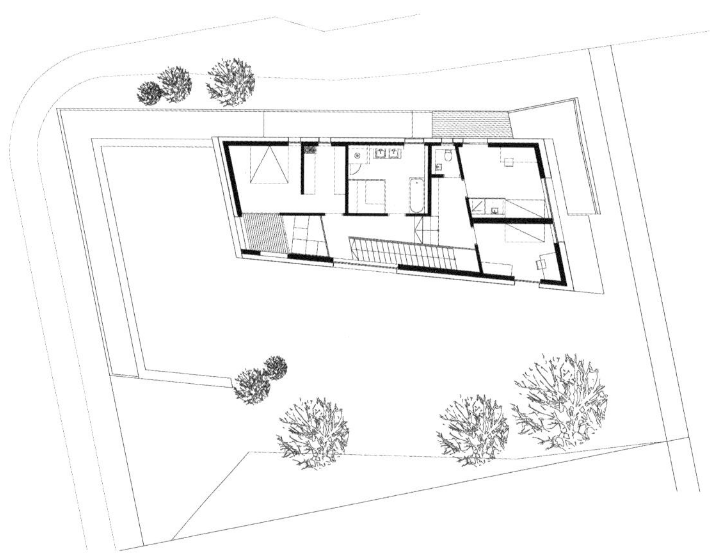

4

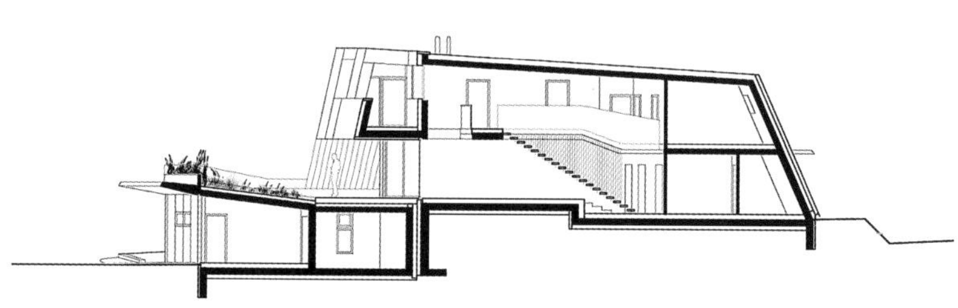

5

6

7

1 First floor plan
2 Basemant floor plan
3 Ground floor plan
4 Longitudinal section
5 Garden view
6 Dining aera
7 Street view at night

1 Grundriss OG
2 Grundriss UG
3 Grundriss EG
4 Längsschnitt
5 Gartenansicht
6 Essbereich
7 Straßenansicht bei Nacht

RUSTY

1

From the outside, the house is slim and fits in with the scale of the neighborhood. Inside, modulated lengths, heights and lighting create a dramaturgically staged sequence of rooms that merge into a whole over four levels. Despite the narrow width of the property, the interior is spacious and wide-ranging. The striking Corten steel façade is complemented by the interior made of exposed concrete. The interior of the building, which is not only used as a residence but also as a gallery, offers an optimal exhibition climate. The façade design, like the staircase, bathrooms and kitchen, is based on designs by the Hungarian artist Zsolt Szalai that give the building an artistic quality. On the top floor is the bedroom, which through its lush glazing offers a panoramic view of the city and a view of the garden, which in addition to a swimming biotope also has a pavilion. The low-energy house is heated and cooled by a heat pump.

Architects: azb – Architekt Zoran Bodrozic
Completion: 2013
Location: Vienna, Austria
Gross floor area: 400 m^2
Number of bedrooms: 4
Main materials / building construction: concrete, Corten steel, oak wood / reinforced concrete construction
Ecological aspects: low-energy house, brine-water heat pump, preparation for the installation of a photovoltaic system

2

3

Architekten: azb – Architekt Zoran Bodrozic
Fertigstellung: 2013
Ort: Wien, Österreich
Bruttogeschossfläche: 400 m²
Anzahl der Schlafzimmer: 4
Hauptmaterialien / Konstruktionsweise: Beton, Cortenstahl, Eichenholz / Stahlbetonkonstruktion
Ökologische Aspekte: Niedrigenergiehaus, Sole-Wasser Wärmepumpe, Vorbereitung für die Einrichtung einer photovoltaischen Anlage

4

1 Garden view
2 Garden, pavilion and house
3 Residential level
4 Residential level with gallery
5 Garden view at dusk

1 Gartenansicht
2 Garten, Pavillon und Haus
3 Wohnebene
4 Wohnebene mit Galerie
5 Gartenansicht bei Dämmerung

Von außen präsentiert sich das Haus schlank und fügt sich in den Maßstab der Nachbarschaft ein. Innen erzeugen modulierte Längen, Höhen und Lichtführungen eine dramaturgisch inszenierte Reihung von Räumlichkeiten, die sich über vier Ebenen zu einem Ganzen fügen. Trotz schmaler Grundstücksbreite verfügt der Raum innen über Großzügigkeit und Weite. Die auffällige Cortenstahlfassade wird durch den in Sichtbeton ausgeführten Innenraum ergänzt. Dieser bietet, in dem nicht nur als Wohnhaus, sondern auch als Galerie genutzten Gebäude, ein optimales Ausstellungsklima. Die Fassadengestaltung basiert genauso wie Treppenhaus, Bäder und Küche auf Entwürfen des ungarischen Künstlers Zsolt Szalai, die dem Gebäude eine künstlerische Qualität verleihen. Im Dachgeschoss befindet sich das Schlafzimmer, das durch die üppige Verglasung einen Rundumblick auf die Stadt und Sicht auf den Garten gewährt, der neben einem Schwimmbiotop auch einen Pavillon bietet. Mittels Wärmepumpe wird das Niedrigenergiehaus beheizt und gekühlt.

5

1

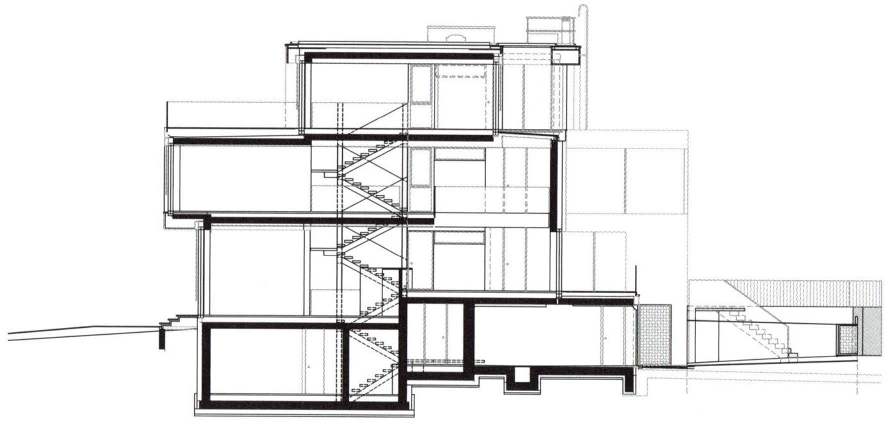

2

3

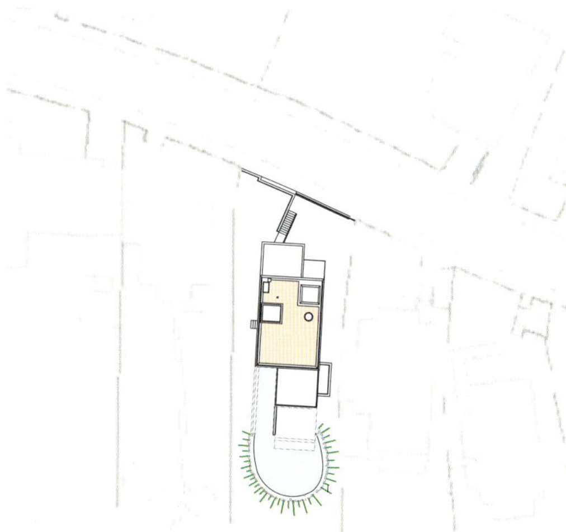

4, 5

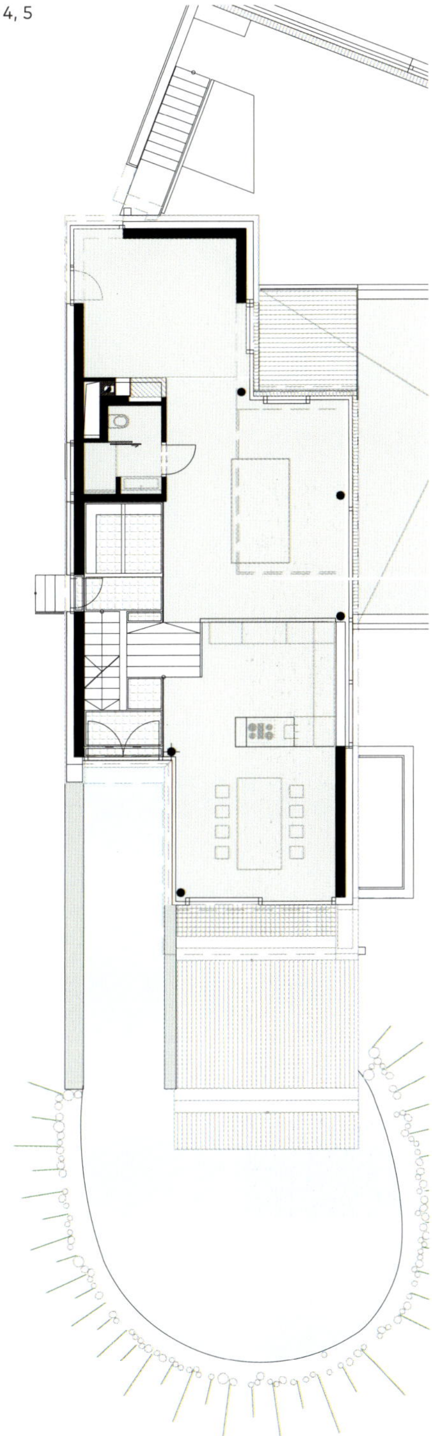

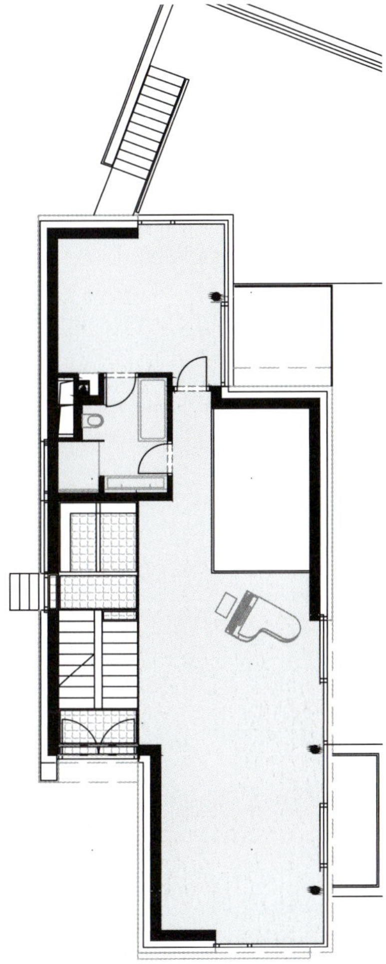

6

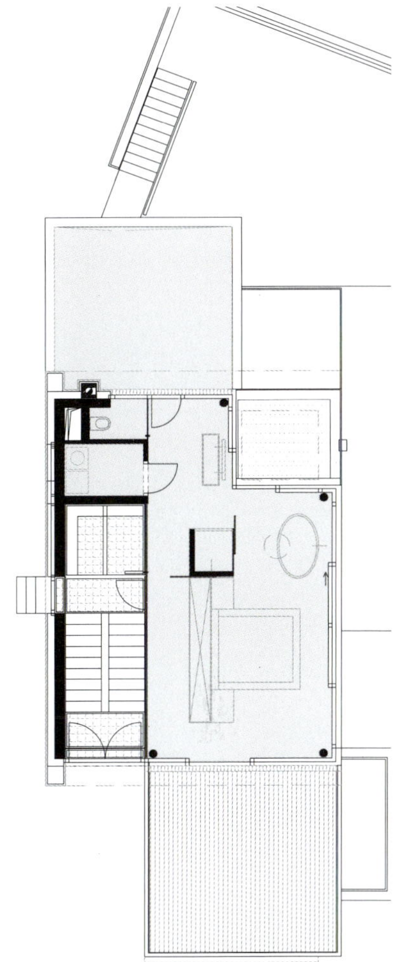

1 Longitudinal section
2 Sketch
3 Site plan
4 Ground floor plan
5 First floor plan
6 Top floor plan

1 Längsschnitt
2 Skizze
3 Lageplan
4 Grundriss EG
5 Grundriss OG
6 Grundriss DG

1

CHALET NANUQ

1 Kitchen and stairs to the mezzanine floor
2 View of the Rhone Valley in wintertime
3 Entrance and terrace
4 Master bedroom

1 Küche und Treppe zum Zwischengeschoss
2 Blick auf das Rhonetal im Winter
3 Eingang und Terrasse
4 Hauptschlafzimmer

2

66

Architects: Atelier Nord Sàrl
Completion: 2016
Location: Saclentse, Nendaz, Switzerland
Gross floor area: 120 m^2
Number of bedrooms: 2
Main materials / building construction: concrete, wood, eternit slate, cement tiles, wooden floor / timber frame construction on concrete base
Ecological aspects: local materials, electricity with photovoltaic roof, heating with heat pump

Architekten: Atelier Nord Sàrl
Fertigstellung: 2016
Ort: Saclentse, Nendaz, Schweiz
Bruttogeschossfläche: 120 m^2
Anzahl der Schlafzimmer: 2
Hauptmaterialien / Konstruktionsweise: Beton, Holz, Eternit-Schiefer, Zementfliesen, Holzboden / Holzrahmenbau auf Betonsockel
Ökologische Aspekte: regionale Materialien, Elektrizität mit Photovoltaik-Dach, Heizen mit Wärmepumpe

Chalet Nanuq offers a beautiful view over the Alps and the Rhone Valley. In contrast to the traditional chalet, the visual identity offers a contemporary silhouette and at the same time blends harmoniously into the surroundings.

The construction made of larch wood of local origin stands on a concrete base. With its horizontal bands protecting the windows, it is inspired by the popular architecture of the region and combines it with modern elements, such as the large windows framing the landscape. On the upper floor, the living room and the directly adjoining kitchen open up, surmounted by a mezzanine that offers additional sleeping space, accessible via a miller's ladder.

One floor below are the two comfortable bedrooms, close to the bathrooms. The living area is extended by outdoor spaces, balcony and terrace, which allow the chalet to constantly interact with the surrounding nature, in summer and winter.

Das Chalet Nanuq bietet eine wunderschöne Aussicht über die Alpen und das Rhonetal. Im Gegensatz zum traditionellen Chalet bietet die visuelle Identität eine zeitgemäße Silhouette und fügt sich gleichzeitig harmonisch in die Umgebung ein.

Die Konstruktion aus Lärchenholz lokaler Herkunft steht auf einem Betonsockel. Sie zeigt sich mit ihren horizontalen Bändern, welche die Fenster schützen, von der volkstümlichen Architektur der Region inspiriert und verbindet diese mit modernen Elementen wie den großen, die Landschaft rahmenden Fenstern. Im Obergeschoss öffnen sich das Wohnzimmer und die direkt angrenzende Küche. Das darüber liegende, über eine Müllerleiter erreichbare Zwischengeschoss bietet zusätzlichen Schlafraum.

Ein Stockwerk tiefer befinden sich die beiden komfortablen Schlafzimmer in unmittelbarer Nähe der Badezimmer. Der Wohnbereich wird durch Außenräume, Balkon und Terrasse erweitert, die dem Chalet eine ständige Interaktion mit der umgebenden Natur, im Sommer wie im Winter, ermöglichen.

3, 4

1

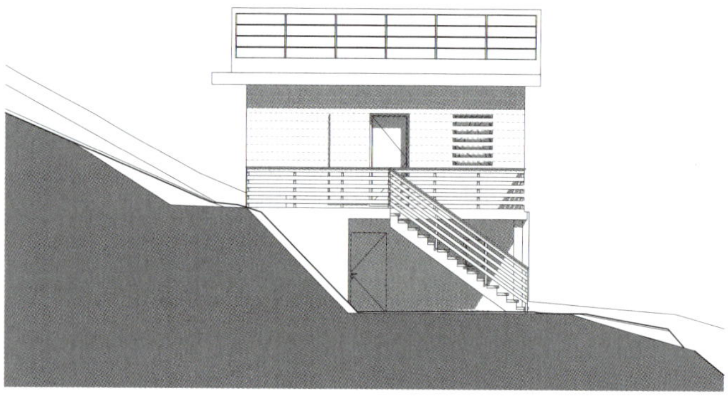

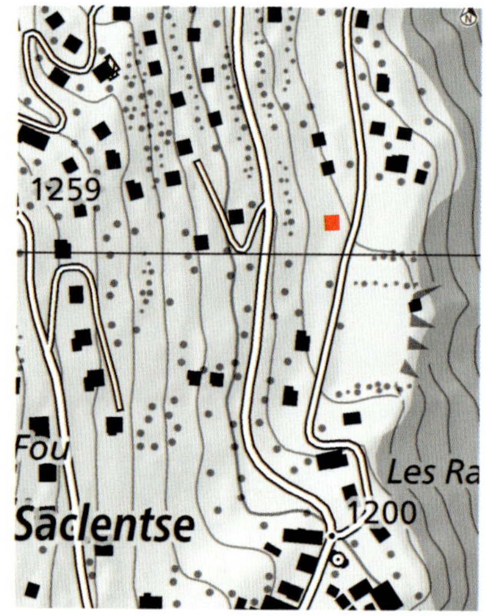

2

3

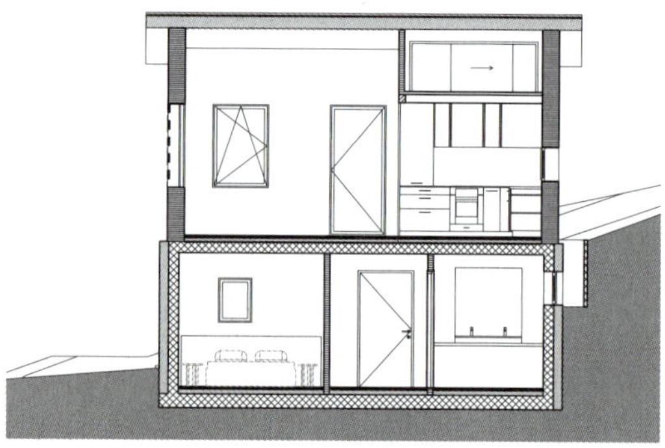

4

5

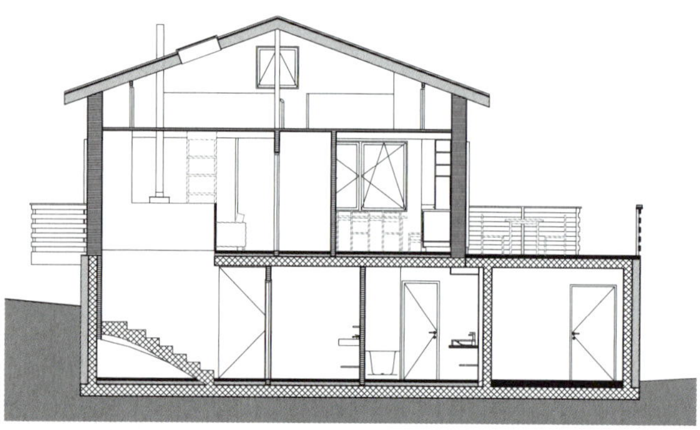

6

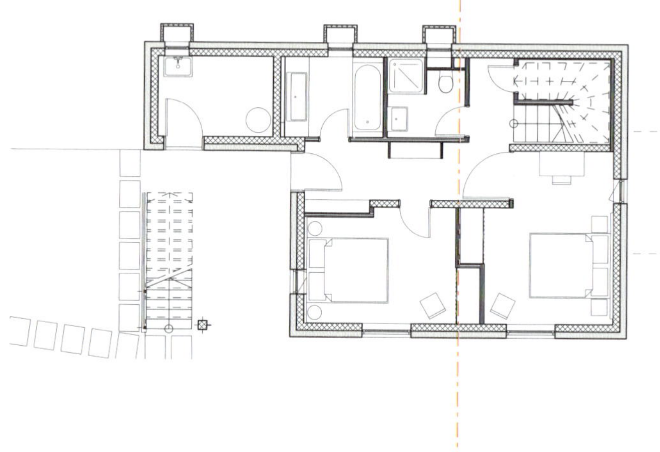

1 South elevation
2 Site plan
3 Longitudinal section
4 First floor plan
5 Frontal section
6 Ground floor plan
7 Exterior view from southeast
8 Dining and living room

1 Aufriss Südseite
2 Lageplan
3 Längsschnitt
4 Grundriss OG
5 Frontalschnitt
6 Grundriss EG
7 Außenansicht von Südosten
8 Ess- und Wohnzimmer

7

8

WOHNHAUS ALTENBERG

In Altenberg, not far from Linz, stands this detached house. It is the residence of a family of four. The owner herself managed the realisation. Her professional connection to building explains the reduction of the design and the use of concrete. It was her wish to create a lot of space on little actually built area.

The property is what the observer suspects at first glance: a remnant, small, pointed and sloping. The ground floor slopes down with the terrain and has three levels. The space therefore becomes higher and higher towards the bottom. Large fixed window fronts create a bright, light-flooded interior. Everything merges seamlessly into one another. The garden is thus also a natural part of the house. But the house remains the actual core of the matter. As soon as the hedge of beech and hazelnut bushes is dense enough, it can be experienced.

1, 2

Architects: Bogenfeld Architektur
Completion: 2016
Location: Altenberg bei Linz, Austria
Gross floor area: 145 m^2
Number of bedrooms: 3
Main materials / building construction: black fiber cement, concrete, wood / solid construction
Ecological aspects: natural building materials

Architekten: Bogenfeld Architektur
Fertigstellung: 2016
Ort: Altenberg bei Linz, Österreich
Bruttogeschossfläche: 145 m^2
Anzahl der Schlafzimmer: 3
Hauptmaterialien / Konstruktionsweise: schwarzer Faserzement, Beton, Holz / Massivbau
Ökologische Aspekte: natürliche Baustoffe

Nicht weit von Linz, in Altenberg, steht dieses Einfamilienhaus. Es ist Wohnort für eine vierköpfige Familie. Die Umsetzung hat die Bauherrin selbst geleitet. Ihr beruflicher Bezug zum Bauen erklärt die Reduktion des Designs und den Einsatz von Beton. Ihr Wunsch war es, auf wenig tatsächlich gebauter Fläche viel Raum zu schaffen.

Das Grundstück ist das, was der Betrachter auf den ersten Blick vermutet: ein Reststück, klein, spitz und schief. Das Erdgeschoss fällt mit dem Gelände ab und hat drei Ebenen. Der Raum wird deshalb nach unten hin immer höher. Große Fensterfronten erzeugen einen hellen, lichtdurchfluteten Innenraum. Alles geht fließend ineinander über. Der Garten ist so auch ganz natürlicher Bestandteil des Hauses, doch das Haus bleibt der eigentliche Kern der Sache. Sobald die Hecke aus Buchen und Haselnusssträuchern dicht genug ist, ist das erlebbar.

3

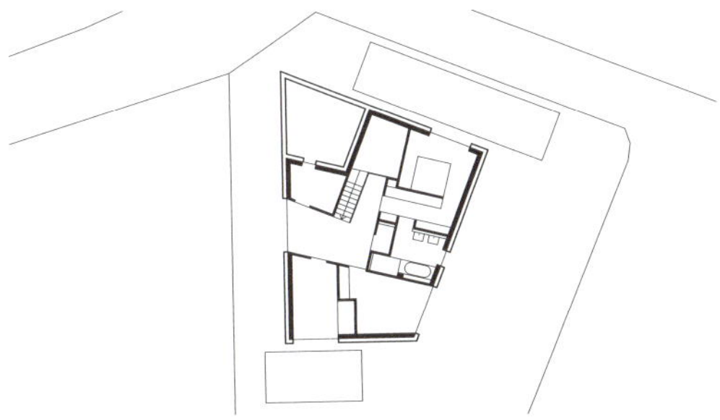

4

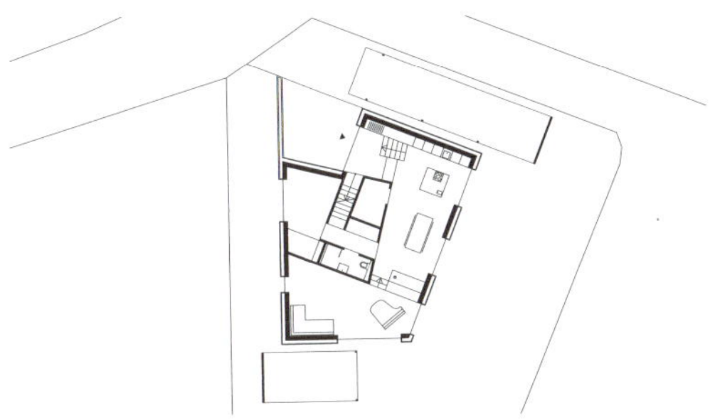

5

1 Dining area
2 Exterior view with garden
3 First floor plan
4 Ground floor plan
5 Living room with garden view

1 Essbereich
2 Außenansicht mit Garten
3 Grundriss OG
4 Grundriss EG
5 Wohnbereich mit Blick in den Garten

STEINHAUS IN VICOSOPRANO

The detached three-story single-family stone house is located at the edge of the mountain village near the edge of the forest on a steep path. The house does not attempt to establish a dialogue in its heterogeneous architectural environment, which consists of single-family homes of different styles. Instead, it builds up a dialogue in harmony with nature. The irregular monolithic building structure moves close to the northeastern boundary of the property, so that on the south side there is enough space for the outdoor space or garden seating area. The shape of the building as well as the broken stones of the massive masonry show the rootedness with the place: a house like a stone as part of nature. The effect of an erratic block or a piece of rock that has always been located there is created. The physicality of the house thus becomes an essential part of living. The old traditional building method is an important element of the design, which refers to the natural environment, tradition and the weather-related changeability of the materials. Statically reduced to the bare essentials, construction and material coincide as a unified appearance.

1, 2

Architects: Renato Maurizio Architekten
Completion: 2012
Location: Vicosoprano, Switzerland
Gross floor area: 220 m^2
Number of bedrooms: 3
Main materials / building construction: natural stone, wood / solid construction
Ecological aspects: Minergie construction

Architekten: Renato Maurizio Architekten
Fertigstellung: 2012
Ort: Vicosoprano, Schweiz
Bruttogeschossfläche: 220 m²
Anzahl der Schlafzimmer: 3
Hauptmaterialien / Konstruktionsweise: Naturstein, Holz / Massivbauweise
Ökologische Aspekte: Minergiebauweise

Das frei stehende dreistöckige Einfamilienhaus steht am Dorfrand des Bergdorfs Vicosoprano nahe dem Waldrand an einem steilen Weg. Das Haus versucht nicht, mit seiner heterogenen baulichen Umgebung, die aus Einfamilienhäusern unterschiedlichster Stilrichtungen besteht, in Dialog zu treten. Es baut stattdessen einen Dialog im Einklang mit der Natur. Der unregelmäßige monolithische Baukörper rückt dicht an die nordöstliche Grundstücksgrenze, sodass auf der Südseite ausreichend Platz für den Außenraum und den Gartensitzplatz entsteht. Die Form des Baukörpers sowie die Bruchsteine des massiven Mauerwerks zeigen die Verwurzelung mit dem Ort: Ein Haus wie ein Stein als Teil der Natur. Es entsteht die Wirkung eines erratischen Blocks oder eines Stücks Fels, der schon immer dort lag. Die Körperlichkeit des Hauses wird so zum wesentlichen Teil des Wohnens. Die alte, traditionelle Bauweise ist ein wichtiges Element des Entwurfs, der sich auf die natürliche Umgebung, auf die Tradition und die wetterbedingte Veränderbarkeit der Materialien bezieht. Statisch auf das Notwendigste reduziert, fallen Konstruktion und Material als eine einheitliche Erscheinungsform zusammen.

3

4

1 Exterior view from northeast
2 Exterior view from north
3 Exterior view from nortwest
4 Exterior view from southeast

1 Außenansicht von Nordosten
2 Außenansicht von Norden
3 Außenansicht von Nordwesten
4 Außenansicht von Südosten

1

2

1 Living and dining room
2 Dining room
3 First floor plan
4 Section
5 Ground floor plan
6 Site plan
7 Basement plan

1 Wohn- und Esszimmer
2 Esszimmer
3 Grundriss OG
4 Schnitt
5 Grundriss EG
6 Lageplan
7 Grundriss UG

3

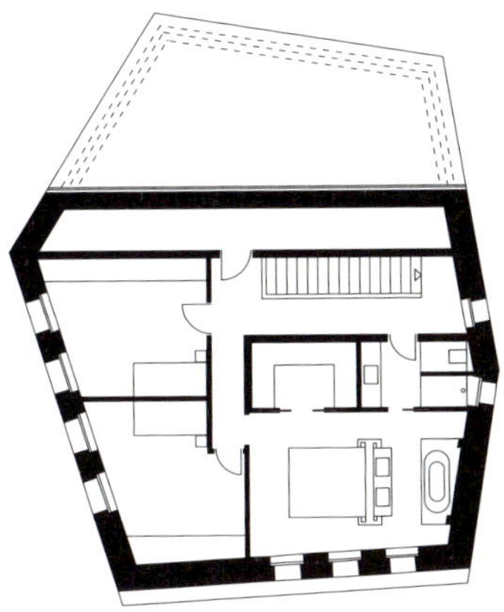

4

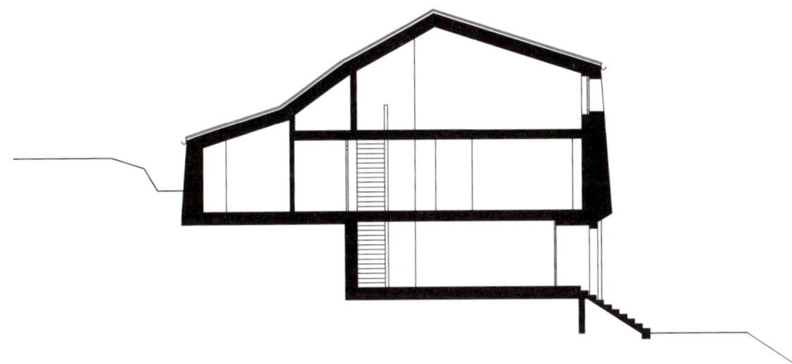

5

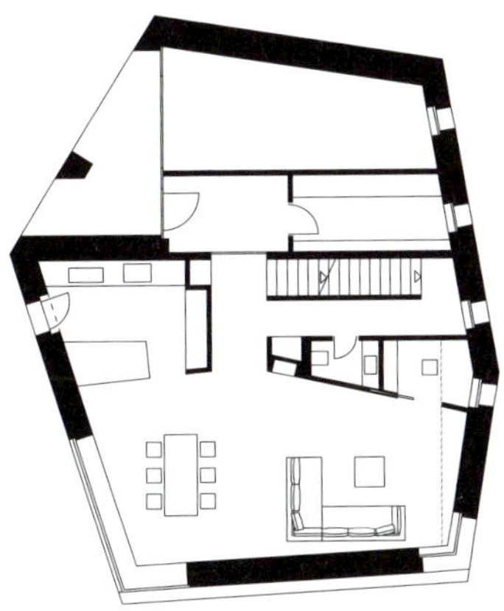

6

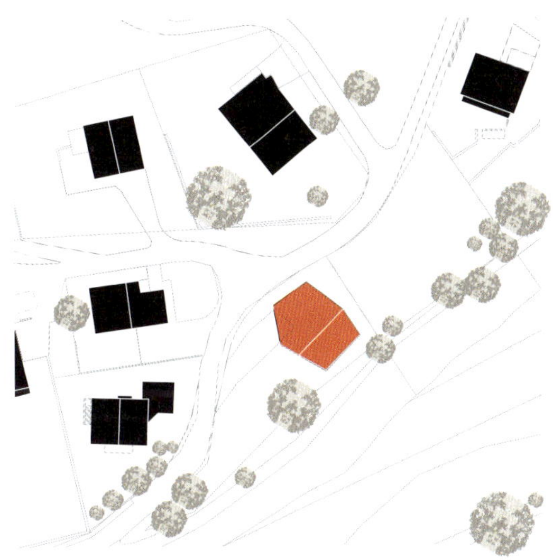

7

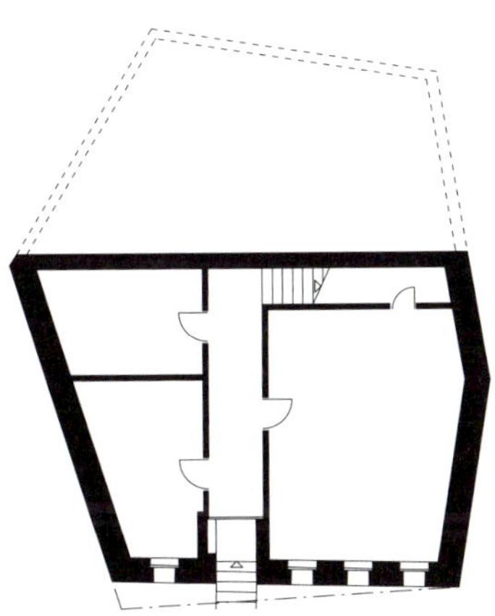

1

ZIEGEL-HAUS

1 Eat-in kitchen
2 Patio
3 Street view

1 Wohnküche
2 Patio
3 Straßenansicht

2

Architects: Triendl und Fessler Architekten
Completion: 2014
Location: Bisamberg, Austria
Gross floor area: 203 m^2
Number of bedrooms: 4
Main materials / building construction: concrete, brick, plaster / solid construction, masonry
Ecological aspects: low-energy house standard

Architekten: Triendl und Fessler Architekten
Fertigstellung: 2014
Ort: Bisamberg, Österreich
Bruttogeschossfläche: 203 m^2
Anzahl der Schlafzimmer: 4
Hauptmaterialien / Konstruktionsweise: Beton, Ziegel, Putz / Massivbau, Mauerwerk
Ökologische Aspekte: Niedrigenergiehaus Standard

The low-budget brick house was designed as a farmhouse type and thus reacts to the local building structure. The hostile attitude of the street-side façade expresses the desire for a retreat on the outskirts of Vienna. The L-shaped floor plan offers a variety of spatial references and, together with the garage and workshop, forms an exciting spatial continuum around the inner courtyard. The high kitchen room on the garden side forms the heart of the residential building and receives a generous extension to the outside through the roofed terrace space. The house was constructed from monolithic brickwork and a conventional timber rafter roof. The brick wall was plastered on the outside and inside and provides an optimal room climate without additional insulation.

Das Low-Budget-Ziegelhaus wurde als Hoftypus konzipiert und reagiert damit auf die ortsübliche Bebauungsstruktur. Die abweisende Haltung der straßenseitigen Fassade drückt den Wunsch nach einem Rückzugsort am Stadtrand Wiens aus. Der L-förmige Grundriss bietet vielfältige Raumbezüge und formt, zusammen mit Garage und Werkstatt, ein spannendes Raumkontinuum um den Innenhof. Der hohe gartenseitige Küchenraum bildet das Herzstück des Wohnhauses und erhält durch den überdachten Terrassenraum eine großzügige Erweiterung nach außen. Konstruiert wurde das Haus aus monolithischem Mauerwerk und einem konventionellen Holzsparrendach. Die Ziegelwand wurde außen und innen verputzt und sorgt für ein optimales Raumklima ohne zusätzliche Dämmung.

3

1

2

1 Garden view
2 Corridor to patio
3 First floor plan
4 Ground floor plan
5 Site plan
6 Cross section

1 Gartenansicht
2 Hausgang zum Patio
3 Grundriss OG
4 Grundriss EG
5 Lageplan
6 Querschnitt

3

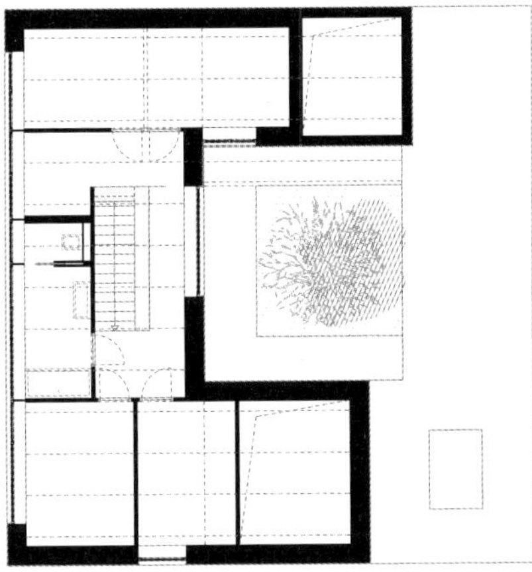

4

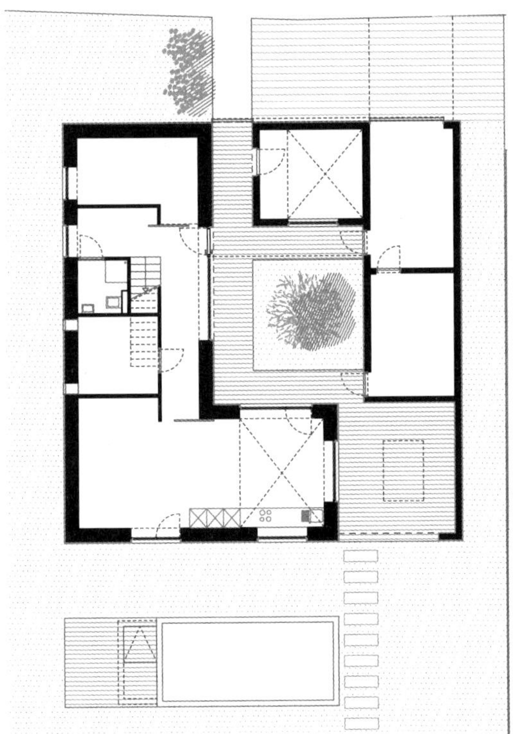

5

6

WOHNHAUS BINDER

1

The pavilion-like residence is formed by a copper roof that rests on a few supports. In keeping with the historical buildings in the townscape, the roof protrudes clearly over the façade on the eaves side, while on the local side the overhang is only slight. Inspired by the buildings in the village, in which the village walls on the outside of the attic were clad in the same color as the roof, the materialization of the residential building is the same all around. The roof as the fifth façade of the house is clad in copper on the outside and appears natural on the inside. The house is a pure timber construction. The modern roof is space-creating and primarily supported by only four pairs of columns inlaid with St. Andrew's crosses. On the slope side, the building, glazed all around, is slightly buried into the terrain. Inside, the offset of the terrain is accompanied by a sideboard along the entire length of the building. An internal core building zones the residential building and at the same time accommodates the adjoining rooms.

Architects: Oliver Christen Architekten
Completion: 2017
Location: Tegerfelden, Switzerland
Gross floor area: 123 m^2
Number of bedrooms: 1
Main materials / building construction: wood, copper, concrete, glass / timber construction
Ecological aspects: external heat generation

2

3

Architekten: Oliver Christen Architekten
Fertigstellung: 2017
Ort: Tegerfelden, Schweiz
Bruttogeschossfläche: 123 m^2
Anzahl der Schlafzimmer: 1
Hauptmaterialien / Konstruktionsweise: Holz, Kupfer, Beton, Glas / Holzkonstruktion
Ökologische Aspekte: externe Wärmeerzeugung

Das pavillonartige Haus wird durch ein kupfernes Dach gebildet, das auf wenigen Stützen aufliegt. Entsprechend den historischen Bauten im Ortsbild, kragt das Dach traufseitig klar über die Fassade aus, während ortseitig der Überstand nur gering ist. Inspiriert von den Gebäuden im Dorf, bei denen die Ortwände im Dachgeschoss außen jeweils in der gleichen Farbigkeit wie das Dach verkleidet wurden, ist die Materialisierung beim Wohnhaus rundherum gleich. Das Dach als fünfte Fassade des Hauses ist außen in Kupfer gekleidet und tritt innen naturbelassen in Erscheinung. Das Wohnhaus wird durch einen reinen Holzbau gebildet. Das moderne Dach ist raumbildend und stützt sich primär auf nur vier Stützenpaaren, ausgefacht mit Andreaskreuzen, auf. Hangseitig gräbt sich das rundum verglaste Gebäude leicht ins Terrain ein. Im Innenraum wird der Terrainversatz durch ein Sideboard über die ganze Gebäudelänge begleitet. Ein innenliegender Kernbau zoniert das Wohnhaus und beherbergt zugleich die Nebenräume.

4

5

1 Garden view
2 Kitchen
3 Living space
4 Sideboard
5 Garden view with surroundings

1 Gartenansicht
2 Küche
3 Wohnraum
4 Sideboard
5 Gartenansicht mit Umgebung

1

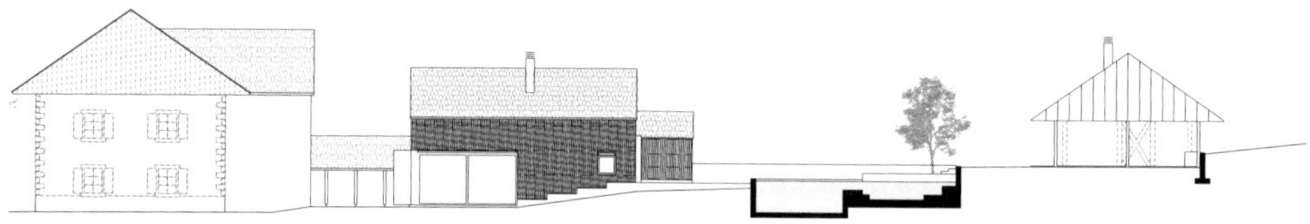

2

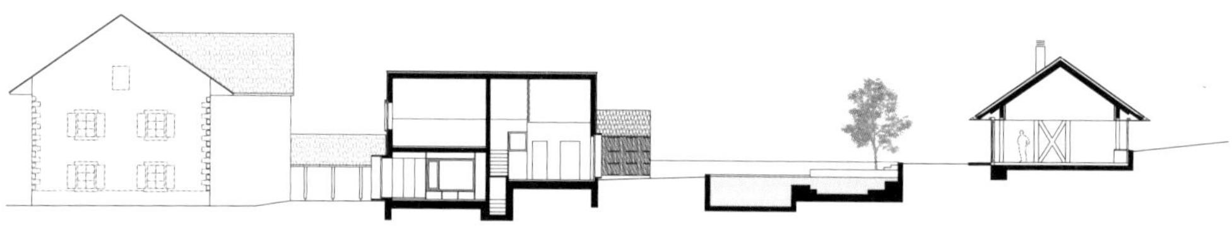

3

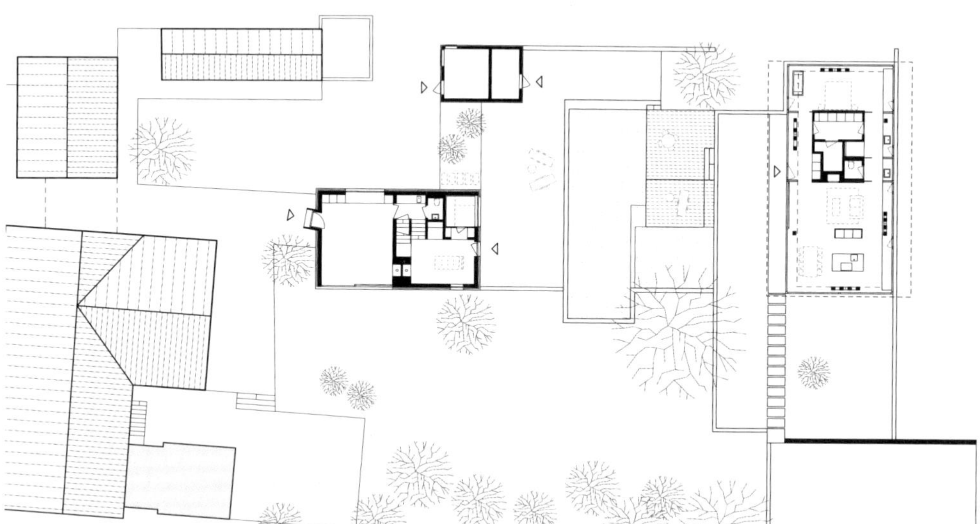

4

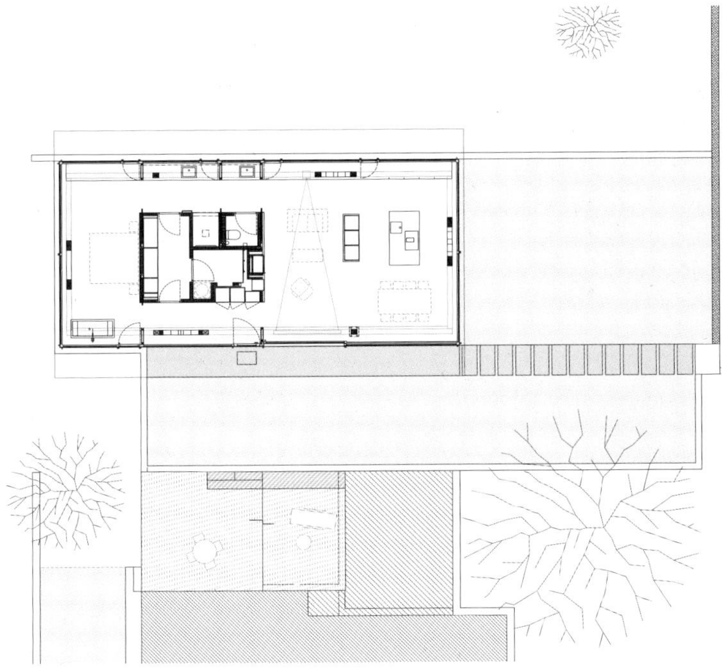

5

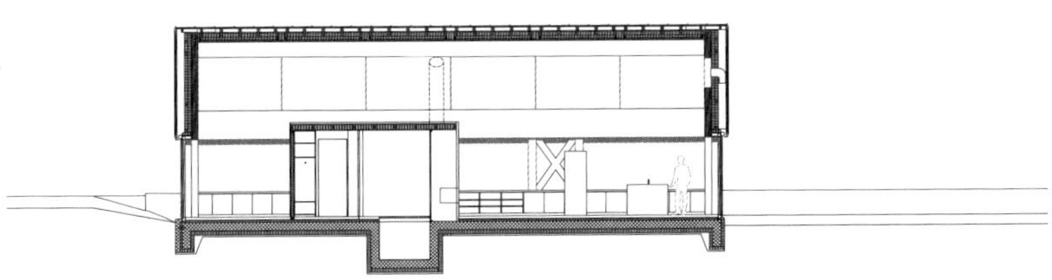

6

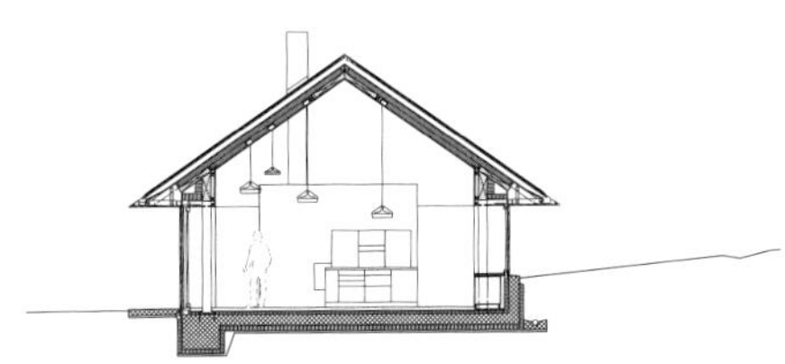

1 South elevation
2 Total cross section south
3 Site plan
4 Ground floor plan
5 Longitudinal section
6 Cross section

1 Aufriss Südseite
2 Gesamtquerschnitt Süd
3 Lageplan
4 Grundriss EG
5 Längsschnitt
6 Querschnitt

BAUERN-HAUS M1

1

The small lined up farm in Jois was converted into a comfortable residential house, including the barn at the rear end of the property. On the one hand the dialogue of old and new elements and on the other hand the spatial interplay between house and yard as well as the different existing levels were the main focus of the planning. For example, a wooden beam ceiling in the current guest room and the roof structure in the air space above the kitchen and living room were retained and integrated into the modern design. Elements such as windows, doors, floors and furniture are made of oak to achieve a harmonious coexistence of old and new. From the gutted barn, the entire front of which can be opened and which houses a swimming pool, among other things, a box in timber frame construction with a cladding of anthracite-colored three-layer panels protrudes. Inside, it has been completely lined with box plywood, with the truss of the old roof construction visibly in front of the wall panels.

Architects: cp architektur
Completion: 2015
Location: Jois, Burgenland, Austria
Gross floor area: 187 m^2 (house); 144 m^2 (barn)
Number of bedrooms: 3 (house); 2 (barn)
Main materials / building construction: oak wood, cement tiles, cast flooring / solid construction (house); larch wood / timber frame construction (barn)
Ecological aspects: air heat pump (house); pure wood construction (barn)

2

3

Architekten: cp architektur
Fertigstellung: 2015
Ort: Jois, Burgenland, Österreich
Bruttogeschossfläche: 187 m^2 (Haus); 144 m^2 (Scheune)
Anzahl der Schlafzimmer: 3 (Haus); 2 (Scheune)
Hauptmaterialien / Konstruktionsweise: Eichenholz, Zementfliesen, Gussböden (Haus); Lärchenholz (Scheune) / Massivbau (Haus); Holzriegelbauweise (Scheune)
Ökologische Aspekte: Luftwärmepumpe (Haus); reiner Holzbau (Scheune)

Der kleine Streckhof in Jois wurde unter Einbeziehung der Scheune am hinteren Ende des Grundstücks zu einem komfortablen Wohnhaus umgebaut. Dabei standen einerseits der Dialog alter und neuer Elemente und andererseits das räumliche Wechselspiel zwischen Haus und Hof sowie den unterschiedlichen vorhandenen Ebenen im Vordergrund der Planung. So wurden zum Beispiel eine Tramdecke, eine Holzbalkendecke, im jetzigen Gästezimmer sowie das Dachtragwerk im Luftraum über Küche und Wohnzimmer erhalten und in die moderne Gestaltung integriert. Elemente wie Fenster, Türen, Böden und Möbel sind in Eiche ausgeführt, um ein harmonisches Miteinander von Alt und Neu zu erreichen. Aus der entkernten Scheune, deren gesamte Vorderfront geöffnet werden kann und die unter anderem ein Schwimmbassin beherbergt, ragt eine Box in Holzriegelbauweise mit einer Verkleidung aus anthrazitfarbenen Dreischichtplatten. Im Inneren wurde sie vollständig mit Kistensperrholz ausgekleidet, wobei das Gebälk des alten Dachstuhls sichtbar vor den Wandscheiben liegt.

4

5

1 Exterior view house and barn
2 Main house kitchen
3 Main house living room
4 Barn with pool area
5 Exterior view barn

1 Außenansicht Haus und Scheune
2 Haupthaus Küche
3 Haupthaus Wohnzimmer
4 Scheune mit Poolbereich
5 Außenansicht Scheune

1

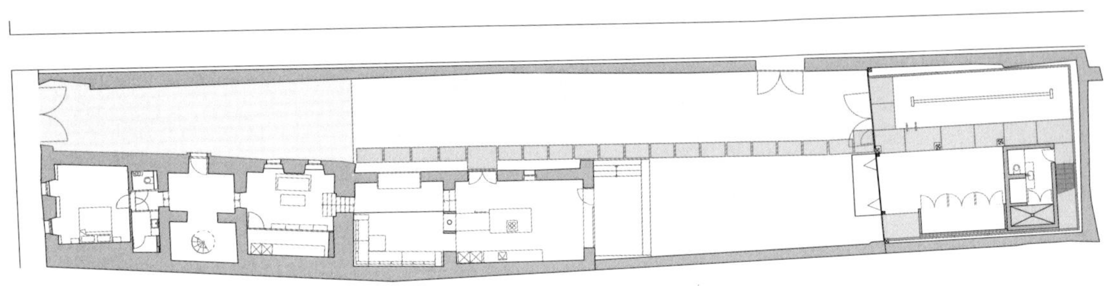

2

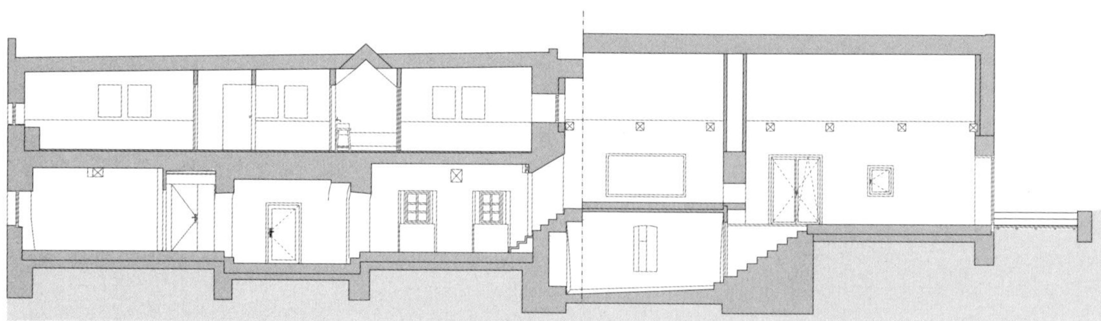

3

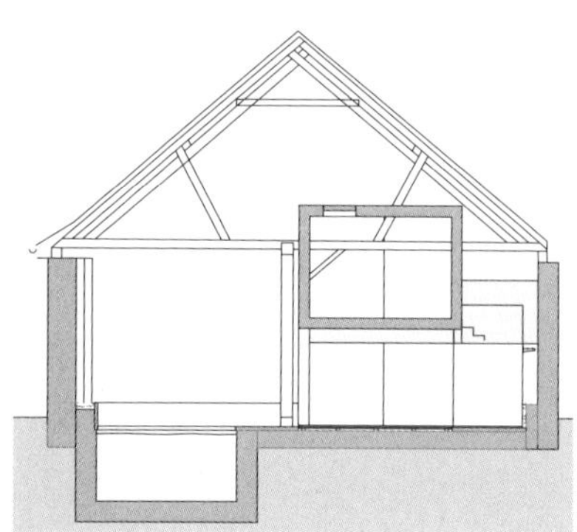

4

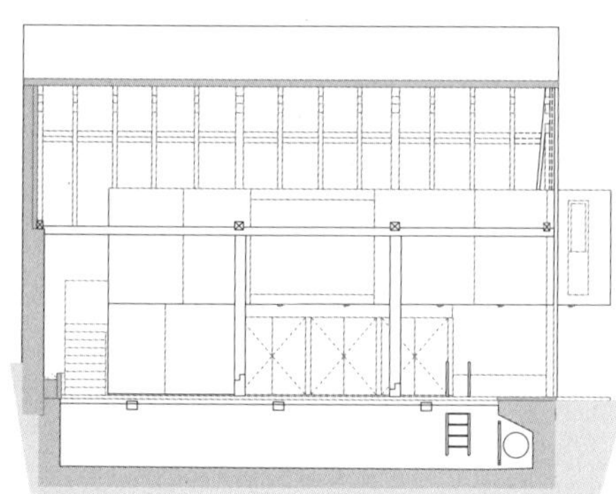

5

6, 7

1 Ground floor plan of main house and barn
2 Section main house
3 Cross section of barn
4 Longitudinal section barn
5 Guest room barn with view of main house and garden
6 Main house reading area
7 Main house entrance area

1 Grundriss EG von Haus und Scheune
2 Schnitt Haupthaus
3 Querschnitt Scheune
4 Längsschnitt Scheune
5 Gästezimmer Scheune mit Blick auf Haupthaus und Garten
6 Haupthaus Lesebereich
7 Haupthaus Eingangsbereich

DOPPELHAUS

1

Architects: MWArchitekten
Completion: 2019
Location: Hohenems, Vorarlberg, Austria
Gross floor area: 170 m²
Number of bedrooms: 3
Main materials / building construction: spruce, cellulose, silver fir, oak / timber frame with intermediate cellulose insulation, prefabricated construction
Ecological aspects: geothermal heat pump, domestic wood, minimal land consumption, compressed construction

Based on the low budget and the desire to create sustainable living space, it was decided to build a semi-detached house consisting of two units. The aim was to create an ecological architecture that would not fall into sterility and artificiality. As a model for this purpose, the architects studied housing typologies developed over generations. The façade design of the semi-detached house on a slope is based on the atmospheric qualities of these traditional buildings. In the interior, the slope makes itself felt in steps leading to the living room and the terrace. Despite its simple timber frame construction insulated with cellulose, the compact volume results in an excellent energy balance of the house. The low-energy house is heated with a geothermal heat pump. Instead of artificial ventilation, there is a fully programmable skylight at the highest point of the staircase, which provides fresh air and night cooling.

2

3

Basierend auf dem geringen Budget und dem Wunsch, nachhaltigen Wohnraum zu schaffen, wurde beschlossen, ein Doppelhaus aus zwei Einheiten zu bauen. Das Ziel war eine ökologische Architektur, die nicht in Sterilität und Künstlichkeit verfällt. Als Modell für diesen Zweck untersuchten die Architekten Wohnbautypologien, die über Generationen entwickelt wurden. Die Fassadengestaltung des Doppelhauses am Hang basiert auf den atmosphärischen Qualitäten dieser traditionellen Bauwerke. Im Innenraum macht sich der Hang in Stufen zum Wohnzimmer und zur Terrasse bemerkbar. Trotz seiner einfachen, mit Zellulose gedämmten Holzrahmenkonstruktion bewirkt das kompakte Volumen eine hervorragende Energiebilanz des Hauses. Das Niedrigenergiehaus wird mit einer Erdwärmepumpe beheizt. Anstelle einer künstlichen Belüftung befindet sich am höchsten Punkt des Treppenhauses ein voll programmierbares Oberlicht, welches für Frischluft und Nachtkühlung sorgt.

Architekten: MWArchitekten
Fertigstellung: 2019
Ort: Hohenems, Vorarlberg, Österreich
Bruttogeschossfläche: 170 m^2
Anzahl der Schlafzimmer: 3
Hauptmaterialien / Konstruktionsweise: Fichte, Zellulose, Weißtanne, Eiche / Holzrahmen mit Zwischendämmung aus Zellulose, Fertigteilbauweise
Ökologische Aspekte: Erdwärmepumpe, heimische Hölzer, minimaler Flächenverbrauch, verdichtete Bauweise

1 Exterior frontal view
2 Exterior view from south
3 Exterior detail
4 Exterior frontal view detail
5 Stairs

1 Außenansicht frontal
2 Außenansicht von Süden
3 Detail Außenansicht
4 Detail Frontansicht
5 Treppe

4, 5

1

2

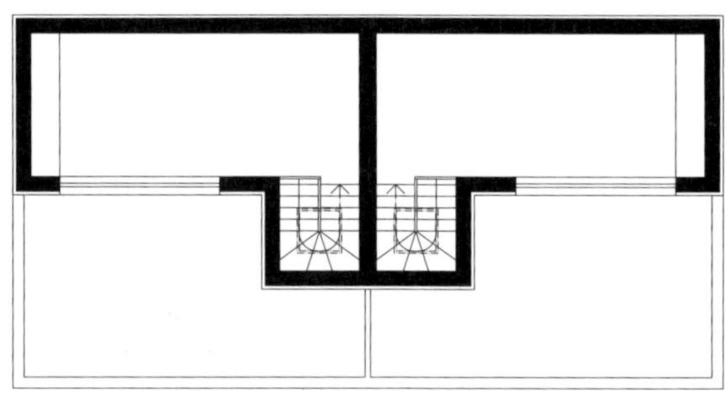

3

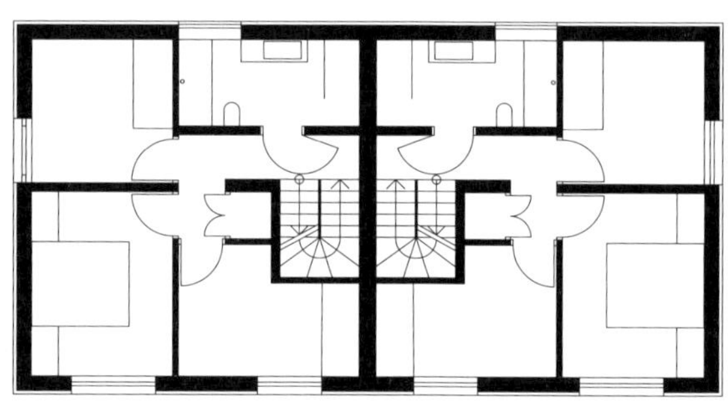

4

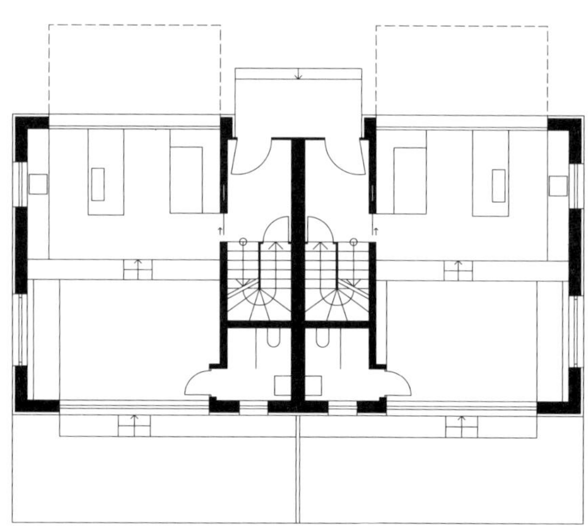

5

6

7

8

1 Site plan
2 Top floor plan
3 First floor plan
4 Ground floor plan
5 Living room
6 Bathroom
7 Living room
8 Bedroom

1 Lageplan
2 Grundriss DG
3 Grundriss OG
4 Grundriss EG
5 Wohnzimmer
6 Badezimmer
7 Wohnzimmer
8 Schlafzimmer

CASA H

1

Casa H is located on a southern slope with an impressive view. It develops its final volume through a process of subtraction of the structure with a gable roof. This creates differentiated spatial situations, resulting in a covered access area and incisions that bring light and views deep into the interior of the building. Functionally, the building is divided into two units. The main apartment extends as a single-family house over three floors. All living rooms face south and towards the valley. A straight staircase between the floors intensifies the focus towards the valley. The choice of materials follows the logic of reduction. The entire building shell is covered with wooden shingles. In addition, stainless steel sheeting is used for all niches. The floor-to-ceiling glazing brings maximum sunlight and views into the interior, where Swiss stone pine and oak create a contrast between light and dark, which is intensified by the use of black steel and dark color accents.

Architects: Plasma Studio
Completion: 2016
Location: Toblach, Aufkirchen, South Tyrol
Gross floor area: 418 m^2
Number of bedrooms: 3 (main house); 2 (granny flat)
Main materials / building construction: concrete, wooden shingle, glass, stainless steel sheet / solid construction, timber roof truss
Ecological aspects: wood fiber insulation, triple glazing, pellet heating, controlled residential ventilation, cooperation with local companies (within a radius of 30 km)

2

3

Architekten: Plasma Studio
Fertigstellung: 2016
Ort: Toblach, Aufkirchen, Südtirol
Bruttogeschossfläche: 418 m²
Anzahl der Schlafzimmer: 3 (Haupthaus). 2 (Einliegerwohnung)
Hauptmaterialien / Konstruktionsweise: Beton, Holzschindel, Glas, Edelstahlblech / Massivbau, Dachstuhl Holz
Ökologische Aspekte: Holzfaserdämmung, Dreifachverglasung, Pelletheizung, kontrollierte Wohnraumlüftung, Zusammenarbeit mit lokalen Firmen (innerhalb eines Radius von 30 km)

Casa H liegt an einem Südhang mit beeindruckender Aussicht. Sie entwickelt ihr endgültiges Volumen durch einen Subtraktionsprozess des Baukörpers mit einem Satteldach. So wurden differenzierte Raumsituationen geschaffen, woraus sich ein überdachter Zugangsbereich sowie Einschnitte ergeben, die Licht und Aussicht tief in das Innere des Hauses bringen. Funktional ist das Gebäude in zwei Einheiten unterteilt. Die Hauptwohnung erstreckt sich als Einfamilienhaus über drei Etagen. Alle Wohnräume sind Richtung Süden und zum Tal hin ausgerichtet. Eine geradläufige Treppe zwischen den Geschossen intensiviert den Fokus zum Tal. Die Materialwahl folgt der Logik der Reduktion: Die gesamte Gebäudehülle wurde mit Holzschindeln eingedeckt. Zusätzlich wurde Edelstahlverblechung für alle Nischen verwendet. Die raumhohen Verglasungen bringen ein Maximum an Sonnenlicht und Aussicht in das Rauminnere, wo Zirbe und Eiche einen Kontrast zwischen hell und dunkel schaffen, der durch die Verwendung von schwarzem Stahl und dunklen Farbakzenten verstärkt wird.

4

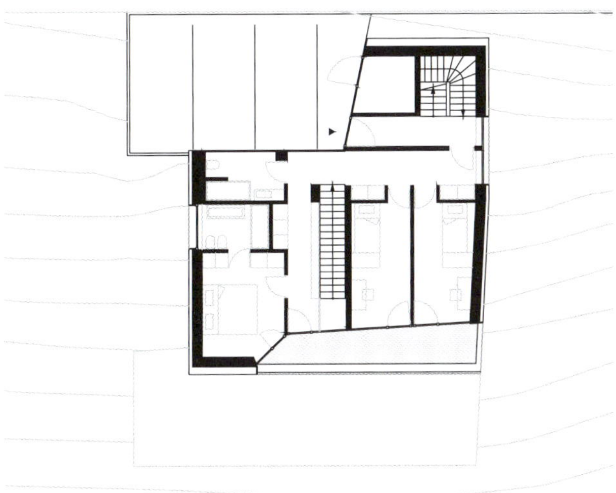

5

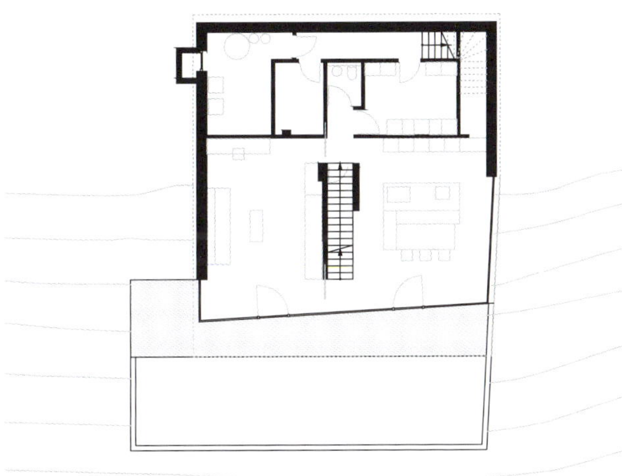

6

1 Exterior view with access road
2 Exterior view from west
3 Living space
4 Access level plan
5 Ground floor plan
6 Stairs

1 Außenansicht mit Zufahrt
2 Außenansicht von Westen
3 Wohnraum
4 Grundriss Zugangsebene
5 Grundriss EG
6 Treppe

1

HAUS DM

1 Street view
2 Garden view
3 Kitchen
4 Living room

1 Straßenansicht
2 Gartenansicht
3 Küche
4 Wohnzimmer

2

Architects: Felix Held Architekt
Completion: 2016
Location: Chur, Switzerland
Gross floor area: 400 m^2
Number of bedrooms: 2
Main materials / building construction: exposed concrete, oak black oiled / standardized wood construction
Ecological aspects: small ecological footprint through good insulation values, heat pump

Architekten: Felix Held Architekt
Fertigstellung: 2016
Ort: Chur, Schweiz
Bruttogeschossfläche: 400 m^2
Anzahl der Schlafzimmer: 2
Hauptmaterialien / Konstruktionsweise: Sichtbeton, Eiche schwarz geölt / Holzbau standardisiert
Ökologische Aspekte: kleiner ökologischer Fußabdruck durch gute Dämmwerte, Wärmepumpe

This house addresses the contradictory demands for public and private life that are made on a residential building on the outskirts of the city. Externally, it is integrated into a tight design plan that defined the building structure and the size of the garden on the hillside. Inside, the rooms develop freely on a three-part floor plan. The large band window of the main floor is set in a dark wooden surface resting on three concrete pillars. Two notched exterior spaces on the ground floor connect it spatially with the neighborhood street, and function as separate entrances. Flat steel stairs divide the elongated structure into two areas on all floors. The music room on the main floor is entered from the intermediate landing of the first staircase, thus separating it from the private area. The bedrooms face the inner courtyard, which doubles the area of the main floor. The access room expands along the façades, creating references to the inner courtyard and the landscape. Black doors and cupboards contrast with the exposed concrete poured between vertical shuttering panels. The residential floor is interpreted as a penthouse, which offers the best views of the local mountain Calanda, the city and the adjoining valley of the Alpine Rhine.

Dieses Haus thematisiert die gegensätzlichen Ansprüche an Öffentlichkeit und Privatheit, die an ein Wohnhaus am Stadtrand gestellt werden. Äußerlich ist es in einen engen Gestaltungsplan eingebunden, der den Baukörper und die Größe des Gartens auf der Hangseite vorgab. Innen entwickeln sich die Räume frei auf einem dreiteiligen Grundriss. Das große Bandfenster des Hauptgeschosses ist in eine dunkle Holzfläche gesetzt, die auf drei Betonpfeilern ruht. Zwei eingekerbte Außenräume im Erdgeschoss verbinden dieses räumlich mit der Quartierstraße, und funktionieren als getrennte Zugänge. Flache Stahltreppen teilen den länglichen Baukörper auf allen Geschossen in zwei Bereiche. Das Musikzimmer im Hauptgeschoss wird vom Zwischenpodest der ersten Treppe betreten und ist damit vom privaten Bereich abgetrennt. Die Schlafräume sind zum Innenhof ausgerichtet, der die Fläche des Hauptgeschosses verdoppelt. Der Erschließungsraum erweitert sich an den Fassaden und schafft Bezüge zu Innenhof und Landschaft. Schwarze Türen und Schränke kontrastieren mit dem Sichtbeton, der zwischen senkrecht stehende Schaltafeln gegossen wurde. Das Wohngeschoss ist als Penthouse interpretiert, das die besten Ausblicke auf den Hausberg Calanda, die Stadt und das anschließende Tal des Alpenrheins bietet.

3, 4

1

2

1 Living room
2 Music room
3 Top floor plan
4 First floor plan
5 Ground floor plan
6 Site plan

1 Wohnzimmer
2 Musikzimmer
3 Grundriss DG
4 Grundriss OG
5 Grundriss EG
6 Lageplan

3

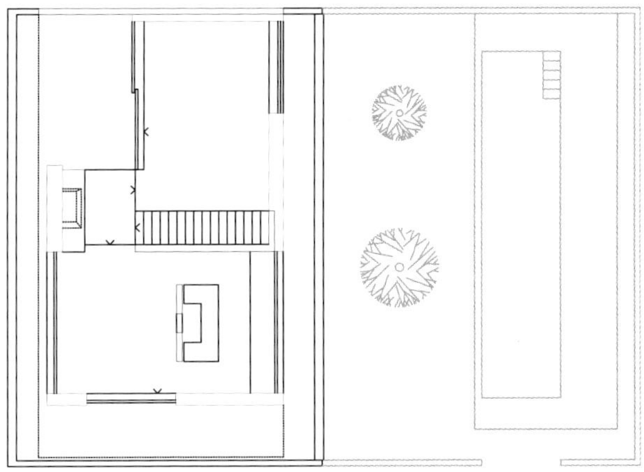

4

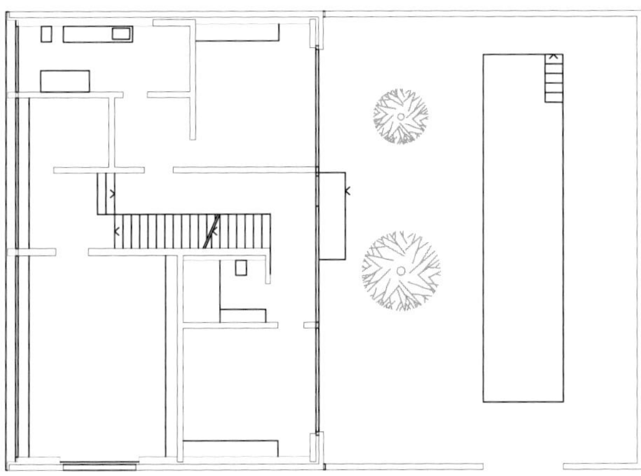

5

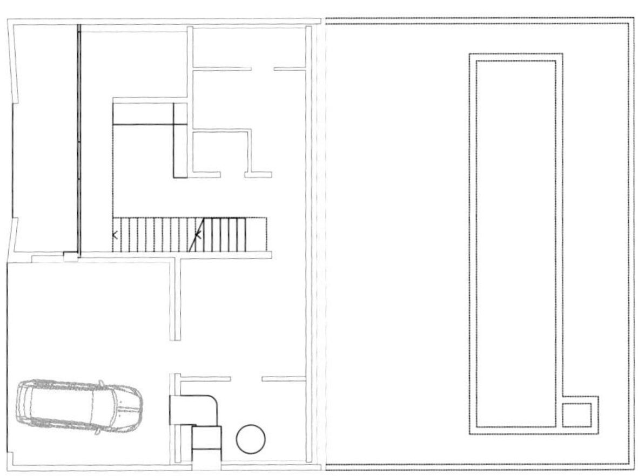

6

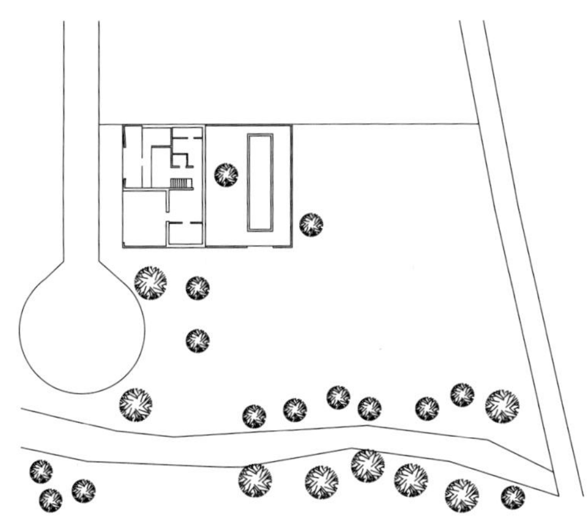

1

6X8 M HAUS

1 Staircase
2 Exterior view from the garden
3 Exterior view from the Lainzer Tiergarten

1 Treppenhaus
2 Außenansicht vom Garten
3 Außenansicht vom Lainzer Tiergarten

2

98

Architects: Tochtermann Wündrich Architekten
Completion: 2015
Location: Vienna, Austria
Gross floor area: 150 m^2
Number of bedrooms: 1
Main materials / building construction: bricks, masonry / solid construction
Ecological aspects: compact building structure, orientation according to solar radiation

Architekten: Tochtermann Wündrich Architekten
Fertigstellung: 2015
Ort: Wien, Österreich
Bruttogeschossfläche: 150 m^2
Anzahl der Schlafzimmer: 1
Hauptmaterialien / Konstruktionsweise: Ziegel, Mauerwerk / Massivbau
Ökologische Aspekte: kompakter Baukörper, Ausrichtung nach Sonneneinstrahlung

Along the stone wall of the enclosure of the Lainzer Tiergarten, which is inhabited by wild boars, one reaches the 6x8 m House. An outside staircase leads to the protected entrance in the basement, which allows the two above-ground floors to be used exclusively for living. The perception of the building's spiral paths is supported by clear rooms, built-in furniture and continuous wooden planks. With the exception of the terrace door, all windows have a square format and thus alternately frame views towards the neighborhood, zoo and the Vienna skyline. The different spatial situations, views and the felt occupation of outside spaces result in a rich and spaciously experienced house on only 150 square meters.

Entlang der Steinmauer des von Wildschweinen belebten Geheges des Lainzer Tiergartens gelangt man zum 6x8 m Haus. Eine Außentreppe führt zum geschützten Hauseingang im Untergeschoss, der es erlaubt, die beiden oberirdischen Geschosse ausschließlich zum Wohnen zu nutzen. Die Wahrnehmung der spiralförmigen Wegverläufe des Gebäudes wird durch klare Räume, Einbaumöbel und durchlaufende Holzdielen unterstützt. Mit Ausnahme der Terrassentür besitzen sämtliche Fenster ein quadratisches Format und rahmen so abwechselnd Ausblicke in Richtung Nachbarschaft, Tiergarten und der Skyline Wiens. Die verschiedenen räumlichen Situationen, Ausblicke und die gefühlte Inbesitznahme von Außenräumen ergeben ein vielseitig und großzügig erlebtes Haus auf nur 150 Quadratmetern.

3

1

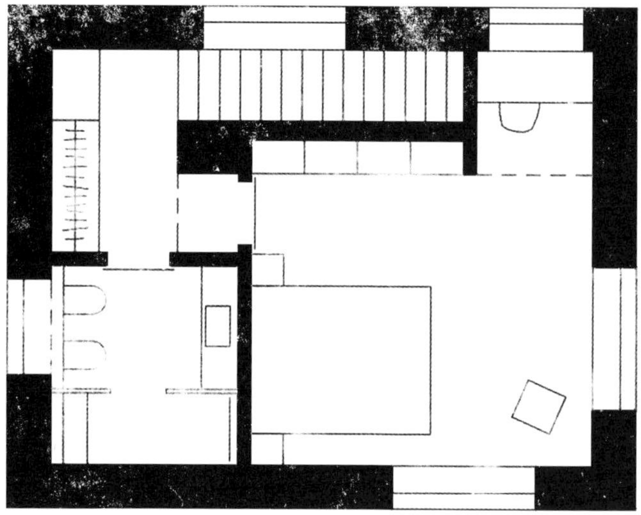

2

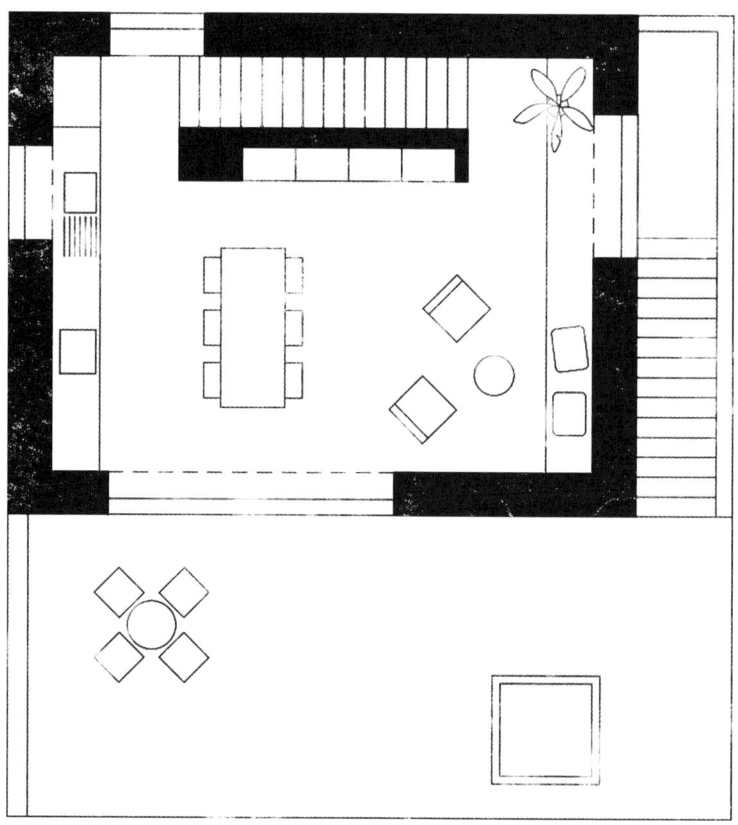

3

4

1 First floor plan
2 Ground floor plan
3 Staircase
4 View towards Vienna

1 Grundriss OG
2 Grundriss EG
3 Treppenhaus
4 Ausblick auf Wien

HAUS MAYER

In the case of the Mayer House, solid wood was used without compromise. The supporting structure consists of five-layer glued cross laminated timber, like the interior walls and the intermediate ceiling do. The entire timber construction is insulated on the outside with wood soft fiber, which not only provides excellent thermal insulation but also effective protection against overheating in summer. The spacious terrace is made entirely of larch wood and can be reached from the inside via various paths. A generous open staircase connects the terrace with the garden. After entering through the front door the rather closed north side of the house immediately reveals its open and permeable opposite on the south side. The spacious, bright living room not only impresses with its warm, friendly wooden surfaces, but also offers views into the nature of the garden and through the expansive terrace it has a flowing transition to the outside. Via a massive oak folding staircase, under which the kitchen is cleverly and compactly arranged, the living area expands into a gallery in the attic, which offers natural light from all directions without allowing unwanted views.

1, 2

Architects: Architekt Michael Nöbauer
Completion: 2018
Location: Schrems, Austria
Gross floor area: 311 m^2
Number of bedrooms: 2
Main materials / building construction: wood (larch, spruce), glass / solid timber construction
Ecological aspects: more than 100 t CO_2 stored in the wood of the project and thus removed from the atmosphere

Architekten: Architekt Michael Nöbauer
Fertigstellung: 2018
Ort: Schrems, Österreich
Bruttogeschossfläche: 311 m^2
Anzahl der Schlafzimmer: 2
Hauptmaterialien / Konstruktionsweise: Holz (Lärche, Fichte), Glas / Holzmassivbauweise
Ökologische Aspekte: über 100 t CO_2 im Holz des Projekts gespeichert und somit der Atmosphäre entzogen

Beim Haus Mayer wurde kompromisslos auf Massivholz gesetzt. Das Tragwerk besteht, wie auch die Innenwände und die Zwischendecke, aus fünfschichtig verleimtem Brettsperrholz. Der gesamte Holzbau ist mit Holzweichfaser außen gedämmt, was nicht nur eine ausgezeichnete Wärmedämmung, sondern auch einen wirksamen Überhitzungsschutz im Sommer gewährleistet. Die großzügige Terrasse besteht zur Gänze aus Lärchenholz und ist über verschiedene Wege aus dem Inneren erreichbar. Eine großzügige Freitreppe verbindet sie mit dem Garten. Die eher geschlossene Nordseite des Hauses offenbart sofort nach dem Eintritt durch die Haustür ihr offenes und durchlässiges Gegenüber auf der Südseite. Der großzügige, helle Wohnraum besticht nicht nur durch die warmen, freundlichen Holzoberflächen. Er bietet zudem Ausblicke in die Natur des Gartens und durch die ausladende Terrasse einen fließenden Übergang ins Freie. Über eine massive Eichenfaltwerktreppe, unter der geschickt und kompakt die Küche angeordnet ist, erweitert sich der Wohnbereich zu einer Galerie im Dachraum, die natürliches Licht aus allen Richtungen bietet, ohne unerwünschte Einblicke zu erlauben.

3

4

1 Terrace west
2 Roof space
3 Exterior view from northeast
4 Living area

1 Terrasse West
2 Dachraum
3 Außenansicht von Nordosten
4 Wohnbereich

1

2

1 Exterior view from southwest
2 Bathroom and living area
3 Section
4 Top floor plan
5 Ground floor plan
6 Site plan

1 Außenansicht von Südwesten
2 Badezimmer und Wohnbereich
3 Gebäudeschnitt
4 Grundriss DG
5 Grundriss EG
6 Lageplan

3

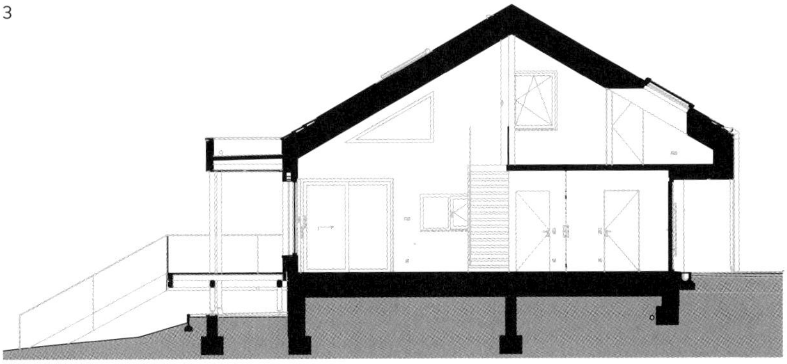

4

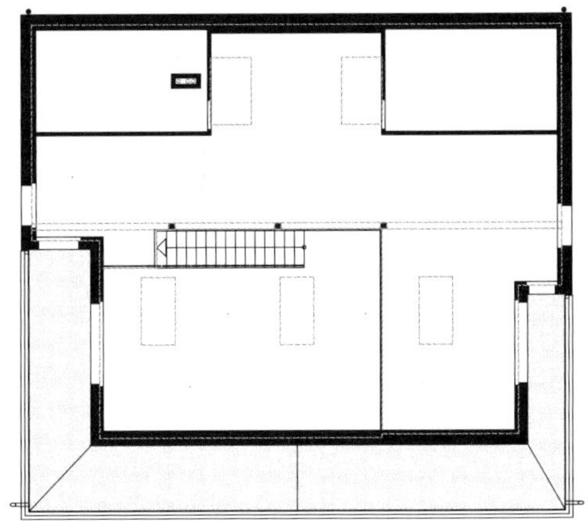

5

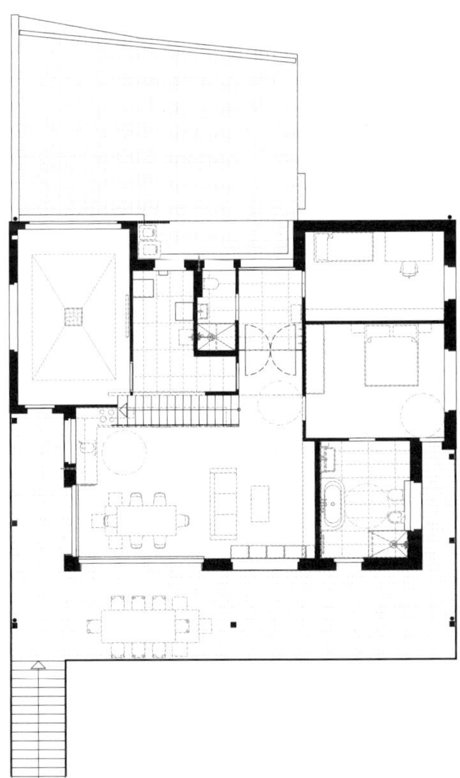

6

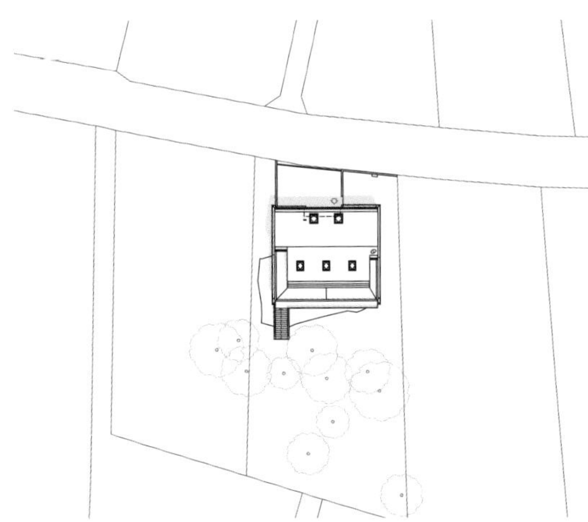

EFH ST. PETER

1

Architects: Bogenfeld Architektur
Completion: 2016
Location: St. Peter in der Au, Austria
Gross floor area: 271.45 m^2
Number of bedrooms: 3
Main materials / building construction: wood, reinforced concrete / reinforced concrete slab, two reinforced concrete cores, timber frame construction
Ecological aspects: natural building materials

The builders of the family home in St. Peter in der Au, a young family, wanted a house made of wood from the very beginning. The property is part of a grown settlement, but very large. In the past the former vicarage was located here. The size protects and creates a loose distance to the neighbors. Accordingly, the house does not directly relate to existing buildings but is purely oriented towards the topography, the shape of the plot, the needs of the family and of course the sun. Thus it stands quite freely in the middle, a small house with a large roof.

Except for the floor slab, the sanitary core and the staircase, only wood was actually used. The floor plan is simple and robust. The development is constructed in such a way that the top and bottom can be seperated at any time. This provides a flexibility that was not only very important to the builders, but is essential especially for single-family homes in order not to appear too large and rigid.

2

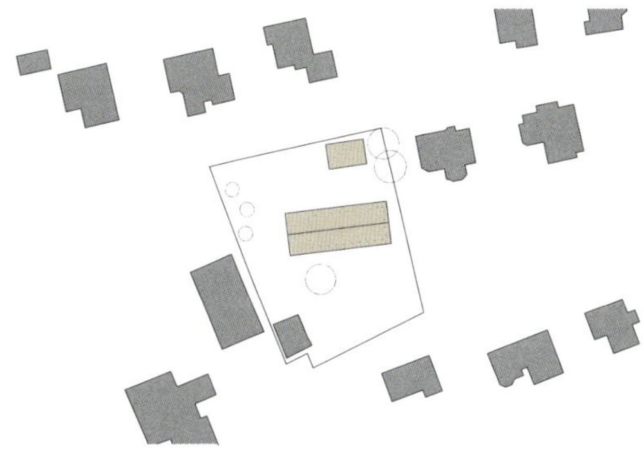

3

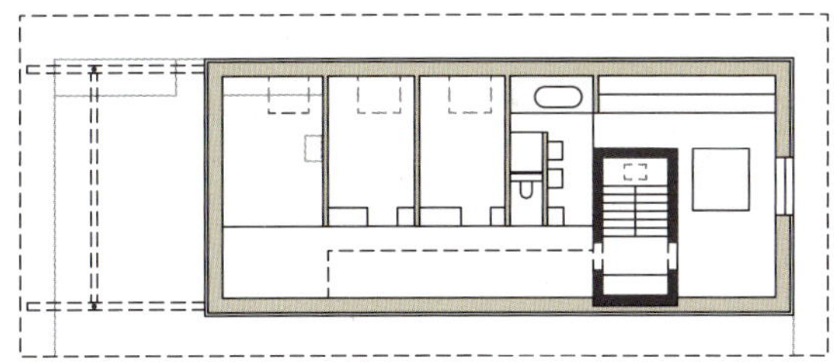

4

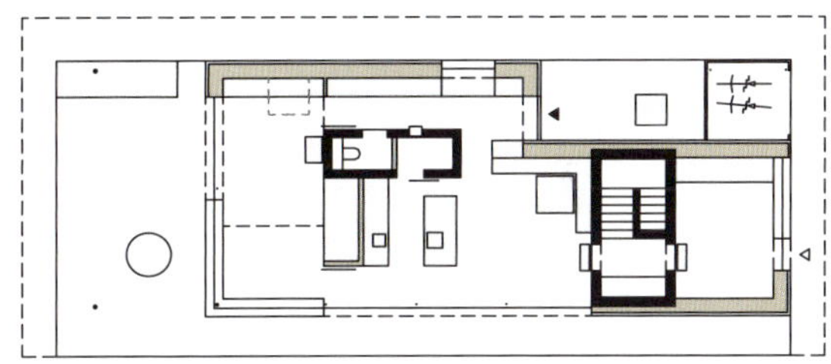

5

Die Bauherren des Wohnhauses St. Peter in der Au, eine junge Familie, wollten von Beginn an ein Haus aus Holz. Das Grundstück ist Teil einer gewachsenen Siedlung, aber sehr groß. Früher befand sich hier der ehemalige Pfarrhof. Die Größe schützt und schafft eine lockere Distanz zu den Nachbarn. Entsprechend nimmt das Haus keinen direkten Bezug zu Bestandsbauten, sondern orientiert sich rein an der Topografie, der Form des Grundstücks, den Bedürfnissen der Familie und natürlich der Sonne. So steht es recht frei in der Mitte, ein kleines Haus mit großem Dach.

Von der Bodenplatte, dem Sanitärkern und dem Treppenhaus abgesehen wurde tatsächlich nur Holz verwendet. Der Grundriss ist einfach und robust. Die Erschließung ermöglicht, dass die Ebenen jederzeit entkoppelt werden können. Das bringt eine Flexibilität, die nicht nur den Bauherren sehr wichtig war, sondern die gerade bei Einfamilienhäusern essenziell ist, um nicht zu groß und starr zu wirken.

Architekten: Bogenfeld Architektur
Fertigstellung: 2016
Ort: St. Peter in der Au, Österreich
Bruttogeschossfläche: 271,45 m^2
Anzahl der Schlafzimmer: 3
Hauptmaterialien / Konstruktionsweise: Holz, Stahlbeton / Stahlbetonplatte, zwei Stahlbetonkerne, Holzriegelkonstruktion
Ökologische Aspekte: natürliche Baustoffe

1 Exterior view from south in summer
2 Exterior view from west
3 Site plan
4 First floor plan
5 Ground floor plan
6 Living area
7 Entry niche
8 Dining area

1 Außenansicht von Süden im Sommer
2 Außenansicht von Westen
3 Lageplan
4 Grundriss OG
5 Grundriss EG
6 Wohnbereich
7 Eingangsnische
8 Essbereich

6, 7, 8

HAUS B

1

House B is strongly related to the surrounding buildings on Schulstraße, which are characterized by gabled façades. This theme is taken up in the northern part of the building, where a two-story, asymmetrical gable façade has been implemented accordingly. While the volume presents itself to the north with a two-story, asymmetrical gable façade, the form towards the south follows an over-high story of the inner function. Through this "form follows function" the expressive and monolithic cubature was crystallized step by step. The northern part of the volume contains a double garage, entrance and bedrooms. In the southern volume is the over-height living area and a working gallery, which offers exciting views and spatial references through precisely placed openings. The building envelope including the roof is made of in-situ concrete. Inside, all horizontal surfaces were also made of concrete. In order to give the rooms additional warmth, all built-in elements such as the kitchen, doors, wardrobe and windows were made of oak.

Architects: moos giuliani herrmann architekten
Completion: 2017
Location: Diessenhofen, Switzerland
Gross floor area: 252 m^2
Number of bedrooms: 5
Main materials / building construction: concrete, aluminum, wood / solid construction
Ecological aspects: heat pump

2

3

Architekten: moos giuliani herrmann architekten
Fertigstellung: 2017
Ort: Diessenhofen, Schweiz
Bruttogeschossfläche: 252 m^2
Anzahl der Schlafzimmer: 5
Hauptmaterialien / Konstruktionsweise: Beton, Aluminium, Holz / Massivbau
Ökologische Aspekte: Wärmepumpe

Haus B bezieht sich stark auf die, von Giebelfassaden geprägten, umliegenden Gebäude an der Schulstraße. Dieses Thema wird im nördlichen Teil des Gebäudes aufgegriffen, wo eine zweistöckige, asymmetrische Giebelfassade entsprechend umgesetzt wurde. Während sich das Volumen nördlich mit einer zweistöckigen, asymmetrischen Giebelfassade präsentiert, folgt die Form gegen Süden einem überhohen Geschoss der inneren Funktion. Durch dieses „form follows function" wurde Schritt für Schritt die expressive und monolithische Kubatur herauskristallisiert. Der nördliche Teil des Volumens beinhaltet eine Doppelgarage, das Entree und Schlafzimmer. Im südlichen Volumen befindet sich der überhohe Wohnbereich und eine Arbeitsgalerie, die durch präzis gesetzte Öffnungen spannende Blick- und Raumbezüge bietet. Die Gebäudehülle inklusive Dach besteht aus Ortbeton. Im Inneren wurden sämtliche horizontale Flächen ebenfalls in Beton gefertigt. Um den Räumen zusätzlich Wärme zu verleihen, wurden alle Einbauelemente wie Küche, Türen, Garderobe und Fenster in Eiche ausgeführt.

4

5

6

1 Garden view from southeast
2 Wardrobe
3 Exterior view from the street
4 Entrance
5 Living space
6 Garden view from southwest

1 Gartenansicht von Südosten
2 Garderobe
3 Außenansicht Straßenseite
4 Eingang
5 Wohnraum
6 Gartenansicht von Südwesten

1

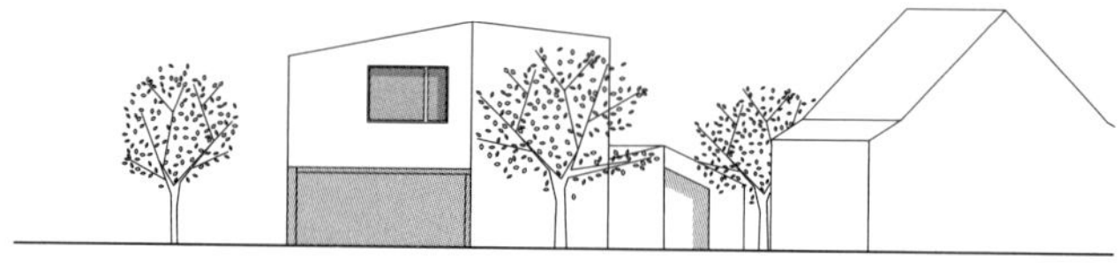

2

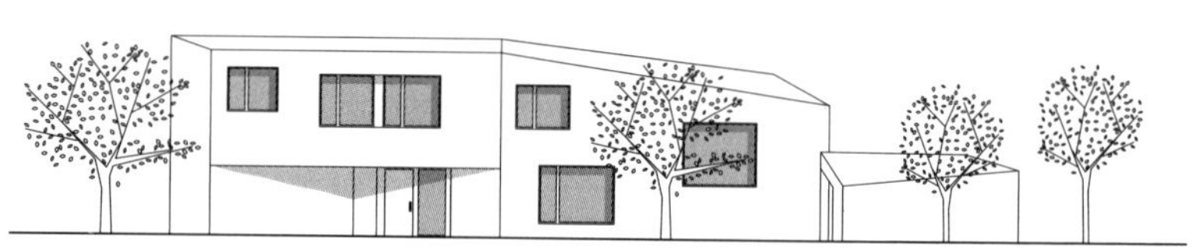

3

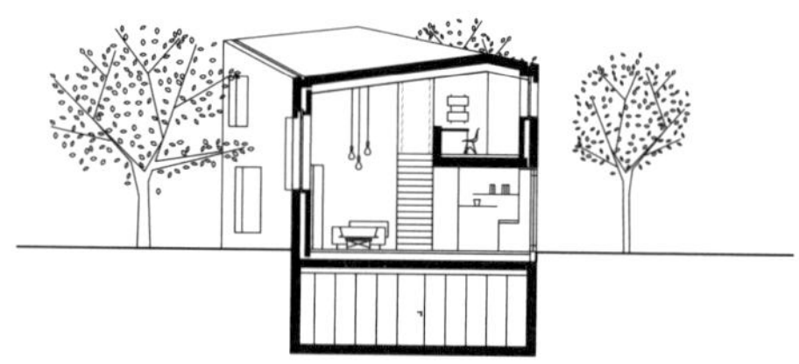

4

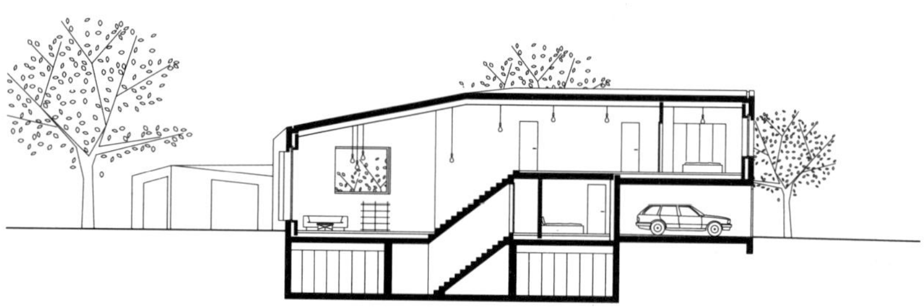

1 Street elevation
2 Garden elevation
3 Cross section
4 Longitudinal section
5 First floor plan
6 Ground floor plan
7 Site plan

1 Ansicht Straßenseite
2 Ansicht Gartenseite
3 Querschnitt
4 Längsschnitt
5 Grundriss OG
6 Grundriss EG
7 Lageplan

5

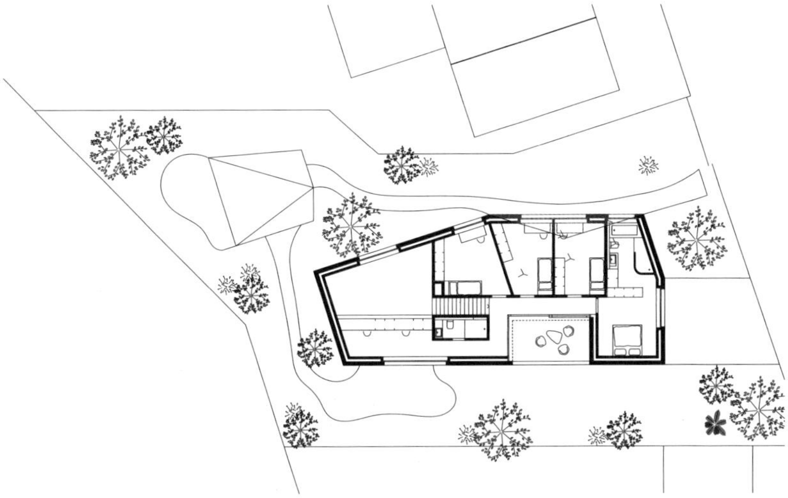

6

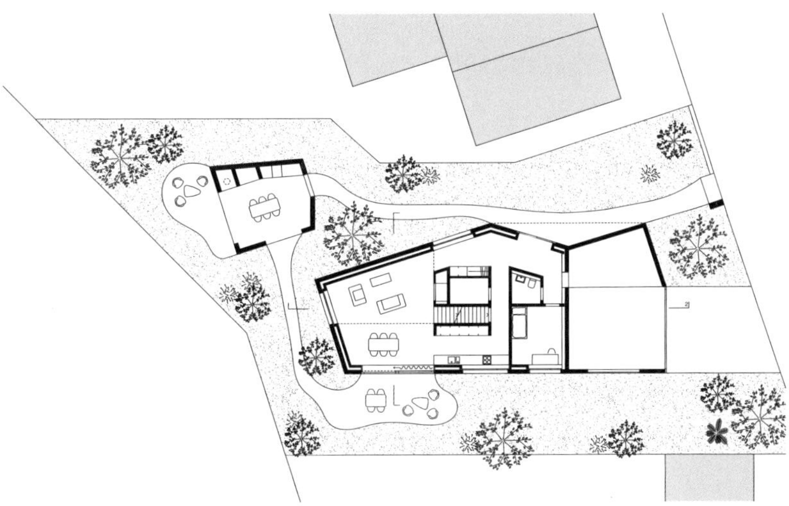

7

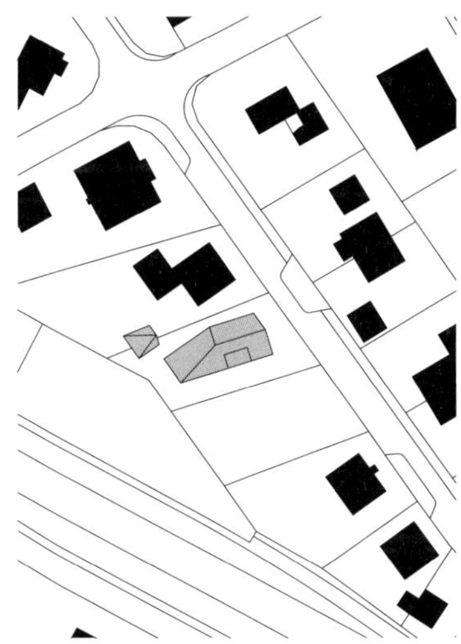

HAUS R

1

In order to reduce the substantial heat losses the existing house dating from 1936 had to be renovated. Moreover, part of the large building was to be rented out in the future, so the architects had to reconfigure the interior with two maisonettes. Both demands resulted in a complete change of architectural expression. Two large roof overhangs, like aeroplane wings, create a spacious shaded terrace to the south and a covered space on the north side. These large overhangs have light tunnel openings oriented according to the sun's path, offering protection from the heat in summer and the possibility to benefit from direct sunlight in winter. The façades have a simple horizontal cladding in pre-grayed wood. Particular attention has been given to the treatment of the window frames, whose opening angles are oriented according to the course of the sun. As an allusion to classic buildings of the early 20th century, the architecture of Scarpa and old cameras the window flanning is made up of narrow wood fluting, created by simply staggering the planks used for the cladding.

Architects: Lacroix Chessex
Completion: 2015
Location: Coppet, Switzerland
Gross floor area: 350 m^2
Number of bedrooms: 5
Main materials / building construction: wood
Ecological aspects: reuse of existing building

2

3

Architekten: Lacroix Chessex
Fertigstellung: 2015
Ort: Coppet, Schweiz
Bruttogeschossfläche: 350 m²
Anzahl der Schlafzimmer: 5
Hauptmaterialien / Konstruktionsweise: Holz
Ökologische Aspekte: Weiternutzung eines Altbaus

Das Haus aus dem Jahr 1936 musste renoviert werden, um die erheblichen Wärmeverluste zu reduzieren. Zudem sollte ein Teil des großen Gebäudes künftig vermietet werden, sodass die Architekten den Innenraum mit zwei Maisonettes ausbauen mussten. Beides führte zu einer völligen Veränderung des architektonischen Ausdrucks. Zwei große Dachüberstände bilden, wie Flugzeugflügel, im Süden eine großzügige, schattige Terrasse, im Norden geschützten Raum. Nach dem Lauf der Sonne ausgerichtet, bieten sie im Sommer Schutz vor Hitze, während im Winter Lichtschächte direkte Sonneneinstrahlung zulassen. Die Fassaden zeigen eine einfache horizontale Verkleidung aus vorvergrautem Holz. Der Öffnungswinkel der Fensterrahmen richtet sich nach dem Lauf der Sonne. Die Fensterlaibungen bestehen aus schmalen Holzrippen, die durch einfaches Versetzen der für die Verkleidung verwendeten Bretter entstehen. Diese Umsetzung ist sowohl eine Anspielung auf klassische Gebäude des frühen 20. Jahrhunderts als auch auf die Architektur von Carlo Scarpa, aber auch auf alte Kameras.

4

5

1 Large roof sheltering open space
2 Original building
3 Contemporary expression
4 Openings provide light under the cantilevering roof
5 Window flanning according to the course of the sun

1 Großes, den Freiraum schützendes Dach
2 Ursprungsbau
3 Zeitgemäße Umformung
4 Öffnungen gewährleisten Licht unterhalb des Dachüberstands
5 Fensterlaibungen dem Sonnenlauf entsprechend

1

2, 3

1 Light-flooded living room
2 Building between dense vegetation
3 Living room
4 West elevation
5 Longitudinal section
6 First floor plan
7 Ground floor plan

1 Lichtdurchflutetes Wohnzimmer
2 Gebäude inmitten der Vegetation
3 Wohnzimmer
4 Aufriss Westseite
5 Längsschnitt
6 Grundriss OG
7 Grundriss EG

4

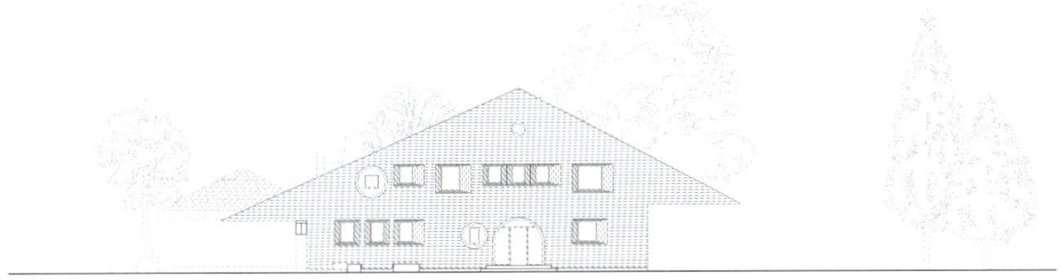

5

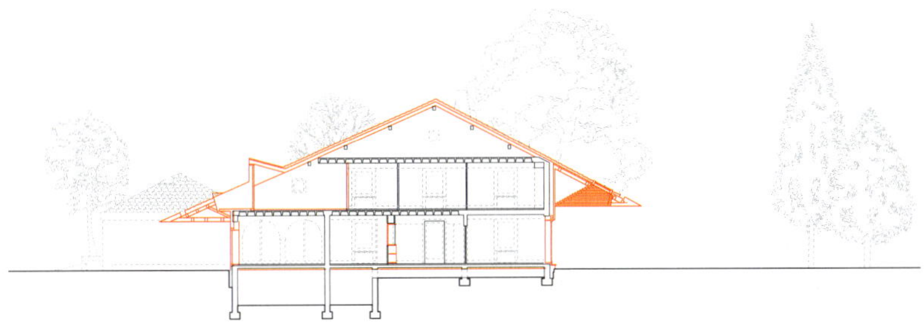

6

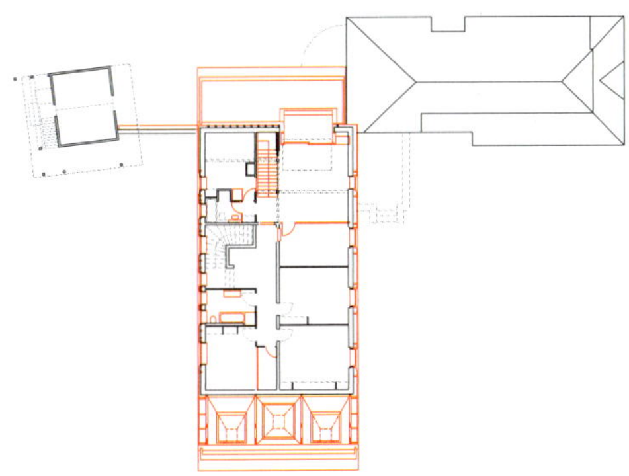

7

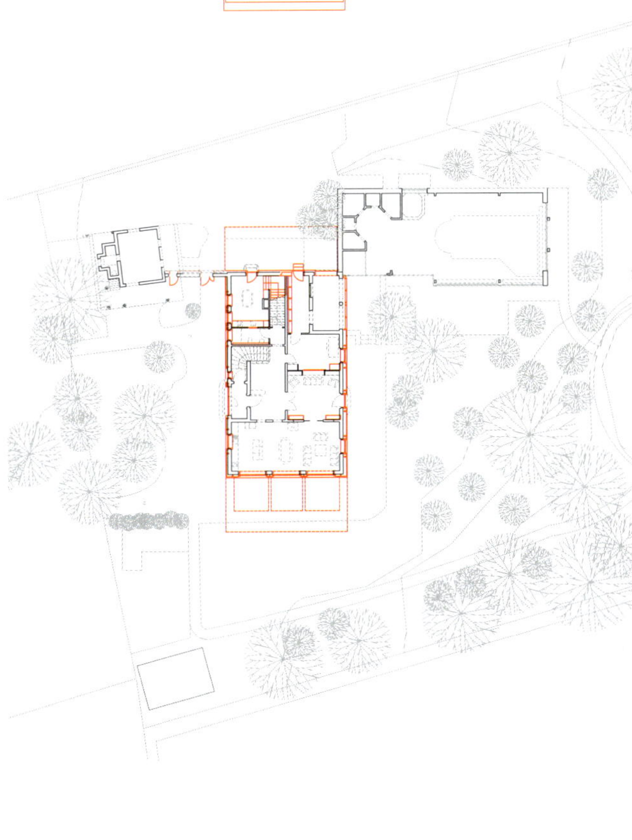

HAUS 3B

To take advantage of the view of the small valley in the canton of Aargau, Haus 3B is situated high up on the steep hillside property. Access is provided by a garage at street level, which is mostly sunken, and an underground staircase connecting the entrance and the residential house. The earth-facing areas are made of exposed concrete and structured with a pine plywood formwork. Above this sits – precisely interlocking in the interior – a timber frame construction, outside with shingles, inside with untreated paneling and rough-sawn planks of silver fir. All levels are inserted into the topography in such a way that direct exterior areas could be assigned. The living level, with a striking incision in the otherwise unobtrusively simple structure, offers a partially covered terrace with a concrete element extending the kitchenette into the open air as a grill and work surface. One floor below, the children's rooms also have direct access to the garden. The attic is reserved for the parents and is partly lit by precisely placed skylights and can be ventilated.

1, 2

Architects: Juri Troy Architects
Completion: 2017
Location: Bottenwil, Aargau, Switzerland
Gross floor area: 285.8 m^2
Number of bedrooms: 3
Main materials / building construction: cedar wood shingles as roof covering, silver fir shingles for the façade, exposed concrete, maritime pine formwork, cellulose blow-in insulation / in-situ concrete, timber frame construction
Ecological aspects: Minergie-P standard (passive house), heat pump with deep drilling, controlled ventilation of living space with heat exchanger

Architekten: Juri Troy Architects
Fertigstellung: 2017
Ort: Bottenwil, Aargau, Schweiz
Bruttogeschossfläche: 285,8 m^2
Anzahl der Schlafzimmer: 3
Hauptmaterialien / Konstruktionsweise: Zedernholzschindeln als Dachdeckung, Weißtannenschindeln für Fassade, Sichtbeton, Seekiefernschalung, Zelluloseeinblasdämmung / Ortbeton, Holzriegelbau
Ökologische Aspekte: Minergie-P Standard (Passivhaus), Wärmepumpe mit Tiefenbohrung, kontrollierte Wohnraumlüftung mit Wärmetauscher

Um die Aussicht in das kleine Tal im Kanton Aargau auszunutzen, sitzt das Haus weit oben auf dem steilen Hanggrundstück. Die Erschließung erfolgt über eine auf Straßenniveau liegende, größtenteils versenkte Garage und eine unterirdische Treppe, die Eingang und Wohnhaus verbindet. Die erdanliegenden Bereiche sind aus Sichtbeton und mit einer Kiefersperrholzschalung strukturiert. Darüber sitzt – sich im Innenraum präzise verzahnend – ein Holzriegelbau, außen mit Schindeln, innen mit unbehandeltem Täfer und sägerauen Dielen aus Weißtanne verkleidet. Alle Niveaus sind so in die Topografie eingesetzt, dass direkte Außenbereiche zugeordnet werden konnten. Jener auf der Wohnebene bietet mit einem markanten Einschnitt in den sonst zurückhaltend einfach gestalteten Baukörper eine teils überdachte Terrasse mit einem die Küchenzeile ins Freie verlängernden Betonelement als Grill und Arbeitsfläche. Ein Stockwerk darunter liegen die Kinderzimmer, ebenfalls mit direktem Ausgang in den Garten. Das Dachgeschoss ist den Eltern vorbehalten und teilweise über präzise gesetzte Oberlichter belichtet und belüftbar.

3

4

1 Exterior view from west
2 View from the loggia into the house
3 Exterior view from southwest
4 Living room

1 Außenansicht von Westen
2 Blick von der Loggia ins Haus
3 Außenansicht von Südwesten
4 Wohnzimmer

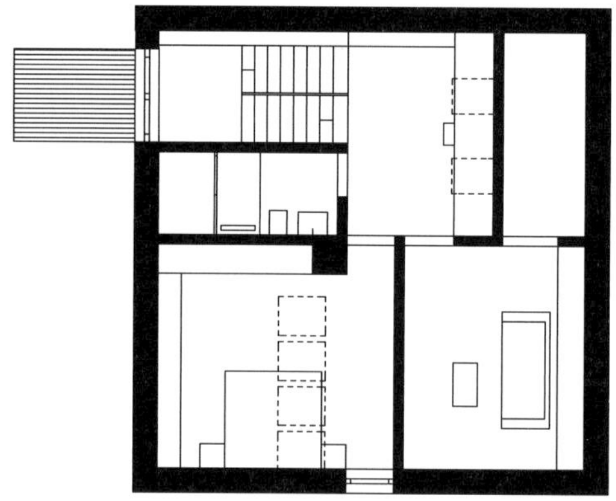

1

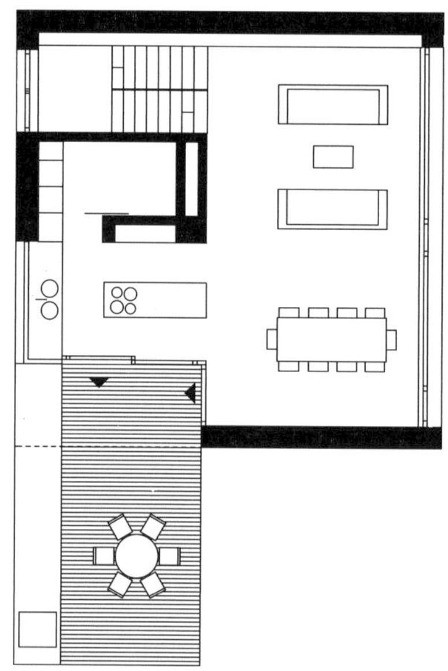

2

3

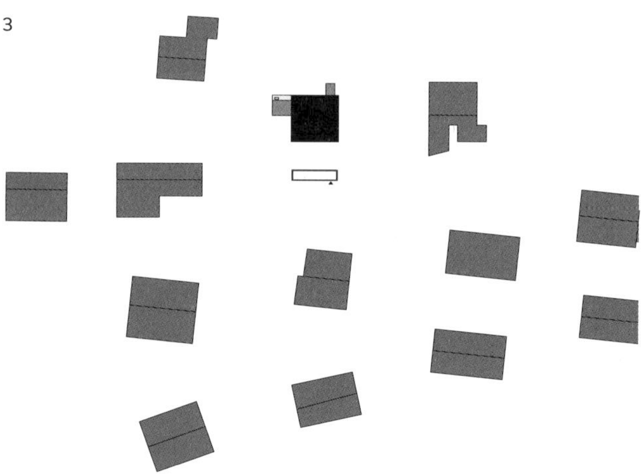

4

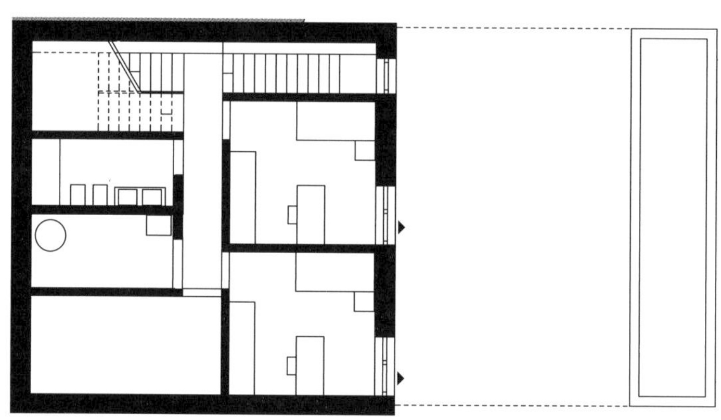

1 Second floor plan
2 First floor plan
3 Site plan
4 Ground floor plan
5 3D view
6 Southeast elevation
7 Cross section

1 Grundriss 2. OG
2 Grundriss 1. OG
3 Lageplan
4 Grundriss EG
5 3-D-Ansicht
6 Aufriss Südostseite
7 Querschnitt

5

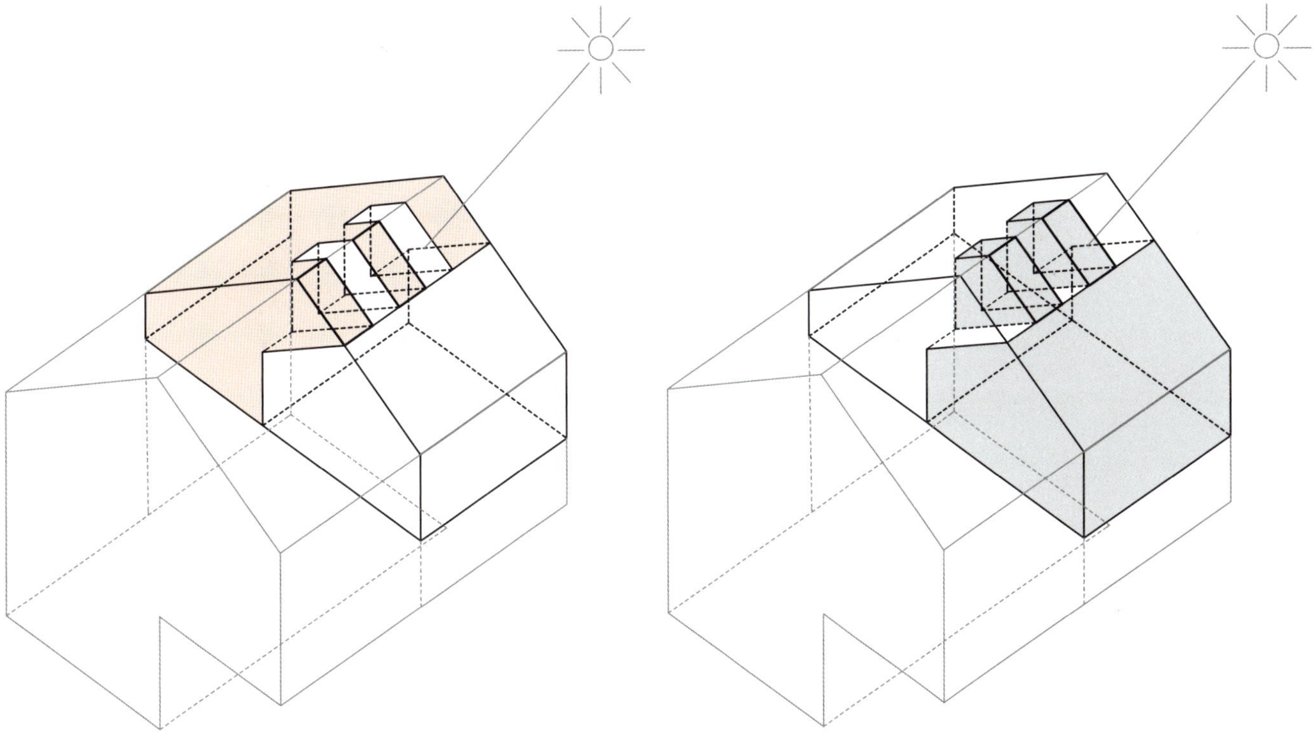

6

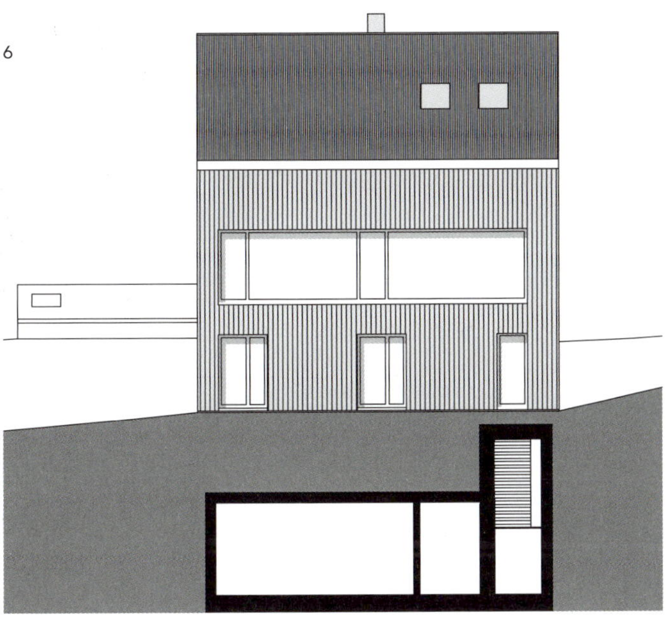

7

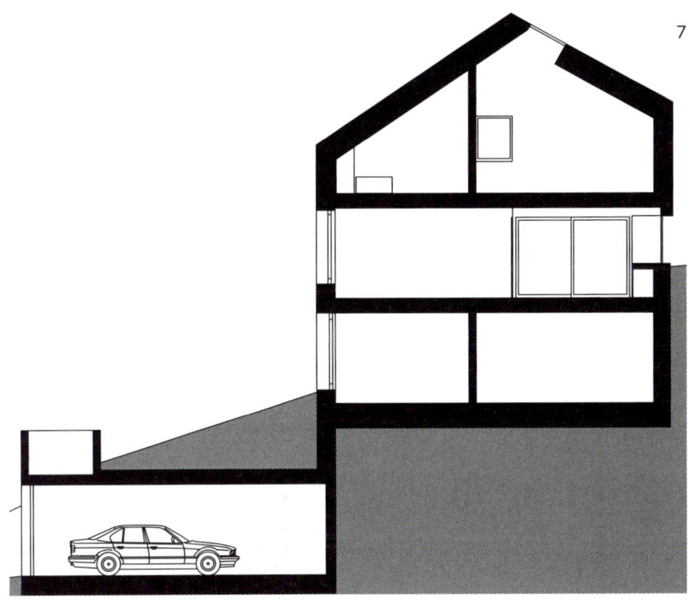

1

EFH MEIER

1 Façade
2 Exterior view from southwest
3 Bathroom

1 Fassade
2 Außenansicht von Südwesten
3 Badezimmer

2

Architects: auer.conte architekten
Completion: 2015
Location: Betschwanden, Glarus, Switzerland
Gross floor area: 85 m^2
Number of bedrooms: 3
Main materials / building construction: wood, concrete / element construction on concrete base with ventilated façade
Ecological aspects: solid concrete core as storage mass, heat pump

Architekten: auer.conte architekten
Fertigstellung: 2015
Ort: Betschwanden, Glarus, Schweiz
Bruttogeschossfläche: 85 m^2
Anzahl der Schlafzimmer: 3
Hauptmaterialien / Konstruktionsweise: Holz, Beton / Elementbauweise auf Betonsockel mit hinterlüfteter Fassade
Ökologische Aspekte: massiver Kern aus Beton als Speichermasse, Wärmepumpe

The house was built as a wooden structure on a concrete base, with traditional elements typical of the Glarnerland. With its soft shell of wood and the hard core of concrete, which is obviously separated and serves as a storage mass, the new building offers a pleasant and homely indoor climate. The base projecting upwards on the north side protects the wooden façade from the weather and houses the kitchen in the bricked part according to the traditional model. The strictly structured and straight-lined exterior forms a strong contrast to the interior of the house, which describes a room plan based on the model of Adolf Loos. Continuous bands structure the façade and at the same time act as window sills and guide rails for the sliding shutters.

Das Haus wurde als Holzbau auf einem Betonsockel mit traditionellen, für das Glarnerland typischen Elementen erstellt. Mit seiner weichen Hülle aus Holz und dem harten Kern aus Beton, welcher offensichtlich entkoppelt ist und als Speichermasse dient, bietet der Neubau ein angenehmes und wohnliches Raumklima. Der nordseitig hochragende Sockel schützt die Holzfassade vor dem Wetter und beherbergt die Küche nach traditionellem Vorbild im gemauerten Bereich. Das streng gegliederte und gradlinige Äußere bildet einen starken Kontrast zum Innenleben des Hauses, das einen Raumplan nach Vorbild von Adolf Loos beschreibt. Umlaufende Bänder gliedern die Fassade und sind zugleich Fensterbank und Führungsschiene für die Schiebeläden.

3

1

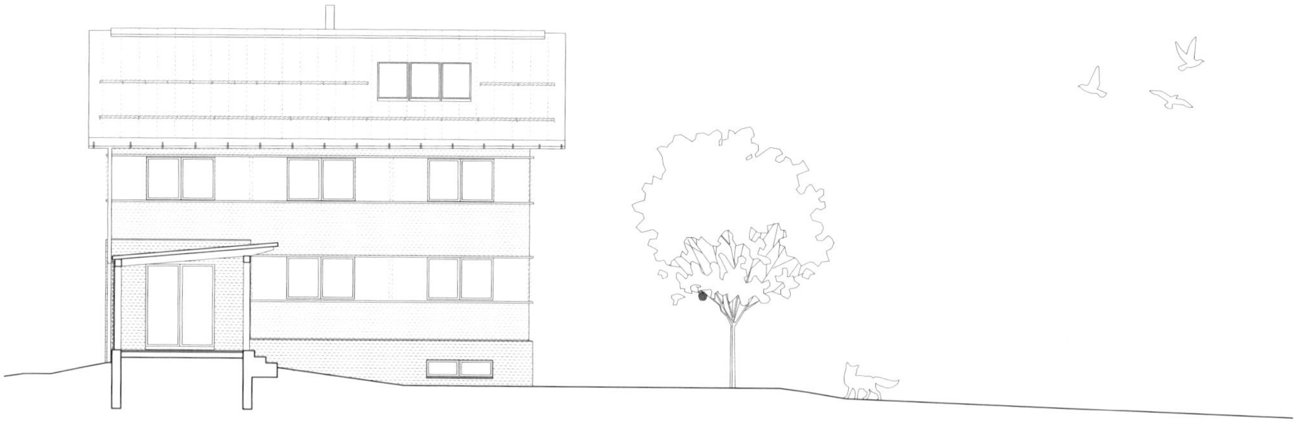

2

3

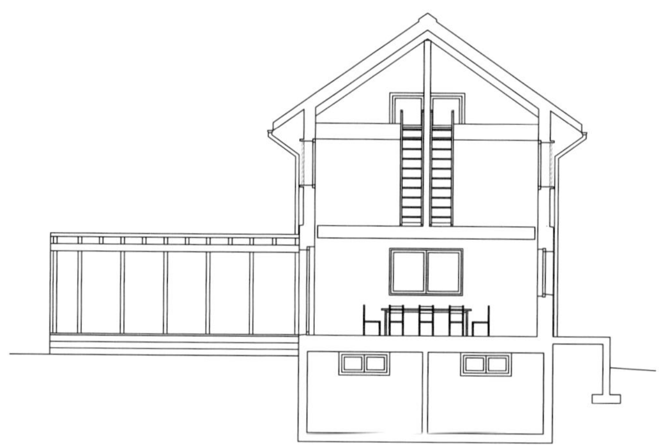

4

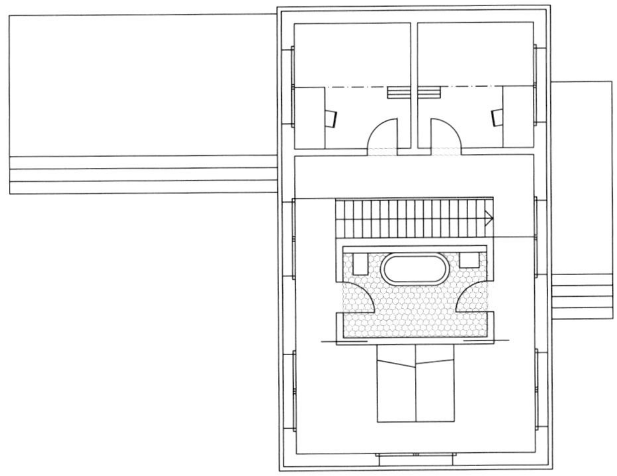

5

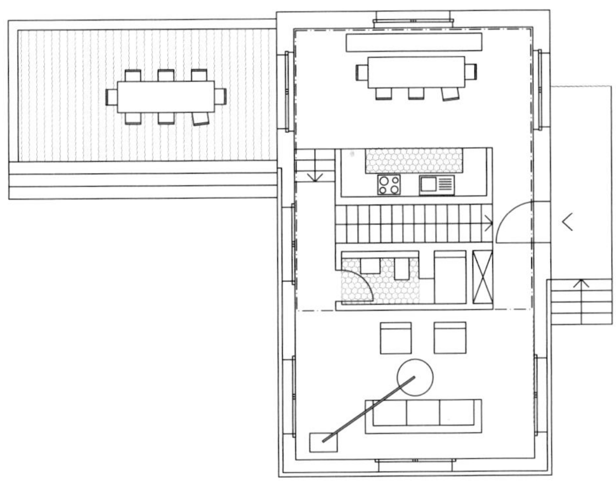

6

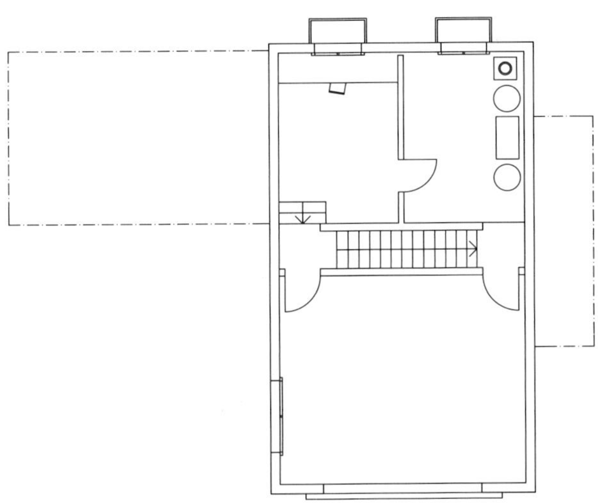

1 West elevation
2 Longitudinal section
3 Cross section
4 First floor plan
5 Ground floor plan
6 Basement floor plan

1 Aufriss Westseite
2 Längsschnitt
3 Querschnitt
4 Grundriss OG
5 Grundriss EG
6 Grundriss UG

EFH IN NÄFELS

1

Architects: Raum B Architektur
Completion: 2018
Location: Näfels, Switzerland
Gross floor area: 242.75 m^2
Number of bedrooms: 4
Main materials / building construction: wooden slats, chalet formwork / prefabricated timber element construction
Ecological aspects: materials can be individually dismantled and recycled according to Eco-Bau

The family home in Näfels closes a gap that has existed for about 40 years in the Villäggen single-family home quarter. Like a puzzle stone, the prefabricated wooden building blends into its surroundings. The north-facing, currently unobstructed agricultural land as well as the east side brook also represent the great quality of the building site. The three storys develop around the central staircase and always allow particularly beautiful views of the surroundings. On the ground floor, the view is directed from the spacious entrance hall to the northern meadow directly adjoining the house. In the living and dining room, a large-format panoramic window with an accompanying bench offers a view of the renaturalized brook with its old birch trees. The attic is a simple but all the more attractive room, which extends over the entire floor area. To the north, a round window frames the poetic view of the meadow, stable and group of trees.

2

3

4

Das Familienhaus in Näfels schließt eine schon seit rund 40 Jahren existierende Baulücke im Einfamilienhausquartier Villäggen. Wie ein Puzzlestein fügt sich das als vorfabrizierter Holzbau erstellte Gebäude in die Umgebung ein. Das nordseitige zurzeit unverbaubare Landwirtschaftsland sowie der ostseitige Bach stellen die großen Qualitäten des Bauplatzes dar. Die drei Geschosse entwickeln sich um die zentrale Treppe herum und lassen immer wieder besonders schöne Ausblicke in die Umgebung zu. Im Erdgeschoss wird der Blick von der großzügigen Eingangshalle auf die nördliche, direkt ans Haus anschließende Wiese gelenkt. Im Wohn- und Esszimmer bietet ein großformatiges Panoramafenster mit zugehöriger Sitzbank Sicht auf den renaturierten Bach mit den alten Birken. Das Dachgeschoss ist ein einfacher, aber umso attraktiverer Raum, der sich über die gesamte Geschossfläche zieht. Gegen Norden rahmt ein rundes Fenster den poetischen Ausblick auf Wiese, Stall und Baumgruppe.

Architekten: Raum B Architektur
Fertigstellung: 2018
Ort: Näfels, Schweiz
Bruttogeschossfläche: 242,75 m^2
Anzahl der Schlafzimmer: 4
Hauptmaterialien / Konstruktionsweise: Holzlamellenplatten, Chaletschalung / vorfabrizierter Holzelementbau
Ökologische Aspekte: Materialien gemäß Eco-Bau einzeln rückbau- und recycelbar

1 Exterior view from northwest with renaturalized brook
2 Exterior view from southeast
3 View from the living room to the brook
4 Living room
5 View from the top floor
6 Bench and panoramic window
7 Top floor

1 Außenansicht von Nordwesten mit renaturiertem Bach
2 Außenansicht von Südosten
3 Blick aus dem Wohnzimmer zum Bach
4 Wohnzimmer
5 Blick aus dem Dachgeschoss
6 Sitzbank und Panoramafenster
7 Dachgeschoss

5, 6, 7

1

2

1 Wardrobe with stairs
2 Staircase
3 Staircase section
4 Ground floor plan
5 Site plan

1 Garderobe mit Treppe
2 Treppenhaus
3 Schnitt durchs Treppenhaus
4 Grundriss EG
5 Lageplan

3

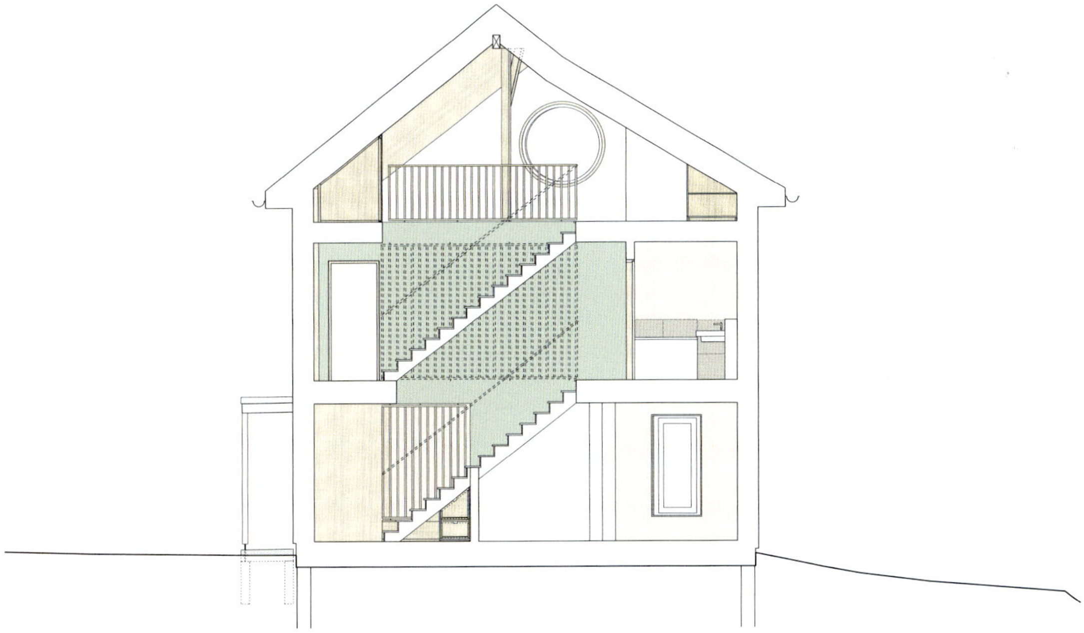

4

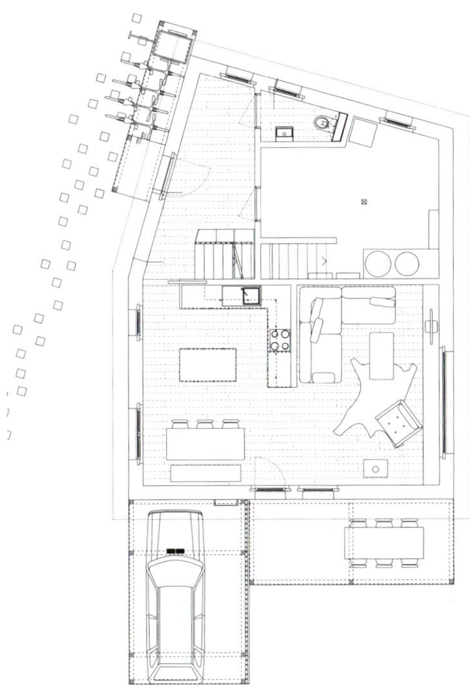

5

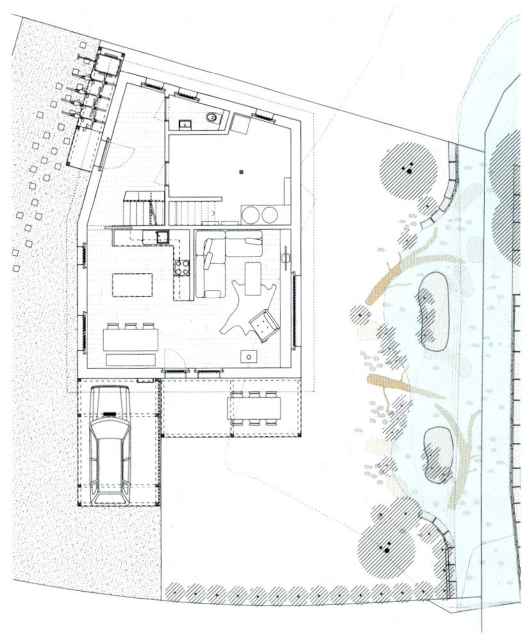

1

KOYO

1 Stairs
2 Exterior view from south
3 Living and dining area

1 Treppe
2 Außenansicht von Süden
3 Wohn- und Essbereich

2

Architects: mahore architekten
Completion: 2018
Location: Tulfes, Austria
Gross floor area: 250 m²
Number of bedrooms: 3
Main materials / building construction: concrete, wood, HPL panels, glass / reinforced concrete construction

Architekten: mahore architekten
Fertigstellung: 2018
Ort: Tulfes, Österreich
Bruttogeschossfläche: 250 m²
Anzahl der Schlafzimmer: 3
Hauptmaterialien / Konstruktionsweise: Beton, Holz, HPL-Platten, Glas / Stahlbetonbauweise

The black, dynamic structure hovers above the edge of the slope. Due to the small and difficult to build on hillside property, the living room and garden are raised to the top level to reveal the unique view of the tree tops and the mountains. The inner development is designed as an open room sculpture and connects the living levels. Natural surfaces were used in the interior, which are reduced to three essential materials – exposed concrete, wood and black steel. The adjoining imposing ash trees have accompanied the design from the very beginning and are reflected both in the wood used and in the project title. "Koyo" means in Japanese as much as discoloring leaves.

Der schwarze, dynamische Baukörper schwebt über der Hangkante. Aufgrund des kleinen und schwer zu bebauende Hanggrundstücks wird der Wohnraum und der Garten auf die oberste Ebene gehoben, um den einzigartigen Ausblick in die Baumkronen und die Bergwelt freizulegen. Die innere Erschließung ist als offene Raumskulptur konzipiert und verbindet die Wohnebenen. Im Innenraum wurden naturbelassene Oberflächen verwendet, diese sind auf drei wesentliche Materialien reduziert – Sichtbeton, Holz und Schwarzstahl. Die angrenzenden imposanten Eschen waren von Beginn an entwurfsbegleitend und spiegeln sich sowohl im verwendeten Holz als auch im Projekttitel wider. „Koyo" bedeutet im Japanischen so viel wie sich verfärbende Blätter.

3

1

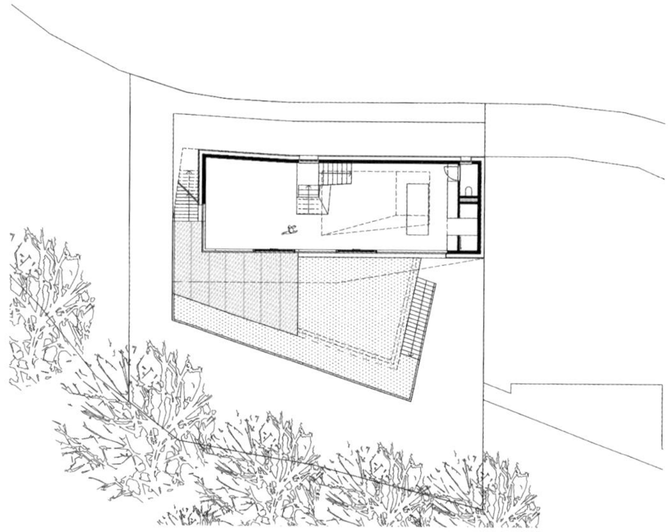

2

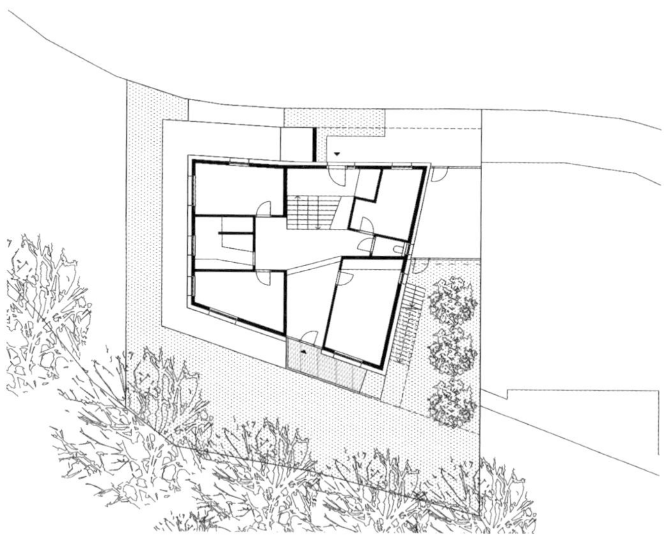

3

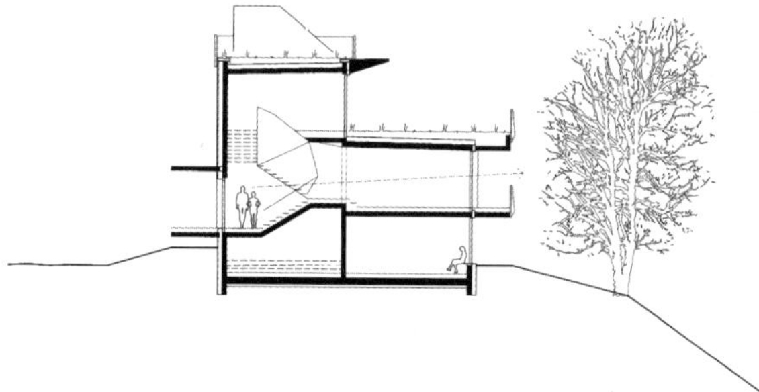

4

5

6

7

1 First floor plan
2 Ground floor plan
3 Cross section
4 Living area and terrace
5 Exterior view from west
6 Stairs detail
7 Entrance

1 Grundriss OG
2 Grundriss EG
3 Querschnitt
4 Wohnbereich und Terrasse
5 Außenansicht von Westen
6 Detail Treppe
7 Eingang

VILLA B

1

Located in a rural area, Villa B adapts to the traditional shape of the surrounding buildings but simultaneously has a dynamic touch due to shifted slopes and folds in the roof that are reflected in the interior spaces. The exterior plaster also covers the interior of the house, while the black-brown varnished larch of the roofing is also used for the windows and door frames. The choice of wood is linked to the traditional architecture in this particular region. Its use can also be found in the sliding shutters that give the project a sense of privacy, but they still can be opened if the user wants to establish contact with the landscape. The plans have different heights depending on the direction of the roof. Large open spaces are divided by a central element, the staircase, which organizes the house. On the upper floor, masonry and roofing merge to become a three-dimensional space. A large triple height space unites the various areas of the house at one glance. The house takes the form of a frame enclosing an intimate space while becoming one with its surrounding landscape.

Architects: bergmeisterwolf
Completion: 2018
Location: Aldrans, Austria
Gross floor area: 340 m^2
Main materials / building construction: plaster, concrete, oak wood / solid construction

2

3

Architekten: bergmeisterwolf
Fertigstellung: 2018
Ort: Aldrans, Österreich
Bruttogeschossfläche: 340 m^2
Hauptmaterialien / Konstruktionsweise: Gips, Beton, Eichenholz / Massivbau

4

1 Exterior view from northwest
2 Kitchen
3 Window with oak wood
4 Under the roof
5 Entrance

1 Außenansicht von Nordwesten
2 Küche
3 Fenster mit Eichenholz
4 Dachspitze
5 Eingang

Die in einer ländlichen Gegend liegende Villa B passt sich der traditionellen Form der umliegenden Gebäude an. Gleichzeitig geben verschobene Neigungen und Faltungen im Dach, die sich auch in den Innenräumen widerspiegeln, ihr eine dynamische Note. Der Außenputz setzt sich im Inneren fort, und die schwarz-braun lackierte Lärche der Dacheindeckung wird auch für die Fenster und Türrahmen verwendet. Dieses Holz entspricht der traditionellen Architektur dieser Region. Es findet sich auch in den Schiebeläden, die Privatsphäre verleihen, aber geöffnet werden können, wenn der Benutzer in Kontakt mit der Landschaft treten möchte. Je nach Richtung des Daches ergeben sich unterschiedliche Raumhöhen. Große offene Räume werden durch das zentrale Element, die Treppe, die das Haus organisiert, geteilt. Im Obergeschoss verschmelzen Mauerwerk und Dach zu einem dreidimensionalen Raum. Ein großer Raum mit dreifacher Höhe vereint die verschiedenen Bereiche des Hauses auf einen Blick. Die Villa B bildet die Form eines Rahmens, der einen intimen Raum umschließt und sich gleichzeitig mit der umgebenden Landschaft vereint.

5

1

2

1 Garden view
2 View of gable and mountains
3 First floor plan
4 Sketch
5 Ground floor plan

1 Gartenansicht
2 Ansicht Giebel und Bergpanorama
3 Grundriss OG
4 Skizze
5 Grundriss EG

3

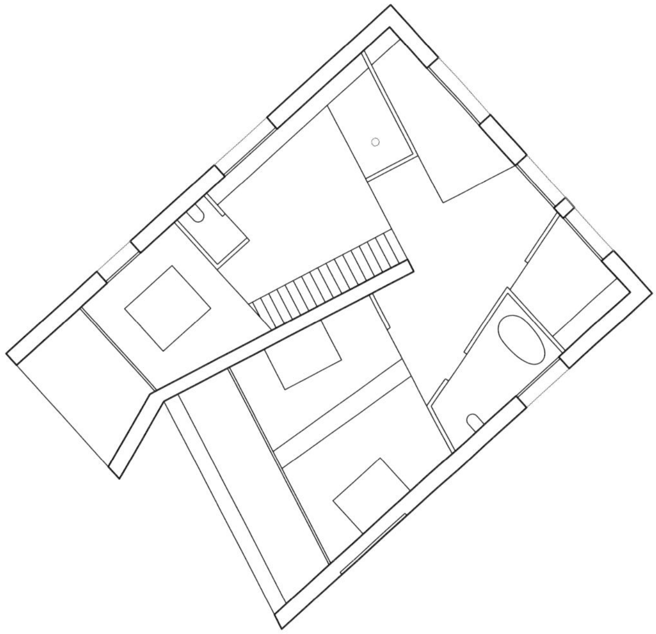

4

5

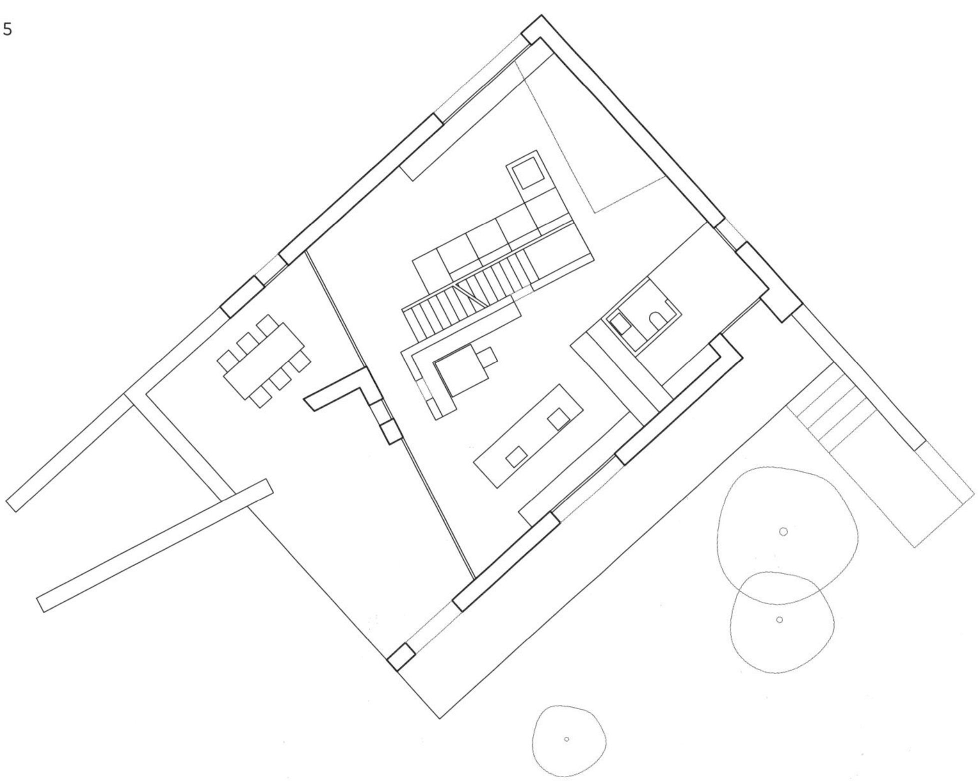

FL9

1

Architects: Polygon Architektur & Design
Completion: 2017
Location: Lenzburg, Aargau, Switzerland
Gross floor area: 215 m²
Number of bedrooms: 3
Main materials / building construction: spruce wood / timber element construction on existing cellar
Ecological aspects: roof covering with photovoltaic system, heat pump, renewable resources

The property is situated in a quiet quarter with detached houses from the 1950s. Supported by the warm and dark color scheme, the two intertwined building bodies – sleeping tower and projecting living room – form an ensemble that stimulates thought and arouses curiosity.

Through the concept of a continuous sequence of rooms, each room reveals its own qualities and offers the most beautiful views of the surroundings.

With the timber element construction, a sustainable, ecological and efficient construction method was chosen. The element walls were merely glazed white on the inside and covered on the outside with ventilated timber formwork. The photovoltaic system covering the entire roof produces one and a half times the energy required annually.

2

Das Grundstück liegt in einem ruhigen Quartier mit Einfamilienhäusern aus den 1950er-Jahren. Von der warmen und dunklen Farbgebung unterstützt, bilden die beiden in sich verschränkten Gebäudekörper – Schlafturm und ausladendes Wohnzimmer – ein Ensemble, das zum Nachdenken anregt und Neugierde weckt.

Durch das Konzept einer kontinuierlichen Raumabfolge offenbart jeder Raum seine eigenen Qualitäten und ermöglicht die jeweils schönsten Ausblicke in die Umgebung.

Mit dem Holzelementbau wurde eine nachhaltige, ökologische und effiziente Bauweise gewählt. Die Elementwände wurden innen lediglich weiß lasiert und außen mit einer hinterlüfteten Holzschalung beplankt. Durch die das gesamte Dach deckende Photovoltaikanlage wird jährlich das Anderthalbfache der benötigten Energie produziert.

3

4

Architekten: Polygon Architektur & Design
Fertigstellung: 2017
Ort: Lenzburg, Aargau, Schweiz
Bruttogeschossfläche: 215 m^2
Anzahl der Schlafzimmer: 3
Hauptmaterialien / Konstruktionsweise: Fichtenholz / Holzelementbau auf bestehendem Keller
Ökologische Aspekte: Dacheindeckung mit Photovoltaikanlage, Wärmepumpe, nachwachsende Rohstoffe

1 Garden view
2 Exterior view from southwest
3 Children's room
4 Bathroom on the first floor
5 Kitchen
6 Inner courtyard
7 Entrance, west façade

1 Gartenansicht
2 Außenansicht von Südwesten
3 Kinderzimmer
4 Badezimmer OG
5 Küche
6 Innenhof
7 Eingang, Westfassade

5, 6, 7

1

2

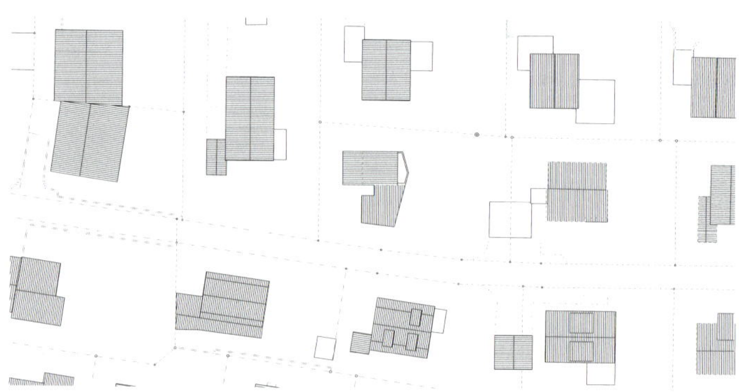

1 Living room with window to the patio
2 Site plan
3 Top floor plan
4 First floor plan
5 Ground floor plan with surroundings

1 Wohnzimmer mit Fenster zum Innenhof
2 Lageplan
3 Grundriss DG
4 Grundriss OG
5 Grundriss EG mit Umgebung

3

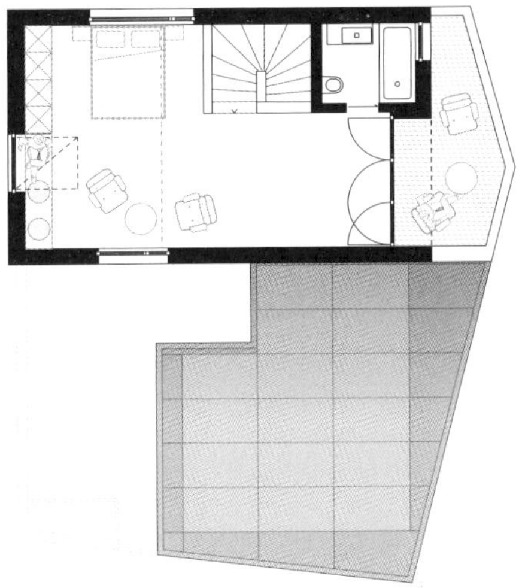

4

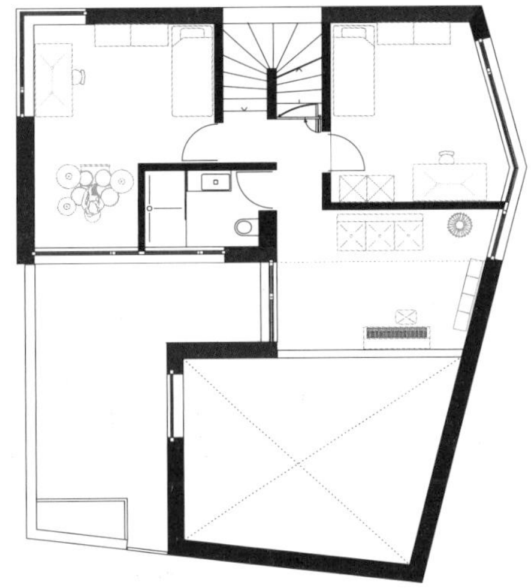

5

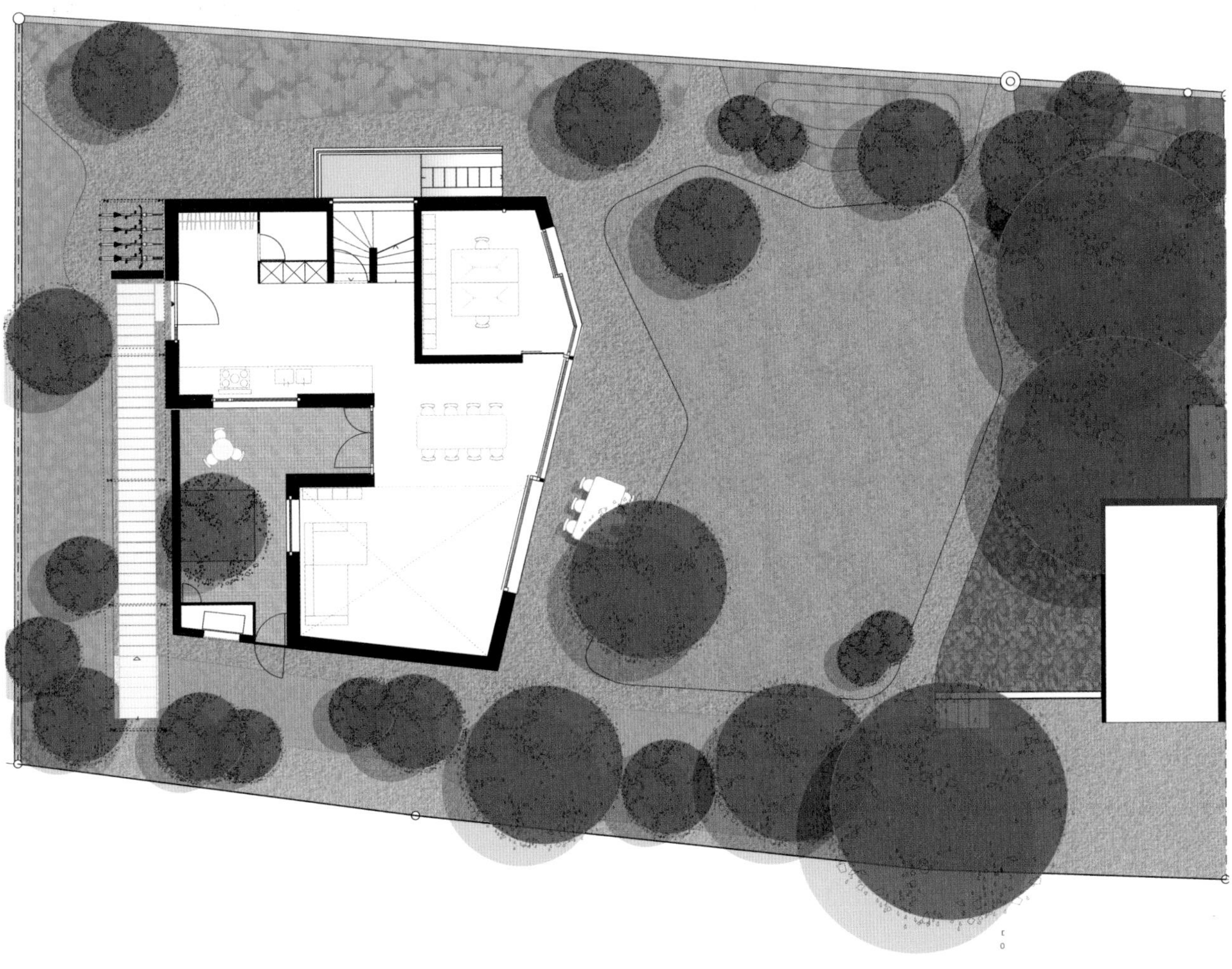

POOLHAUS

1

The client wanted a house with a pool next to his existing home. The steep hillside location and the weight restriction of the access road led to a consistent lightweight steel construction. Uncovered steel girders, delicate round tube supports, trapezoidal sheet metal ceilings, large format fiber cement panels and extensive glazing enabled prefabrication at the factory and rapid assembly on site. The concrete pool and the basement form a constructive edge on which the light steel house rests and cantilevers downhill. A steel walkway connects the existing house with the basement of the new Pool House in a short distance, thus allowing easy access. On the upper floor, the adjoining rooms such as the kitchen, technical room, bathroom and the anteroom for access from the street were grouped on the slope. The living room and the bedroom were glazed to room height and offer a generous view over the Wiental and the city.

Architects: Architekt Jürgen Radatz
Completion: 2015
Location: Vienna, Austria
Gross floor area: 108.87 m^2
Number of bedrooms: 1
Main materials / building construction: steel, concrete, fiber cement, glass / structural steel construction
Ecological aspects: air-to-water heat pump, recyclable steel construction

2

Architekten: Architekt Jürgen Radatz
Fertigstellung: 2015
Ort: Wien, Österreich
Bruttogeschossfläche: 108,87 m^2
Anzahl der Schlafzimmer: 1
Hauptmaterialien / Konstruktionsweise: Stahl, Beton, Faserzement, Glas / konstruktiver Stahlbau
Ökologische Aspekte: Luft-Wasser-Wärmepumpe, recycelbarer Stahlbau

Der Auftraggeber wünschte sich neben seinem bestehenden Wohnhaus ein Haus mit einem Pool. Die steile Hanglage und die Gewichtsbeschränkung der Zufahrtsstraße führten zu einem konsequenten Stahlleichtbau. Unverkleidete Stahlträger, zarte Rundrohrstützen, Trapezblechdecken, großformatige Faserzementplatten und großflächige Verglasungen ermöglichten die werkseitige Vorfertigung und die rasche Montage auf der Baustelle. Der betonierte Pool und das Untergeschoss bilden eine konstruktive Kante, auf der das leichte Stahlhaus ruht und hangabwärts auskragt. Ein Stahlsteg verbindet das bestehende Haus mit dem Untergeschoss des neuen Poolhauses auf kurzem Weg und ermöglicht damit einen bequemen Zugang. Im Obergeschoss wurden hangseitig die Nebenräume wie Küche, Technikraum, Badezimmer und der Vorraum für den straßenseitigen Zugang gruppiert. Der Wohnraum und das Schlafzimmer wurden raumhoch verglast und bieten einen großzügigen Ausblick über das Wiental und die Stadt.

3

4

1 Garden view
2 Glazing living room
3 Entrance
4 Street view

1 Gartenansicht
2 Verglasung Wohnraum
3 Zugang
4 Straßenansicht

1

2

1 Living room
2 Garden view at dusk
3 Northern elevation
4 Ground floor plan

1 Wohnzimmer
2 Gartenansicht bei Dämmerung
3 Aufriss Nordseite
4 Grundriss EG

3

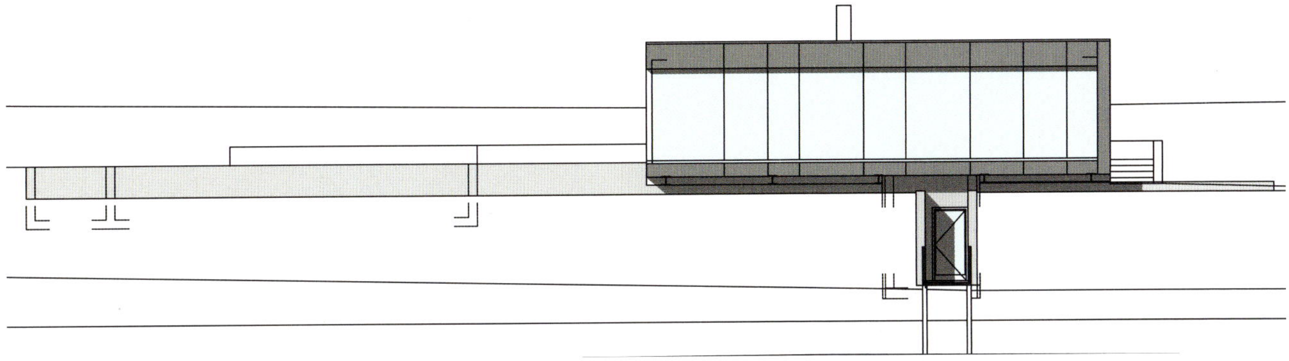

4

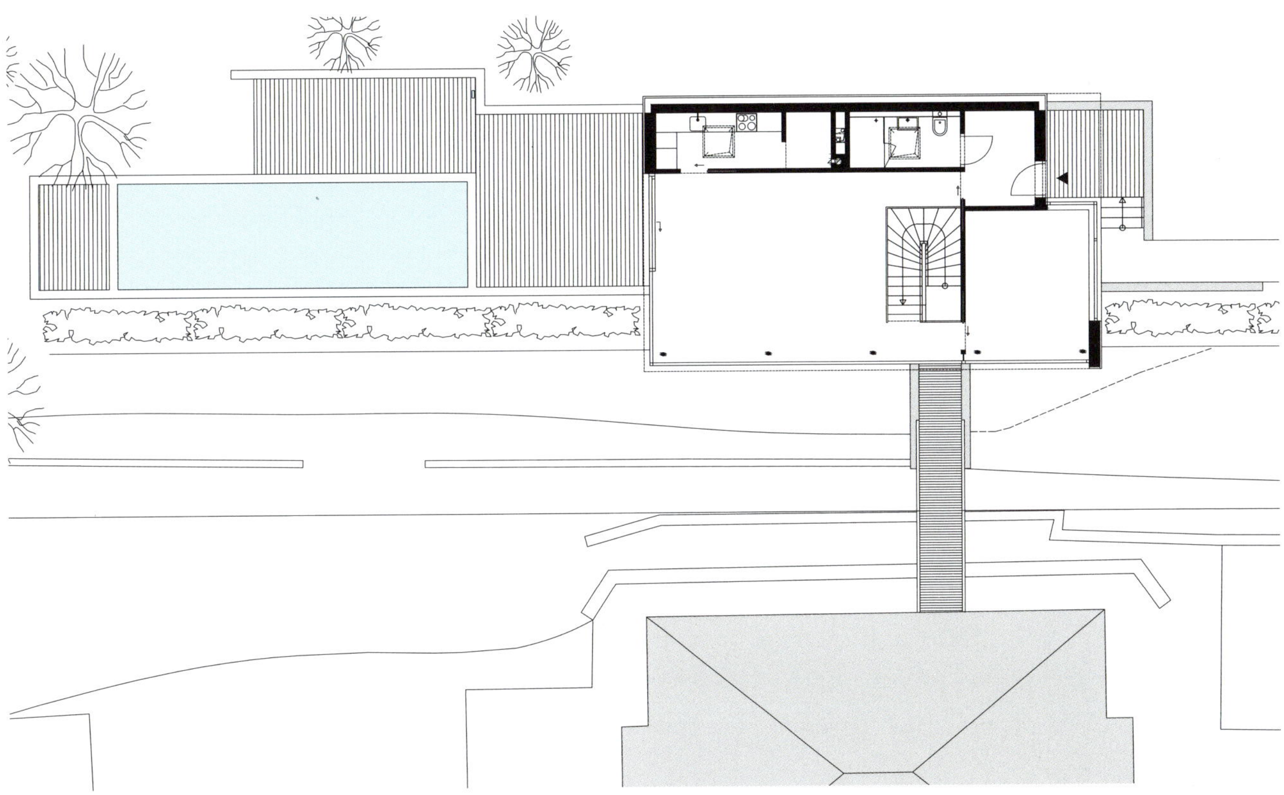

VILLA MOLIGNON

This villa is located in the small historic village of Molignon, near Sion, the capital of the Valais. Set in the middle of the vineyards, it overlooks the Val d'Hérens to the south and the castles of Sion to the west. In order to integrate into the built environment, the construction is defined by a two-sided volume. The project has an L-shaped plan that allows it to open up completely to the views to the south and west without being disturbed by the adjacent road. A mezzanine under the roof provides a retreat area and ensures optimal use of space both horizontally and vertically. A uniform concrete monolith forms the main body of the villa and is only interrupted by indentations in the north to mark the entrance and in the south to create bay windows. The use of wooden elements in the interior and exterior highlights the contrast between cold, in the natural environment, and warmth, in the cosy interior. The materials used are mainly wood and concrete, which allow the contemporary building to adapt perfectly to the rural environment.

1, 2

Architects: Atelier d'architecture Michel Follonier
Completion: 2014
Location: Molignon, Sion, Switzerland
Gross floor area: 165 m^2
Number of bedrooms: 4
Main materials / building construction: exposed concrete, wood / solid construction
Ecological aspects: heat pump

Architekten: Atelier d'architecture Michel Follonier
Fertigstellung: 2014
Ort: Molignon, Sion, Schweiz
Bruttogeschossfläche: 165 m²
Anzahl der Schlafzimmer: 4
Hauptmaterialien / Konstruktionsweise: Sichtbeton, Holz / Massivbau
Ökologische Aspekte: Wärmepumpe

Diese Villa befindet sich in dem kleinen historischen Dorf Molignon, in der Nähe von Sion, der Hauptstadt des Wallis. Mitten in den Weinbergen gelegen, überblickt sie das Val d'Hérens im Süden und die Schlösser von Sion im Westen. Um sich in die gebaute Umgebung zu integrieren, wird die Konstruktion durch ein zweiseitiges Volumen definiert. Das Projekt hat einen L-förmigen Grundriss, der es erlaubt, sich ganz den Ansichten im Süden und Westen zu öffnen, ohne dabei von der angrenzenden Straße gestört zu werden. Ein Zwischengeschoss unter dem Dach bietet einen Rückzugsbereich und sorgt für eine optimale Raumnutzung horizontal wie vertikal. Ein einheitlicher Betonmonolith bildet den Hauptkörper der Villa. Er wird nur durch Einkerbungen im Norden, um den Eingang zu markieren, und im Süden, um Erkerfenster zu schaffen, unterbrochen. Der Einsatz von Holzelementen im Innen- und Außenbereich verdeutlicht den Kontrast zwischen Kälte, in der natürlichen Umgebung, und Wärme, im behaglichen Innenraum. Die verwendeten Materialien sind hauptsächlich Holz und Beton, die dem zeitgenössischen Gebäude eine perfekte Anpassung an die ländliche Umgebung ermöglichen.

3

4

1 Corridor
2 Room
3 Mezzanine
4 Entrance

1 Flur
2 Zimmer
3 Zwischengeschoss
4 Eingang

1

2

1 Living room
2 View from south
3 Section
4 First floor plan
5 Southwest elevation
6 Ground floor plan
7 Southeast elevation

1 Wohnzimmer
2 Ansicht von Süden
3 Gebäudeschnitt
4 Grundriss OG
5 Aufriss Südwestseite
6 Grundriss EG
7 Aufriss Südostseite

3

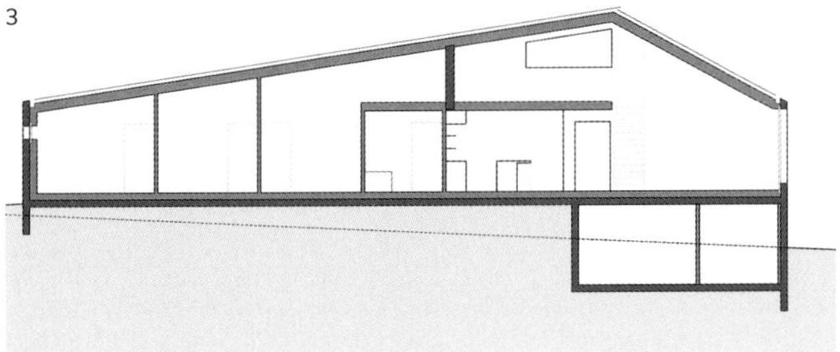

4

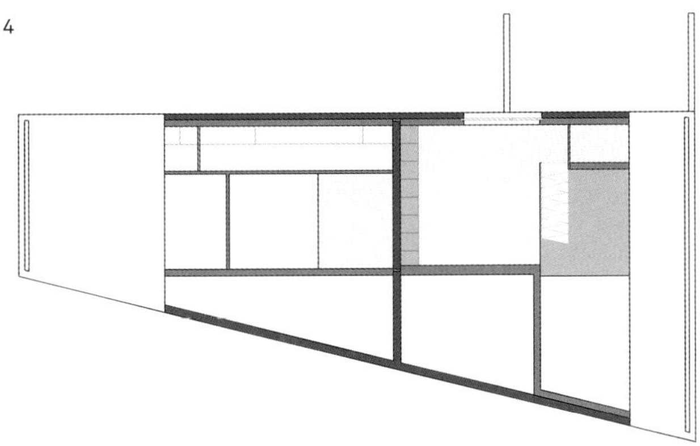

5

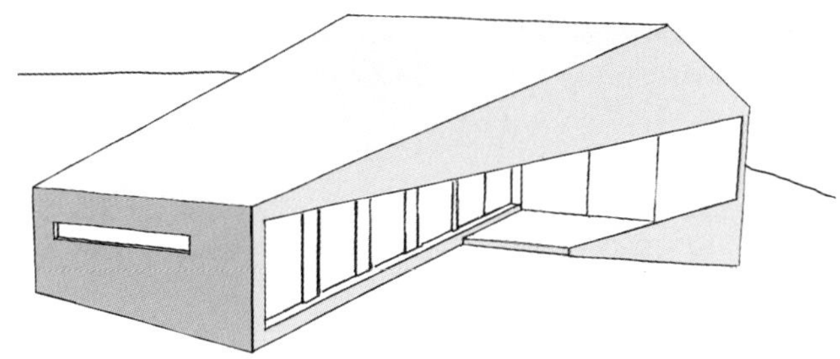

6

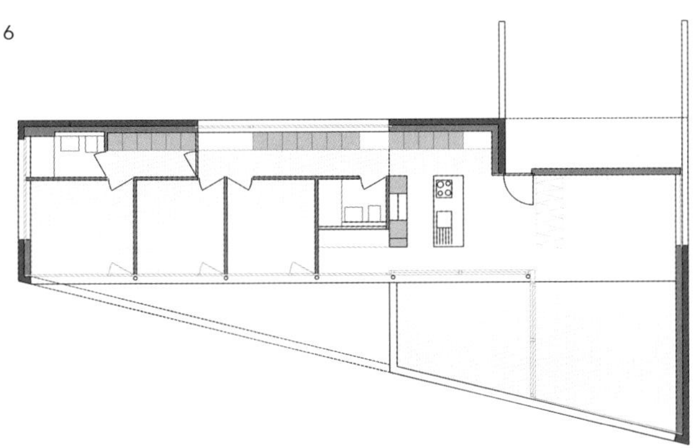

7

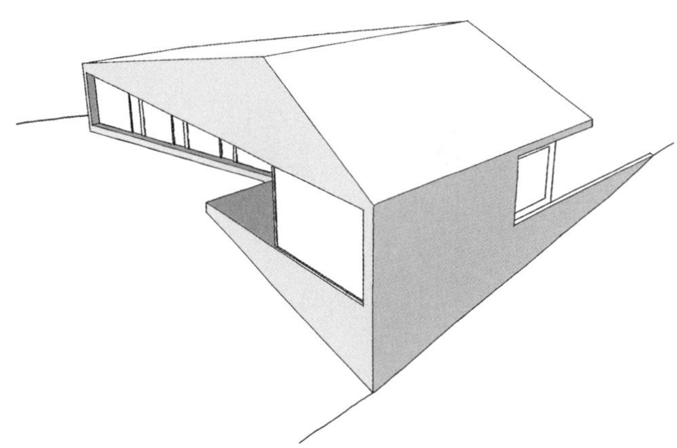

HAUS AM SEE

1

Architects: Backraum Architektur
Completion: 2015
Location: Thurnberg storage reservoir, Austria
Number of bedrooms: 1
Main materials / building construction: wood / solid timber construction
Ecological aspects: wood soft fiber insulation

The design process of the House Near the Lake was based on the rural barns and stables of the surrounding area, which characterize the landscape due to their appearance: a gabled roof, compact form, windowless. Thus the house was very carefully integrated into the topography and the landscape. The wood of the façade and the roof was charred and embedded with oil to make it less sensitive to the weather on the one hand and to obtain the desired black color on the other. In the interior, the solid spruce walls were only oiled. This makes the building look homely and warm inside even in harsh weather and in winter. The building is heated by means of a wood log stove, which provides direct heat as well as hot water for the underfloor heating. Wooden boards were chosen for the fair-faced concrete formwork in accordance with and in contrast to the wood. For the floor, sanded screed was sealed colorless. The interior, which impresses with its clarity, offers a beautiful view of the lake.

2

Als Vorlage für den Designprozess des Hauses am See dienten die bäuerlichen Scheunen und Stallungen der Umgebung, die aufgrund ihres Erscheinungsbilds die Landschaft prägen: Satteldach, kompakte Form, fensterlos. So wurde das Haus sehr behutsam in die Topografie und das Landschaftsbild eingefügt. Das Holz der Fassade und des Dachs wurde angekohlt und mit Öl eingelassen, um es einerseits witterungsunempfindlicher zu machen, andererseits, um den gewünschten schwarzen Farbton zu erhalten. Im Innenbereich wurden die Fichtenmassivwände nur geölt. So wirkt das Gebäude auch bei harschem Wetter und im Winter innen wohnlich warm. Beheizt wird das Gebäude mit einem Holzscheitofen, der neben direkter Wärme auch die Fußbodenheizung mit Warmwasser versorgt. Entsprechend und im Kontrast zum Holz wurden für die Sichtbetonschalung Holzbretter gewählt. Als Boden wurde geschliffener Estrich farblos versiegelt. Der durch seine Klarheit bestechende Innenraum bietet einen schönen Blick auf den See.

3

4

Architekten: Backraum Architektur
Fertigstellung: 2015
Ort: Thurnberger Stausee, Österreich
Anzahl der Schlafzimmer: 1
Hauptmaterialien / Konstruktionsweise: Holz / Holzmassivbau
Ökologische Aspekte: Holzweichfaserdämmung

1 Exterior view at dusk
2 Exterior view with view of the lake
3 The monolithic appearance of the house with view of the lake
4 Terrace with bench and dining table
5 Detail of the lockable façade
6 Bed- and bathroom

1 Außenansicht in der Abenddämmerung
2 Außenansicht mit Blick auf den See
3 Das monolithische Erscheinungsbild des Hauses mit Blick auf den See
4 Terrasse mit Bank und Esstisch
5 Detail der verschließbaren Fassade
6 Bade- und Schlafzimmer

5, 6

1

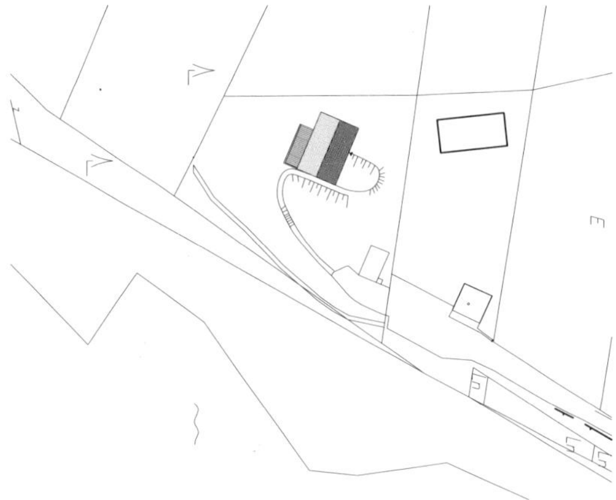

2

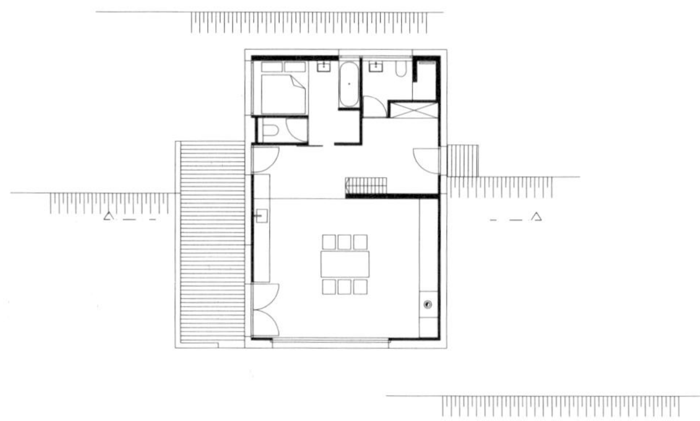

3

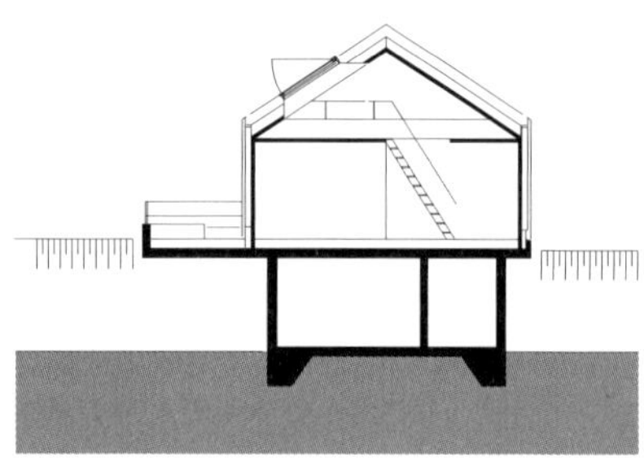

4

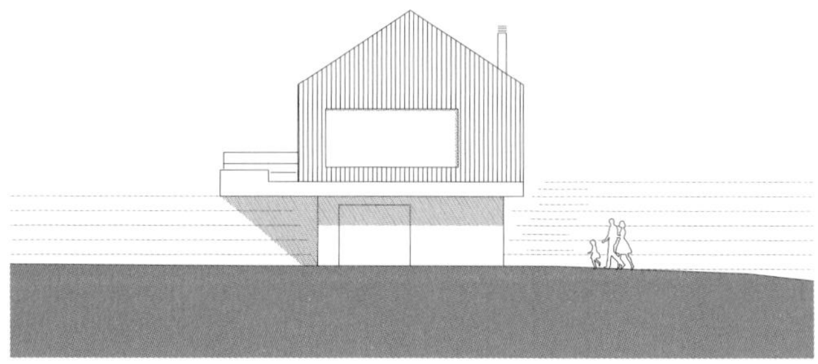

5

6

7

8

1 Site plan
2 Floor plan
3 Section
4 Elevation sea side
5 View from the living room towards the lake
6 Gallery
7 Entrance area and stairs to the gallery
8 Living room

1 Lageplan
2 Grundriss
3 Schnitt
4 Aufriss Seeseite
5 Blick aus dem Wohnraum in Richtung See
6 Galerie
7 Eingangsbereich und Treppe zur Galerie
8 Wohnraum

EFH HUWILER-MURANTA

The single-family house, which was built using only regional woods, combines a north façade of concrete, which has a wooden structure surface, with a massive wooden complex to form a harmonious unit.

Important to the client were large and bright common rooms, such as the sports studio or the utility room. In return, the bedrooms were allowed to be a little smaller. This is compensated by a large corridor, which functions as a playroom or office.

The surroundings should invite to play, rest or gardening. Thus, towards the street a pavement made of local quartzite is used and in the private outdoor space one floor above there is a beautiful meadow.

The house is heated with an outdoor air heat pump and has collectors on the roof for hot water. For controlled room ventilation, the ventilation center is located on the middle floor and can supply all floors with fresh air with a very short pipe run.

1, 2

Architects: Albertin Partner Architekten
Completion: 2015
Location: Chur, Switzerland
Number of bedrooms: 4
Main materials / building construction: exposed concrete, larch wood / solid timber construction
Ecological aspects: ecological timber construction, sustainable materials, solar energy

Architekten: Albertin Partner Architekten
Fertigstellung: 2015
Ort: Chur, Schweiz
Anzahl der Schlafzimmer: 4
Hauptmaterialien / Konstruktionsweise: Sichtbeton, Lärchenholz / Massivholzsystem
Ökologische Aspekte: ökologischer Holzbau mit einheimischem Holz, nachhaltige Materialien, Sonnenenergie

Das Haus, das nur mit regionalen Hölzern gefertigt wurde, verbindet eine Nordfassade aus Beton, deren Oberfläche die Holzstruktur zeigt, mit einem massiven Holzkomplex zu einer harmonischen Einheit.

Wichtig waren der Bauherrschaft große und helle Gemeinschaftsräume, wie das Sportstudio oder der Hauswirtschaftsraum. Dafür durften die Schlafzimmer etwas kleiner sein. Kompensiert wird dies mit einem großen Korridor, der als Spielzimmer oder Büroraum fungiert.

Die Umgebung soll zum Spielen, Verweilen oder zur Gartenarbeit einladen. So wird zur Straße hin mit einem Pflasterbelag aus einheimischem Quarzit reagiert und im privaten Außenraum, ein Geschoss höher, gibt es eine schöne Wiese.

Das Haus wird mit einer Außenluftwärmepumpe beheizt und hat zur Gewinnung von Warmwasser Kollektoren auf dem Dach. Für die kontrollierte Raumlüftung liegt die Lüftungszentrale im Mittelgeschoss und kann mit einer sehr kurzen Leitungsführung alle Geschosse mit Frischluft bedienen.

3

4

1 Terrace first floor
2 View of the concrete façade
3 View outside
4 Courtyard in evening mood

1 Terrasse OG
2 Ansicht Betonfassade
3 Ausblick
4 Vorplatz in der Abendstimmung

1

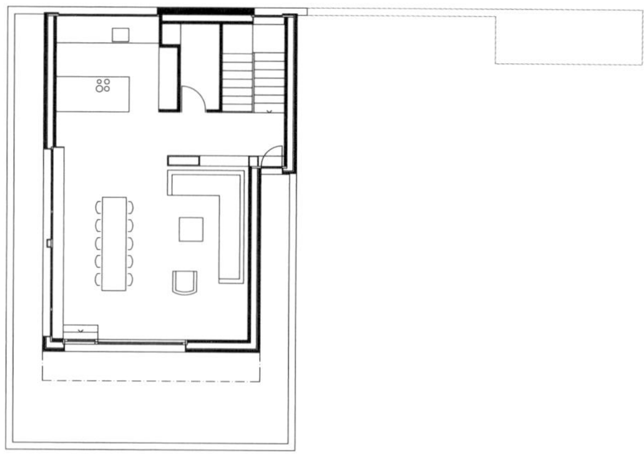

2

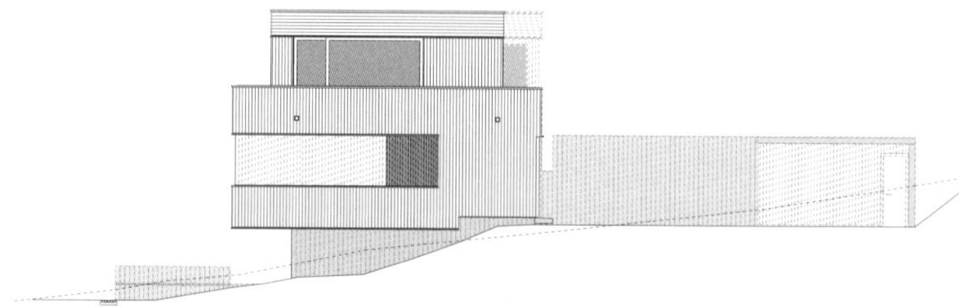

3

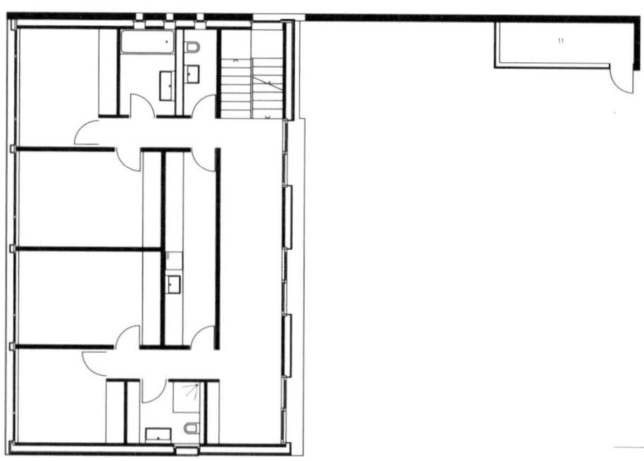

4

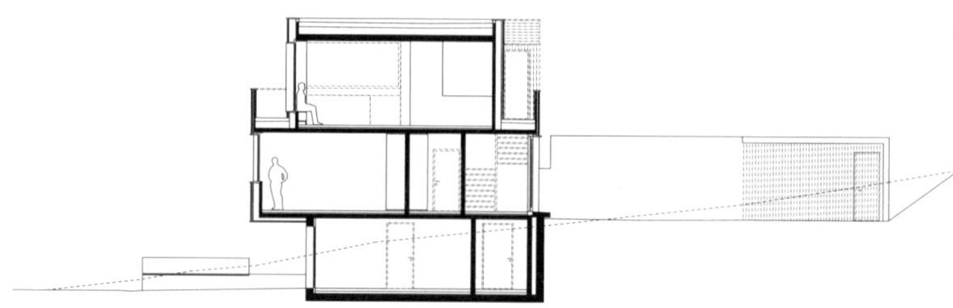

5

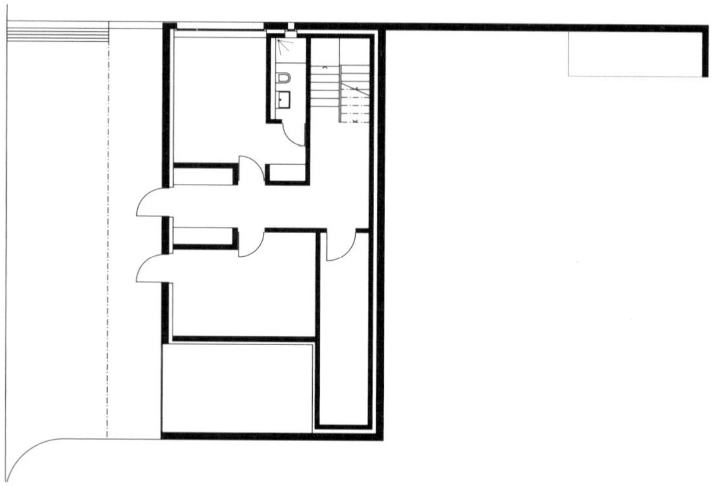

6

7, 8

1 Attic floor plan
2 South elevation
3 First floor plan
4 Section
5 Ground floor plan
6 Dining and living area
7 Corridor
8 Detail window, concrete façade

1 Grundriss DG
2 Aufriss Südseite
3 Grundriss OG
4 Gebäudeschnitt
5 Grundriss EG
6 Ess- und Wohnzimmer
7 Korridor
8 Detail Fenster der Betonfassade

1

HAUS SCH

1 Exterior view with entrance area
2 Exterior view from east
3 Exterior view with entrance area at dusk

1 Außenansicht mit Eingangsbereich
2 Außenansicht von Osten
3 Außenansicht mit Eingangsbereich bei Dämmerung

2

Architects: Dietrich | Untertrifaller Architekten
Completion: 2015
Location: Bregenz, Austria
Gross floor area: 179 m²
Number of bedrooms: 2
Main materials / building construction: wood, exposed concrete, glass / timber construction with reinforced concrete core
Ecological aspects: regional material silver fir, controlled aeration and ventilation

Architekten: Dietrich | Untertrifaller Architekten
Fertigstellung: 2015
Ort: Bregenz, Österreich
Bruttogeschossfläche: 179 m²
Anzahl der Schlafzimmer: 2
Hauptmaterialien / Konstruktionsweise: Holz, Sichtbeton, Glas / Holzkonstruktion mit Stahlbetonkern
Ökologische Aspekte: regionales Baumaterial Weißtanne, kontrollierte Be- und Entlüftung

In the northeast of Bregenz, a black-painted wooden prism juts out from a steep southern slope. What at first glance appears to be a freely formed building sculpture is actually the result of an economic calculation. In order to obtain the greatest possible cubature from the extremely steep site, a maximum body with a widely projecting soffit was designed. The development of the slope requires four levels. The four-story reinforced concrete core on the uphill side was structurally preceded by a two-story timber construction projecting to the valley side. The surfaces inside follow the constructive division – exposed concrete walls and polished screed in the concrete component, paneling and floor boards of brushed silver fir in the wooden body.

Im Nordosten von Bregenz kragt ein schwarz gestrichenes, hölzernes Prisma aus einem steilen Südhang ins Freie. Was auf den ersten Blick wie eine frei geformte Bauskulptur erscheint, ist tatsächlich das Resultat einer ökonomischen Kalkulation. Um dem extrem steilen Grundstück eine größtmögliche Kubatur abzugewinnen, wurde ein Maximalkörper mit weit auskragender Untersicht entworfen. Die Erschließung der Hangneigung erfordert vier Ebenen. Konstruktiv wurde dem viergeschossigen, bergseitigen Stahlbetonkern ein talseitig auskragender, zweigeschossiger Holzbau vorgehängt. Die Oberflächen im Inneren folgen der konstruktiven Zweiteilung – Sichtbetonwände und geschliffener Estrich im Betonbauteil, Vertäfelungen und Bodendielen aus gebürsteter Weißtanne im Holzkörper.

3

1

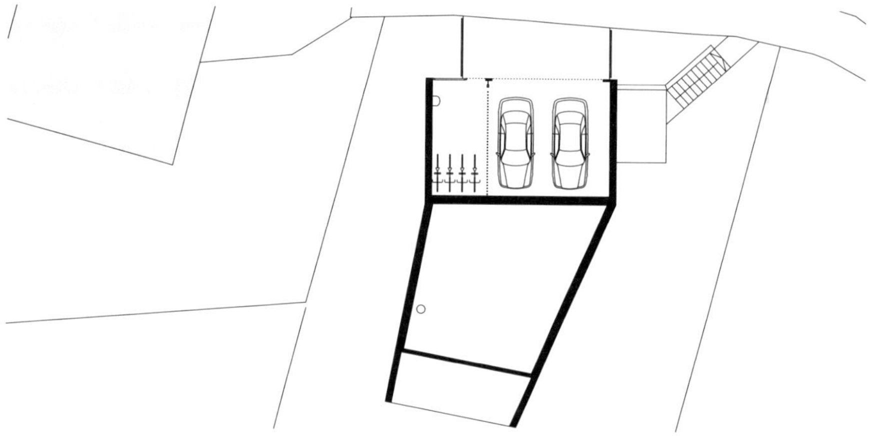

2

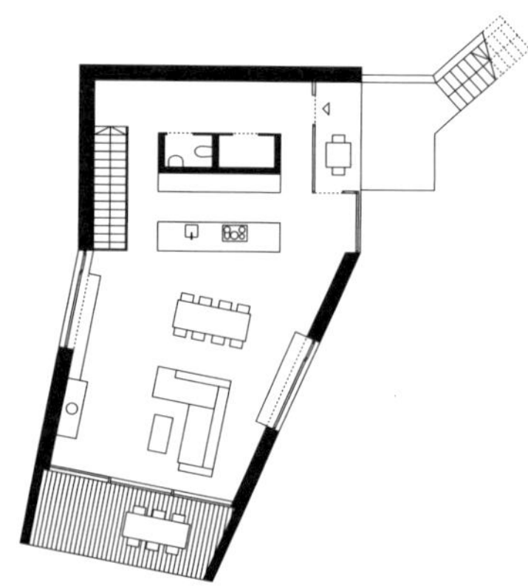

3

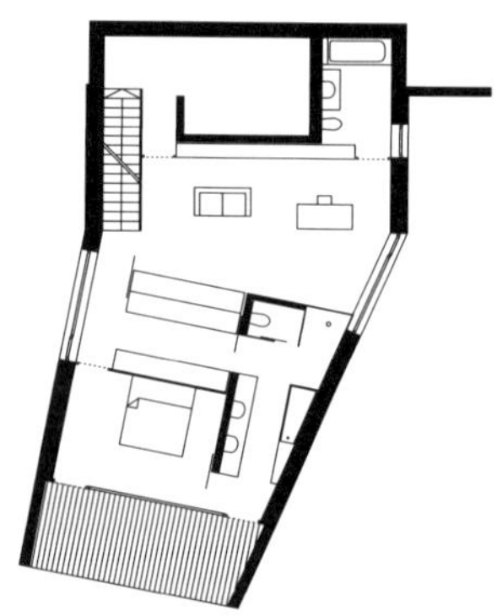

4

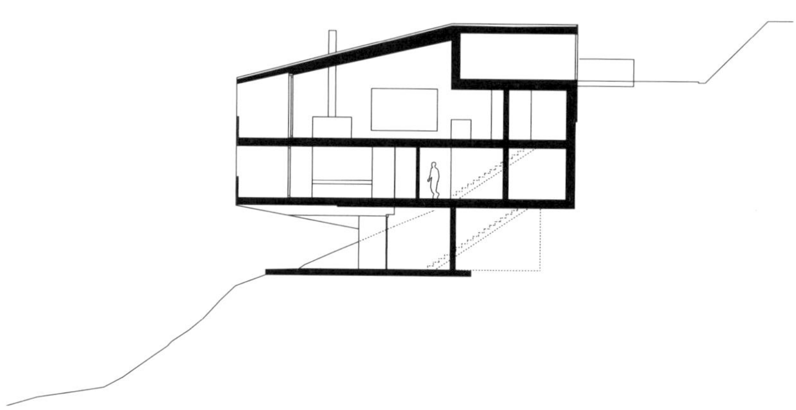

5 

 6

 7

8 

1 Ground floor plan with garage
2 First basement floor plan with living area
3 Second basement floor plan with bedroom, bathroom and office
4 Section
5 Living area with view to the balcony
6 Bathroom
7 Access living area
8 Living area with view into the kitchen

1 Grundriss EG mit Garage
2 Grundriss 1. UG mit Wohnbereich
3 Grundriss 2. UG mit Schlafzimmer, Bad und Büro
4 Schnitt
5 Wohnbereich mit Blick auf den Balkon
6 Bad
7 Erschließung Wohnbereich
8 Wohnbereich mit Blick in die Küche

CASA L

1

Architects: Plasma Studio
Completion: 2019
Location: Gsies, South Tyrol
Gross floor area: 218 m²
Number of bedrooms: 3
Main materials / building construction: larch wood formwork / solid construction, timber roof truss
Ecological aspects: wood fiber insulation, geothermal energy, controlled ventilation of living space, cooperation with local companies (within a radius of 15 km)

The property of Casa L lies protected in a small terrain depression with an old silver fir in its center. Around, an L-shaped bungalow-like structure was built. At the access level is the part of the building that is used during the day. The spatial center is arranged around a stove. The position of the kitchen is chosen so that it is touched by the morning sun, while the position of the living room brings the evening sun into the room. These rooms are almost two storys high, with a gallery stretched between them and the roof surface put over it, creating a great spatial tension. The building is designed in a reduced range of materials. A vertical rough-sawn plank formwork extends as a continuum over the sloping roof surface, which is perceived as a gabled roof surface when viewed from the north and south sides. The interior is dominated by larch and Swiss stone pine.

2

3

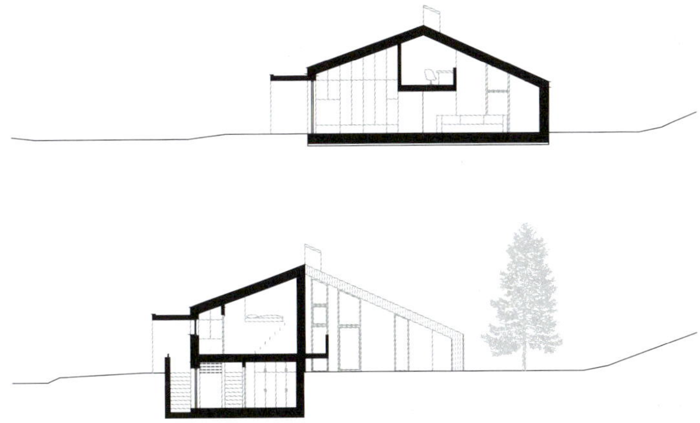

Das Grundstück von Casa L liegt geschützt in einer kleinen Geländesenke, in deren Mitte eine alte Silbertanne steht. Um diese herum wurde ein L-förmiger, bungalowartiger Baukörper errichtet. Auf Zugangsniveau befindet sich jener Teil des Gebäudes, der tagsüber genutzt wird. Das räumliche Zentrum ist um einen Ofen arrangiert. Die Position der Küche ist so gewählt, dass sie von der Morgensonne profitiert, die des Wohnraums lässt die Abendsonne in den Raum scheinen. Diese Räume sind fast zweigeschossig, eine dazwischen gespannte Galerie und die darübergestülpte Dachfläche verleihen eine große räumliche Spannung. Das Gebäude ist in einer reduzierten Materialpalette ausgeführt. Eine vertikale sägeraue Bretterschalung zieht sich als Kontinuum auch über die geneigte Dachfläche, die von der Nord- und Südseite betrachtet als Satteldachfläche wahrgenommen wird. Im Innenraum dominieren Lärchen- und Zirbenholz.

Architekten: Plasma Studio
Fertigstellung: 2019
Ort: Gsies, Südtirol
Bruttogeschossfläche: 218 m^2
Anzahl der Schlafzimmer: 3
Hauptmaterialien / Konstruktionsweise: Lärchenschalung / Massivbau, Holzdachstuhl
Ökologische Aspekte: Holzfaserdämmung, Geothermie, kontrollierte Wohnraumlüftung, Zusammenarbeit mit lokalen Firmen (innerhalb eines Radius von 15 km)

4

1 Exterior view from the street
2 Exterior view from the garden
3 Sections
4 Exterior view of the garden and surroundings
5 Kitchen
6 Entrance

1 Außenansicht von der Straße
2 Außenansicht vom Garten
3 Schnitte
4 Außenansicht vom Garten mit Umgebung
5 Küche
6 Eingang

5, 6

HARTE SCHALE, WEISSER KERN

1

In order to fulfill the function of a protective shell, but also as an adaptation of the existing material hierarchy of neighboring buildings, the architects opted for a concrete body as a hard shell with completely closed side walls. As soon as one enters the building, the color of the concrete, which is true to the material, turns into a brilliant, surprising white. The shell becomes the core, becomes the interior resting place, as a counterweight to the view of the sweeping nature. The large sun terrace resembles a viewing platform. Sublime and with a generous panoramic view, it invites to linger, look and enjoy. Some of the special qualities of the integrated outdoor spaces are to provide open, mutually usable connections to the atrium, to the living, cooking and sleeping areas, as well as daylight deep into the interior of all adjoining room zones. A special feature here is the possible room extension by opening the glass façade to the inner courtyard, so that a private life outdoors and sleeping under the starry sky become possible.

Architects: Wannerpartner Architekten
Completion: 2014
Location: Münchenstein, Switzerland
Gross floor area: 217 m^2
Number of bedrooms: 2
Main materials / building construction: concrete, glass / compact façade with exposed concrete

2

3

Architekten: Wannerpartner Architekten
Fertigstellung: 2014
Ort: Münchenstein, Schweiz
Bruttogeschossfläche: 217 m²
Anzahl der Schlafzimmer: 2
Hauptmaterialien / Konstruktionsweise: Beton, Glas / Kompaktfassade mit Sichtbeton

Um der Funktion einer Schutzhülle gerecht zu werden, aber auch als Adaption der bestehenden Materialhierarchie benachbarter Bauten, entschied sich das Architektenteam für einen Betonkörper als harte Schale mit komplett geschlossenen Seitenwänden. Sobald man das Haus betritt, kehrt sich die materialgetreue Farbgebung des Betons in ein strahlendes, überraschendes Weiß. Die Hülle wird zum Kern, zum innenliegenden Ruhepol, als Gegengewicht zum Ausblick in die weitschweifende Natur. Die große Sonnenterrasse gleicht einer Aussichtsplattform. Erhaben und mit großzügigem Rundumblick lädt sie zum Verweilen, Schauen und Genießen ein. Offene, wechselseitig nutzbare Verbindungen zum Atrium, zum Wohn-, Koch- und Schlafbereich sowie Tageslicht bis tief ins Innere aller angrenzenden Raumzonen zählen zu den besonderen Qualitäten der integrierten Außenräume. Die Besonderheit hier ist die mögliche Raumerweiterung über das Öffnen der Glasfassade zum Innenhof, sodass ein privates Leben im Freien und ein Schlafen unterm Sternenhimmel möglich sind.

4

5

1 Exterior view from south at night
2 Exterior view from east
3 Exterior view from south
4 Inner courtyard with stairs to the living floor
5 Bathroom with view over atrium to kitchen

1 Außenansicht von Süden bei Nacht
2 Außenansicht von Osten
3 Außenansicht von Süden
4 Innenhof mit Treppe ins Wohngeschoss
5 Badezimmer mit Sicht über Atrium zu Küche

1

2

1 Dining room with large panorama window
2 Living room with view to the courtyard
3 Floor plan carport
4 First floor plan
5 Ground floor plan
6 Base floor plan
7 Section

1 Esszimmer mit großem Panoramafenster
2 Wohnzimmer mit Sicht zum Innenhof
3 Grundriss Carport
4 Grundriss OG
5 Grundriss EG
6 Grundriss Sockelgeschoss
7 Schnitt

3

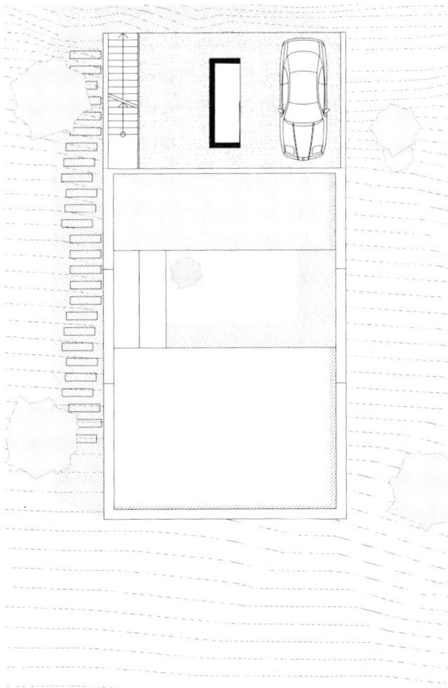

4

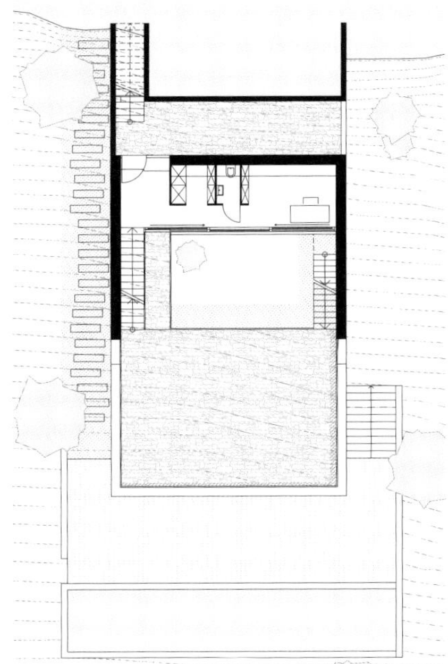

5

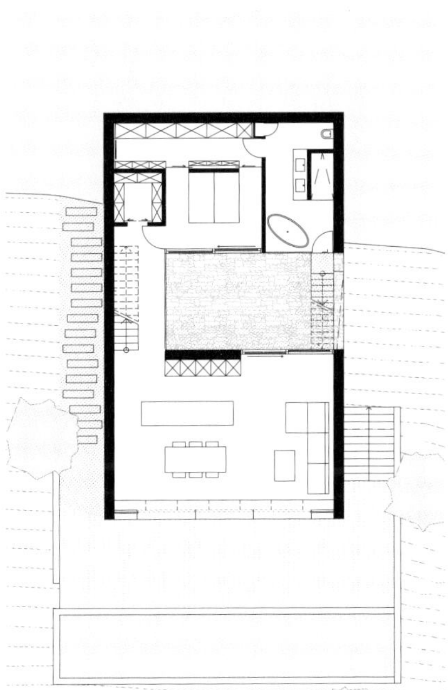

6

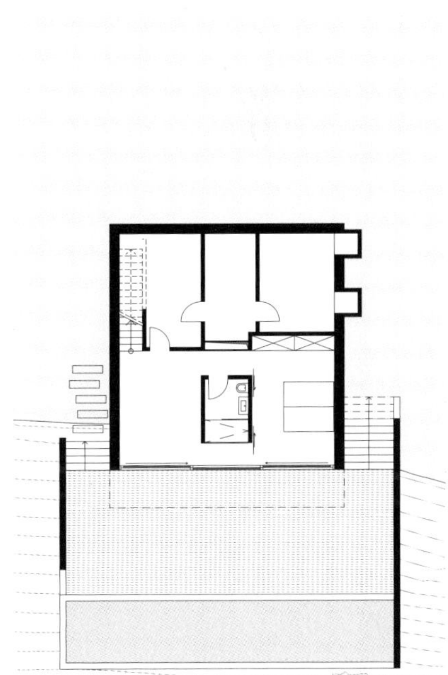

7

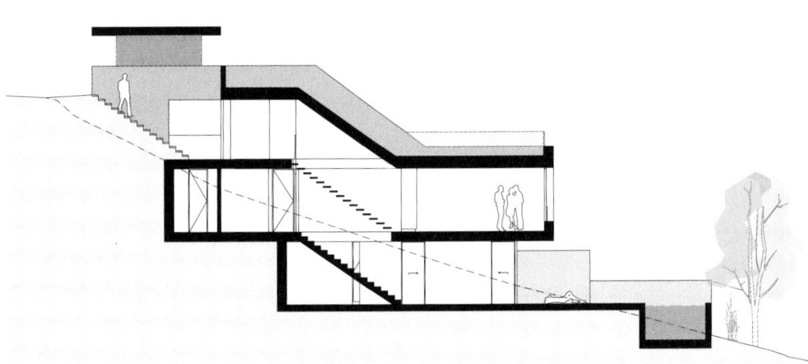

MAISON TERRASSE

Maison Terrasse is located on the highest point of the property, with views of the Rhone Valley and the Alps. It is situated on a slope without changing the topography or character. Organized on three levels, the building takes up the elongated shape of the surroundings and shows a clear orientation on the plain.

The entrance hall on the ground floor provides access to the living rooms. The kitchen opens to the dining room and the living room with a higher ceiling height and provides access to a large terrace with a swimming pool, all facing southeast. The large openings allow continuity from the interior to the exterior. Upstairs are the bedrooms and downstairs are the technical rooms, the cellar and a music room. On the ground floor there are large sandstone tiles that extend outwards onto the terrace, enhancing the feeling of a single continuous space between inside and outside.

1, 2

Architects: François Meyer architecture
Completion: 2017
Location: Grimisuat, Switzerland
Gross floor area: 310 m^2
Number of bedrooms: 3
Main materials / building construction: concrete / metal structure
Ecological aspects: minimum impact on natural slope

Architekten: François Meyer architecture
Fertigstellung: 2017
Ort: Grimisuat, Schweiz
Bruttogeschossfläche: 310 m²
Anzahl der Schlafzimmer: 3
Hauptmaterialien / Konstruktionsweise: Beton / Metalltragwerk
Ökologische Aspekte: minimaler Eingriff in den Naturhang

Die Maison Terrasse befindet sich auf dem höchsten Punkt des Grundstücks mit Blick auf das Rhonetal und die Alpen. Es liegt an einem Hang, ohne die Topografie oder den Charakter zu verändern. Auf drei Ebenen organisiert, nimmt das Gebäude die längliche Form der Umgebung auf und zeigt eine klare Orientierung in der Ebene.

Die Eingangshalle im Erdgeschoss bietet Zugang zu den Wohnräumen. Die Küche öffnet sich zum Esszimmer und zum Wohnzimmer mit höherer Deckenhöhe und bietet Zugang zu einer großen Terrasse mit Swimmingpool. Sie alle sind nach Südosten ausgerichtet. Die großen Öffnungen ermöglichen eine Verbindung von innen und außen. Im Obergeschoss befinden sich die Schlafzimmer und im Untergeschoss die Technikräume, der Keller und ein Musikzimmer. Große Sandsteinfliesen erstrecken sich vom Erdgeschoss auf die Terrasse und verstärken auf diese Weise den Eindruck eines einzigen durchgehenden Raums zwischen innen und außen.

3

4

1 Exterior view with pool
2 Terrace at the pool
3 Exterior view from east
4 Exterior view with surroundings

1 Außenansicht mit Pool
2 Terrasse am Pool
3 Außenansicht von Osten
4 Außenansicht mit Umgebung

1

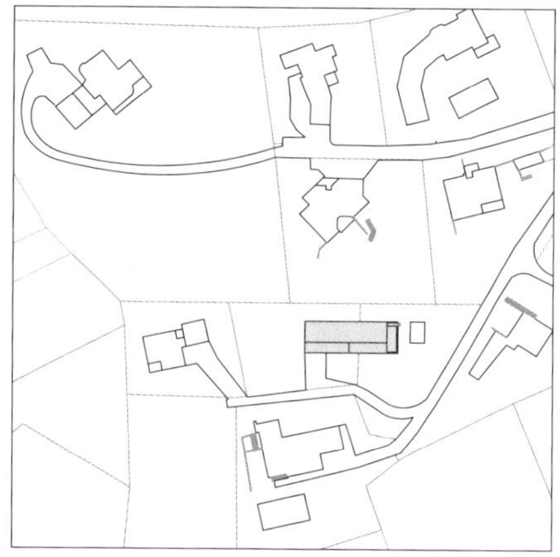

2

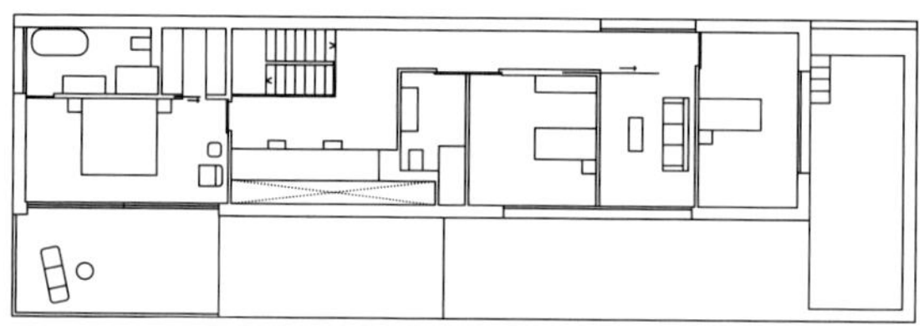

3

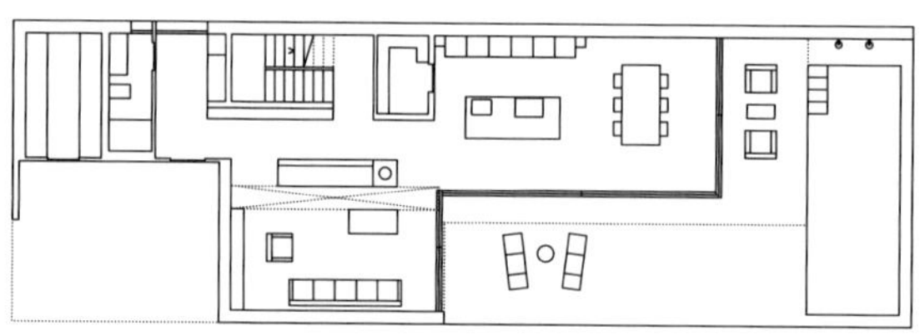

4

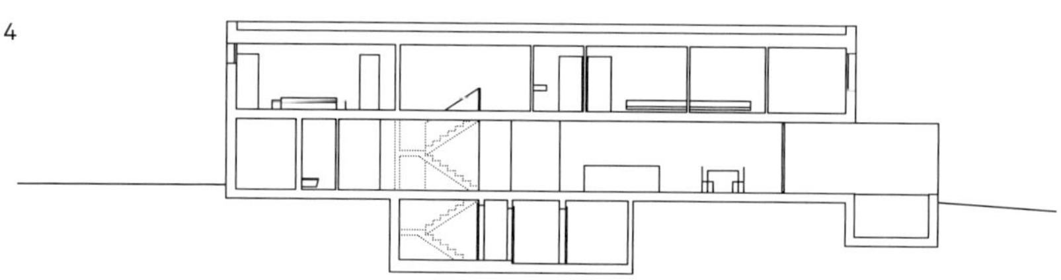

5

6

7

8

1 Site plan
2 First floor plan
3 Ground floor plan
4 Section
5 Dining area
6 Living area with view outside
7 Living area with bookshelf
8 Bedroom

1 Lageplan
2 Grundriss OG
3 Grundriss EG
4 Gebäudeschnitt
5 Essbereich
6 Wohnbereich mit Ausblick
7 Wohnbereich mit Bücherregal
8 Schlafzimmer

1

HAUS FÜR JULIA

1 Exterior view from west with terrace
2 Exterior view from west
3 Exterior view from south

1 Außenansicht von Westen mit Terrasse
2 Außenansicht von Westen
3 Außenansicht von Süden

2

Architects: firm Architekten
Completion: 2016
Location: Lustenau, Vorarlberg, Austria
Gross floor area: 75 m^2
Number of bedrooms: 1
Main materials / building construction: wood / timber construction on solid base plate
Ecological aspects: wooden house, heated only with solar energy and Swedish stove

Architekten: firm Architekten
Fertigstellung: 2016
Ort: Lustenau, Vorarlberg, Österreich
Bruttogeschossfläche: 75 m^2
Anzahl der Schlafzimmer: 1
Hauptmaterialien / Konstruktionsweise: Holz / Holzbau auf massiver Bodenplatte
Ökologische Aspekte: Holzhaus, beheizt nur mit Solarenergie und Schwedenofen

As Julia could not find a suitable apartment for herself on the housing market, she decided to build a house in her parents' garden that would suit her needs. Unique to the property is its quiet location close to the city center. The plot is bordered to the north and south by two residential streets with hardly any traffic. To the east and west it is flanked by gardens with fruit trees. The interior of Haus für Julia is as spacious as possible. The two outer walls, which are parallel to the existing building, and the gable roof resting on them form a large space. The necessary fixtures are placed in this room in such a way that the remaining area is as large as possible, allowing for flexible use.

Nachdem Julia auf dem Wohnungsmarkt keine geeignete Wohnung für sich finden konnte, beschloss sie, ein für ihre Bedürfnisse passendes Haus im Garten der Eltern zu errichten. Einzigartig an diesem Grundstück ist die ruhige Lage in unmittelbarer Nähe zum Stadtzentrum. Das Grundstück wird im Norden und Süden von zwei kaum befahrenen Wohnstraßen begrenzt. Im Osten und Westen wird es von Gärten mit Obstbäumen flankiert. Der Innenraum des Hauses für Julia ist so großzügig wie möglich. Die zwei parallel zum Bestand gestellten Außenwände und das darauf ruhende Satteldach bilden einen Großraum. In diesem wurden die notwendigen Einbauten so platziert, dass eine möglichst große Restfläche flexible Nutzungen zulässt.

3

1

2

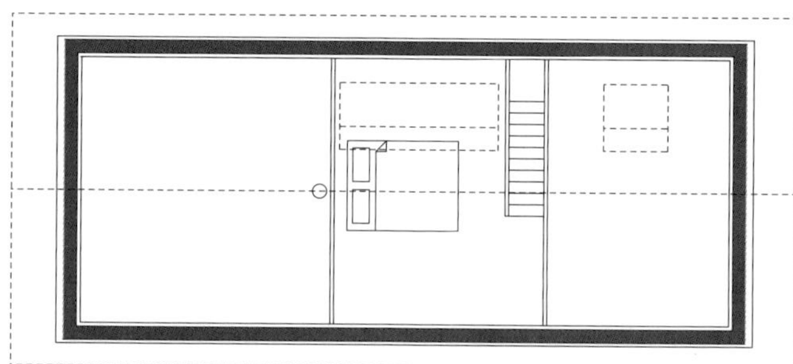

3

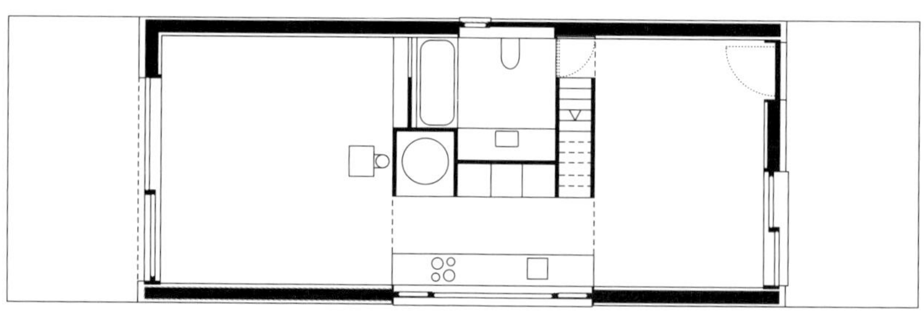

4

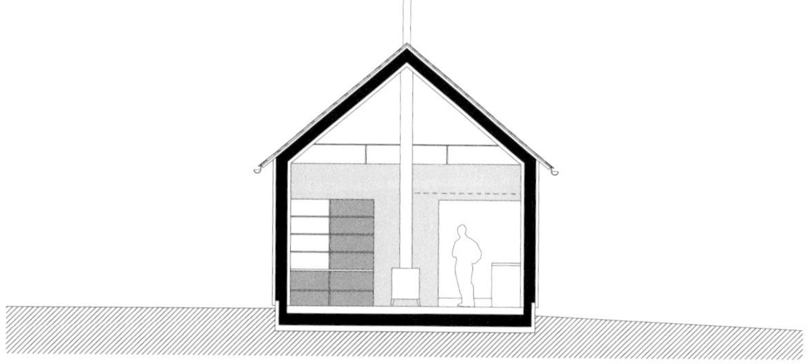

5

6

7

8

1 Site plan
2 Gallery floor plan
3 Ground floor plan
4 Section through the living area
5 Dining area
6 View of the entrance and dining area from the gallery
7 Gallery
8 Living area

1 Lageplan
2 Grundriss Galerie
3 Grundriss EG
4 Schnitt durch den Wohnbereich
5 Essbereich
6 Blick auf Eingangs- und Essbereich von der Galerie
7 Galerie
8 Wohnbereich

FLUH 34G

1

Fluh 34g is in line with modern architecture in Vorarlberg. The existing topography should be changed as little as possible and the house should be carefully placed on the site. The elongated structure is clearly oriented to the south and reveals little of its interior on the north side. The windows on the entrance side are only visible at night because the vertical wooden cladding made of pre-patinated silver fir consistently runs through. As an exception, only the entrance is cut out. On the valley side, the house opens up through large window elements that extend the floor plan to the outside. The single-family house was designed with a partial basement on a solid exposed concrete base in timber construction. The positioning of the residential house and outbuilding creates courtyard situations on both sides of the property with a high quality of stay. Exposed concrete, pre-patinated silver fir and the wood-aluminum windows are the materials of the outer skin. The interior of the building is designed with spruce wood, smooth white wall surfaces and a sanded screed.

Architects: Fischer Rüdenauer Architekten
Completion: 2017
Location: Bregenz-Fluh, Vorarlberg, Austria
Gross floor area: 207 m^2
Number of bedrooms: 1
Main materials / building construction: concrete, wood, glass / timber construction on an exposed concrete base
Ecological aspects: use of local silver fir, heat pump

2

3

Architekten: Fischer Rüdenauer Architekten
Fertigstellung: 2017
Ort: Bregenz-Fluh, Vorarlberg, Österreich
Bruttogeschossfläche: 207 m^2
Anzahl der Schlafzimmer: 1
Hauptmaterialien / Konstruktionsweise: Beton, Holz, Glas / Holzbau auf einem Sichtbetonsockel
Ökologische Aspekte: Verwendung heimischer Weißtanne, Wärmepumpe

Fluh 34g folgt der modernen Architektur in Vorarlberg. Die vorhandene Topografie sollte so wenig wie möglich verändert und das Haus behutsam auf dem Grundstück platziert werden. Der längliche Baukörper ist eindeutig nach Süden ausgerichtet und gibt auf der Nordseite nur wenig von seinem Inneren preis. Die Fenster sind auf der Eingangsseite nur bei Nacht sichtbar, weil die vertikale Holzverschalung aus vorpatinierter Weißtanne konsequent durchläuft. Einzig der Eingang bildet als Einschnitt eine Ausnahme. Auf der Talseite öffnet sich das Haus durch große Fensterelemente, die den Grundriss ins Freie erweitern. Das Einfamilienhaus wurde teilunterkellert auf einem massiven Sichtbetonsockel in Holzbauweise konzipiert. Die Positionierung von Wohnhaus und Nebengebäude ergibt auf beiden Grundstücksseiten Hofsituationen mit hoher Aufenthaltsqualität. Sichtbeton, vorpatinierte Weißtanne und die Holz-Alu-Fenster sind die Materialien der Außenhaut. Das Gebäudeinnere ist mit Fichtenholz, glatten weißen Wandflächen und einem geschliffenen Sichtestrich gestaltet.

4

5

1 Exterior view from southwest
2 Exterior view from north
3 Living and dining area
4 View from the outside into the living room
5 Kitchen

1 Außenansicht von Südwesten
2 Außenansicht von Norden
3 Wohn- und Essbereich
4 Blick von außen in den Wohnraum
5 Küche

1

2

3

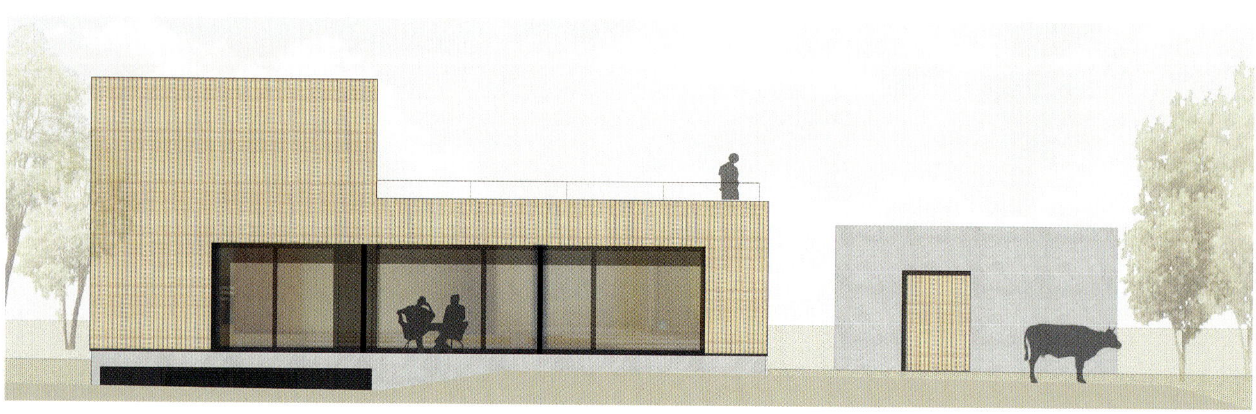

1 North elevation
2 East elevation
3 South elevation
4 First floor plan
5 Ground floor plan
6 Basement plan

1 Aufriss Nordseite
2 Aufriss Ostseite
3 Aufriss Südseite
4 Grundriss OG
5 Grundriss EG
6 Grundriss UG

4

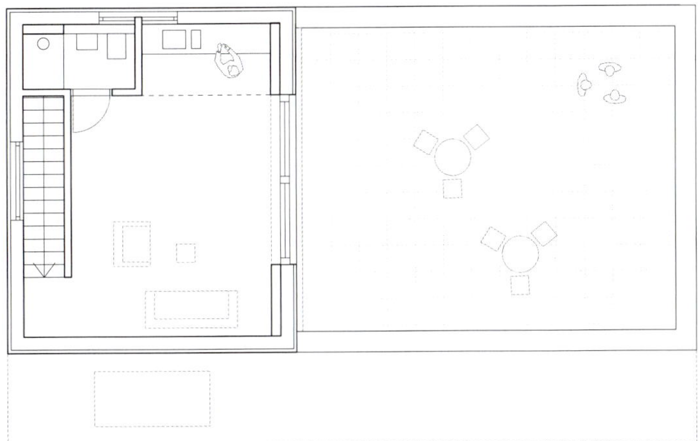

5

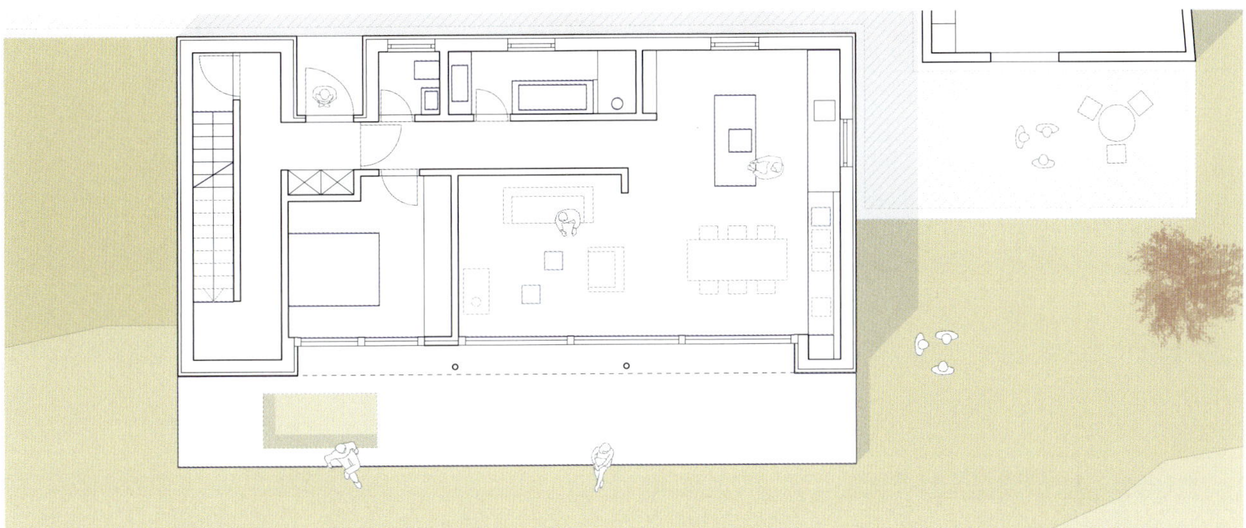

6

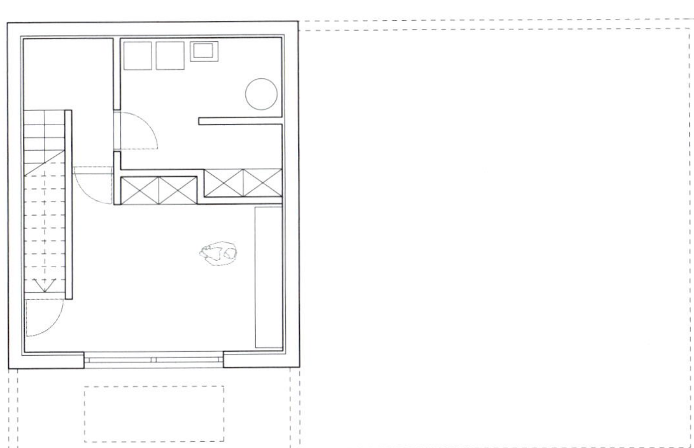

1

EFH IN RIEIN

1 Exterior view from south
2 Living room
3 Exterior view from northwest

1 Außenansicht von Süden
2 Wohnzimmer
3 Außenansicht von Nordwesten

2

Architects: Andreas Fuhrimann Gabrielle Hächler Architekten
Completion: 2015
Location: Riein, Canton of Grisons, Switzerland
Gross floor area: 250 m^2
Number of bedrooms: 4
Main materials / building construction: 3-laminated sheet spruce, anhydrite floor / prefabricated timber construction

Architekten: Andreas Fuhrimann Gabrielle Hächler Architekten
Fertigstellung: 2015
Ort: Riein, Graubünden, Schweiz
Bruttogeschossfläche: 250 m^2
Anzahl der Schlafzimmer: 4
Hauptmaterialien / Konstruktionsweise: 3-Schichtplatte Fichte, Anhydritboden / vorfabrizierter Holzelementbau

The house faces southwest from the slightly set-back entrance towards the valley. There a terrace, which extends over the entire width of the façade on the ground floor, emphasizes the orientation towards the unique landscape view. The basement remains unheated and is used to house the heating system as well as a simple materials store. Similarly, the attic remains unheated and openly ventilated, the insulation layer forms the flat ceiling of the upper living floor. The glazing of the living and dining area on the ground floor covers the entire width of the façade towards the terrace and is protected by the slight cantilever of the upper floor. The outer façade is planked on all sides with rough-sawn conifer wood.

Das Haus richtet sich vom leicht zurückversetzten Eingang südwestlich in Richtung Tal. Dort betont eine Terrasse, die sich im Erdgeschoss über die gesamte Fassadenbreite erstreckt, die Ausrichtung zur landschaftlich einzigartigen Aussicht. Das Untergeschoss bleibt unbeheizt, dient der Unterbringung der Heizungsanlage und als einfaches Materiallager. Analog dazu bleibt auch der Dachraum ohne Heizung und offen belüftet, die Isolationsschicht bildet die flache Decke des oberen Wohngeschosses. Die Verglasung des Wohn- und Essbereiches im Erdgeschoss bedeckt die gesamte Fassadenbreite hin zur Terrasse und wird über die leichte Auskragung des oberen Geschosses geschützt. Die Außenfassade ist allseitig mit sägerauem Nadelholz beplankt.

3

1

2

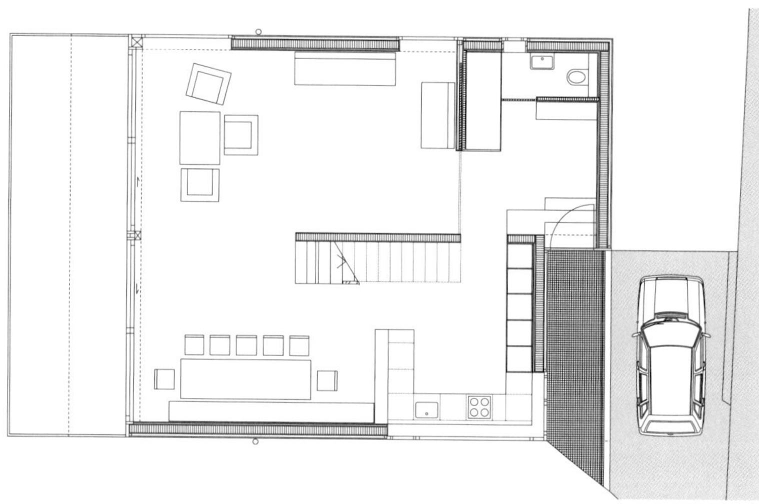

3

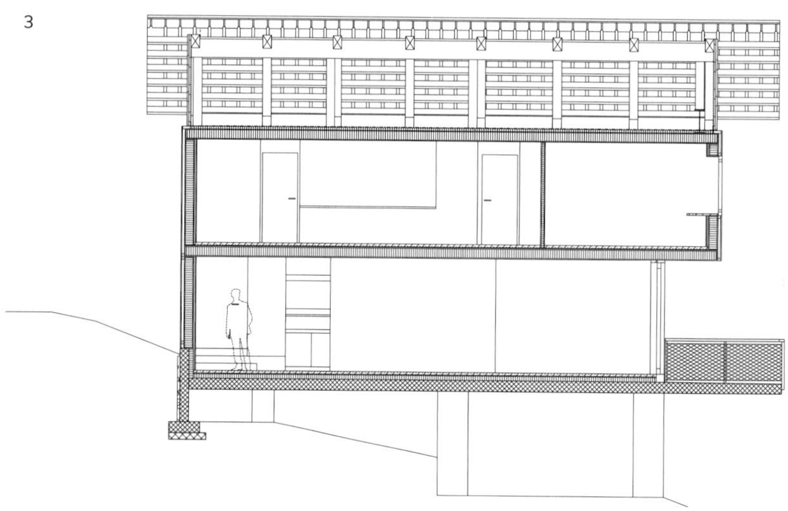

4

5

6

7

1 First floor plan
2 Ground floor plan
3 Longitudinal section
4 Living and dining room
5 First floor stairs and corridor
6 Exterior view from southwest
7 Exterior view from east

1 Grundriss OG
2 Grundriss EG
3 Längsschnitt
4 Wohn- und Esszimmer
5 Treppe und Flur OG
6 Außenansicht von Südwesten
7 Außenansicht von Osten

37 M

1

The single-family house, located in the Vorarlberg Rhine Valley between Schattenwald and the Rheinauen, is 37 meters long. The slender, long figure is the result of the shape of the property and appears as a clear line among the multitude of surrounding single-family homes. The ground plan is organized as an enfilade of rooms, which is then broken down at both ends into spacious, open living and working spaces. On the one hand, the block accommodates the home of a young family and on the other hand a graphic design office. Living and working are thus united under one roof, but are clearly separated by the entrance area and car park, as well as a protected roof terrace on the upper floor. Graphic design was also the inspiration for the façade, which is made of an anthracite-colored polyethylene mesh and can thus be used and redesigned as advertising space at will. Along the longitudinal façades, windows and openings are precisely positioned, and their size and format are adapted to special views of the surroundings.

Architects: Juri Troy Architects
Completion: 2014
Location: Hohenems, Austria
Gross floor area: 285 m^2
Number of bedrooms: 3
Main materials / building construction: polyethylene mesh, wood / pile foundation, timber frame construction
Ecological aspects: low-energy house, heat pump

2

3

Architekten: Juri Troy Architects
Fertigstellung: 2014
Ort: Hohenems, Österreich
Bruttogeschossfläche: 285 m²
Anzahl der Schlafzimmer: 3
Hauptmaterialien / Konstruktionsweise: Polyethylennetz, Holz / Pfahlgründung, Holzriegelbau
Ökologische Aspekte: Niedrigenergiehaus, Wärmepumpe

Das Einfamilienhaus, das im Vorarlberger Rheintal zwischen Schattenwald und den Rheinauen liegt, ist 37 Meter lang. Die schlanke, lange Gestalt ist der Grundstücksform zu verdanken und nimmt sich als klare Linie unter der Vielzahl der umgebenden Einfamilienhausbebauung aus. Der Grundriss ist als Enfilade von Räumen organisiert, die an beiden Enden in großzügige, offene Wohn- und Arbeitsräume aufgelöst wird. Der Riegel beherbergt einerseits das Heim einer jungen Familie und andererseits ein Grafikbüro. Wohnen und Arbeiten sind somit unter einem Dach vereint, jedoch durch den Eingangsbereich und den Parkplatz sowie einer geschützten Dachterrasse im Obergeschoss klar getrennt. Die Tätigkeit der grafischen Gestaltung war auch Inspiration für die Fassade, die aus einem anthrazitfarbenen Polyethylennetz gefertigt wurde und so nach Belieben als Werbefläche genutzt und umgestaltet werden kann. Entlang der Längsfassaden sind Fenster und Öffnungen präzise positioniert und richten sich in Größe und Format nach besonderen Ausblicken in der Umgebung.

4

5

1 Longitudinal view at twilight
2 Bedroom
3 Longitudinal view
4 Dining room
5 Front view

1 Längsansicht in der Dämmerung
2 Schlafzimmer
3 Längsansicht
4 Esszimmer
5 Frontalansicht

1

2

1 Front view at twilight
2 Terrace on the first floor
3 First floor plan
4 Ground floor plan
5 Longitudinal section

1 Frontalansicht in der Dämmerung
2 Terrasse im OG
3 Grundriss OG
4 Grundriss EG
5 Längsschnitt

3

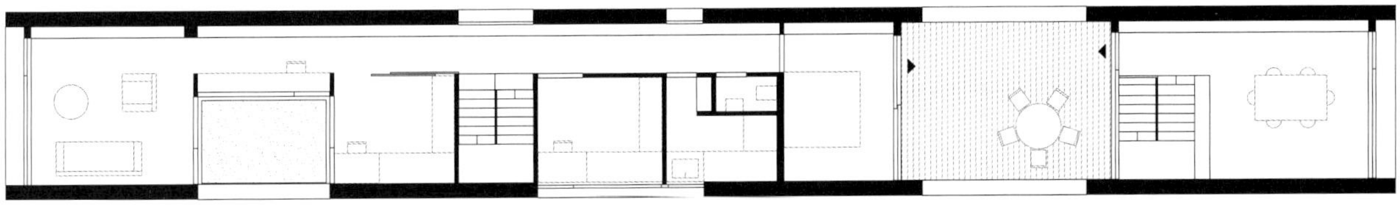

4

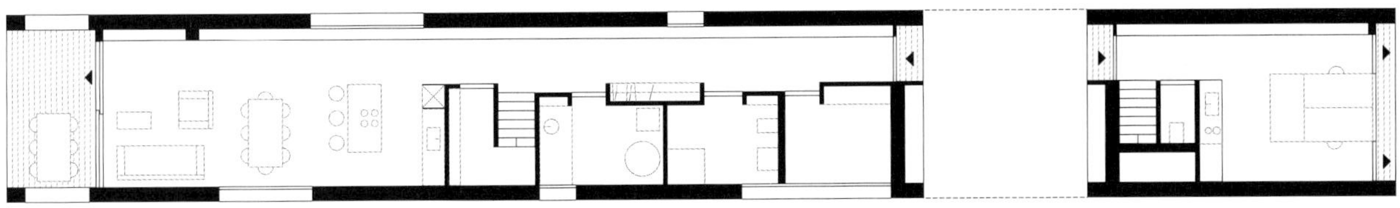

5

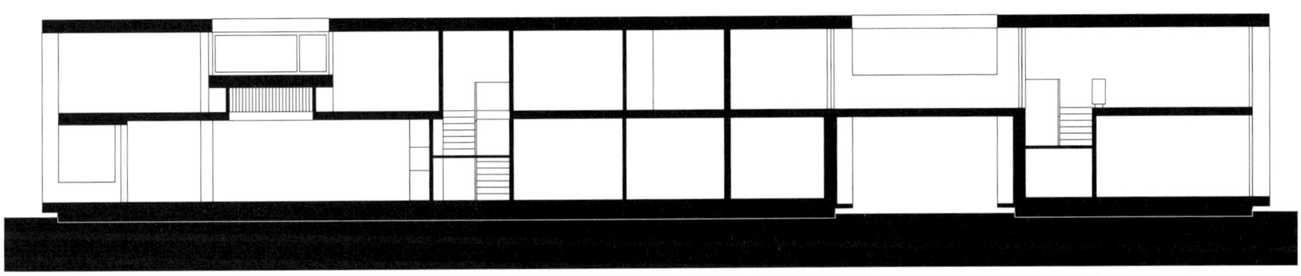

EFH BEI ZÜRICH

1 Building corner and entrance
2 Garden view
3 Kitchen, living and dining room

1 Gebäudeecke und Hauszugang
2 Gartenansicht
3 Küche, Wohn- und Esszimmer

Architects: m3 Architekten
Completion: 2018
Location: near Zurich, Switzerland
Gross floor area: 460 m^2
Number of bedrooms: 4
Main materials / building construction: concrete, wood, glass, steel / solid construction with compact façade and rough plaster (casting plaster)
Ecological aspects: Minergie standard (without certificate)

Architekten: m3 Architekten
Fertigstellung: 2018
Ort: bei Zürich, Schweiz
Bruttogeschossfläche: 460 m^2
Anzahl der Schlafzimmer: 4
Hauptmaterialien / Konstruktionsweise: Beton, Holz, Glas, Stahl / Massivbauweise mit Kompaktfassade und groben Putz (Kellenwurf)
Ökologische Aspekte: Minergiestandard (ohne Zertifikat)

The property is located in a residential quarter from the 1950s, where houses with front gardens are lined up parallel along the streets. The new building deliberately deviates from this pattern. It stands at right angles to the street and is therefore south-facing, as is the garden. Together with the garden pavilion in exposed concrete, an intimate world is created. The residential building has four floors, each with its own type and function. The upper floors offer a view of the Alps. A sculptural staircase creates interesting vertical references. Cores structure the floor plans. Façade projections, bay window-like roof structures, skylights and a sculptural roof design give the gabled roof house a unique expression with the intention of disrupting the key stimuli of the traditional "Hüsli".

Das Grundstück befindet sich in einem Wohnquartier aus den 1950er-Jahren, Häuser mit Vorgärten reihen sich parallel entlang der Straßen auf. Der Neubau weicht bewusst von diesem Muster ab, steht quer zur Straße und ist somit wie der Garten südorientiert. Zusammen mit dem Gartenpavillon in Sichtbeton wurde eine intime Welt geschaffen. Das Wohnhaus verfügt über vier Etagen, jede in ihrer Art und Funktion eigen; die oberen mit Alpensicht. Ein skulpturales Treppenhaus schafft interessante Vertikalbezüge. Kerne gliedern die Grundrisse. Fassadenvorsprünge, erkerartige Dachaufbauten, Dachflächenfenster und eine plastische Dachgestaltung verleihen dem Satteldachhaus einen eigenwilligen Ausdruck mit der Absicht, die Schlüsselreize des traditionellen „Hüsli" zu stören.

3

1

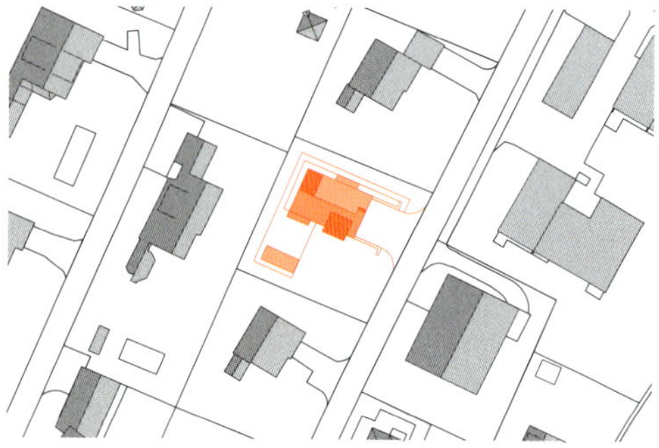

2

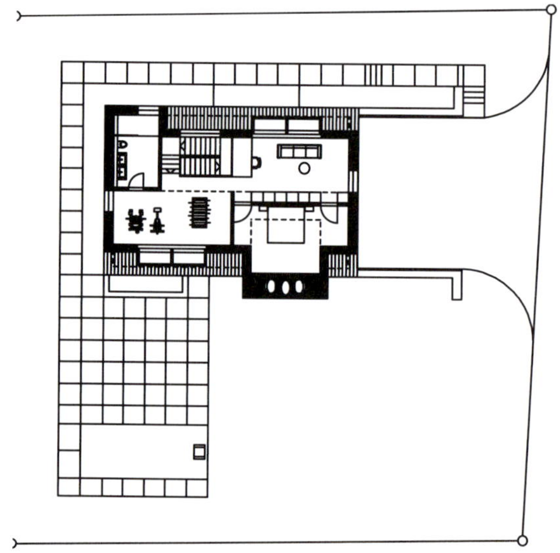

3

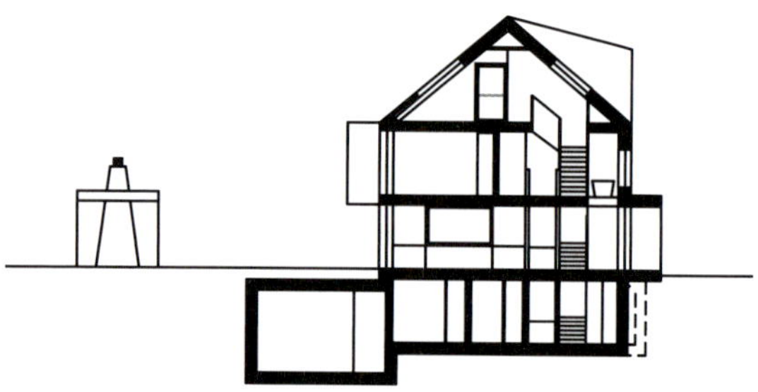

4

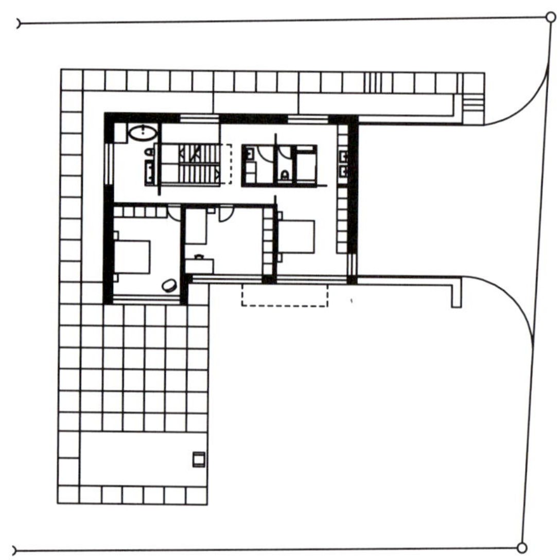

5

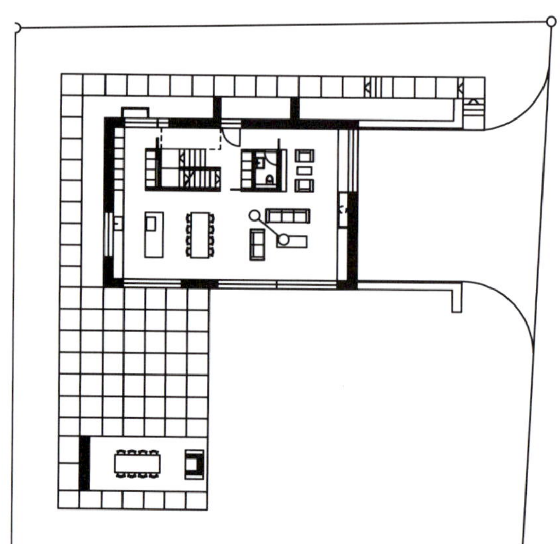

6

7, 8

1 Site plan
2 Top floor plan
3 Cross section
4 First floor plan
5 Ground floor plan
6 Pavilion with outdoor chimney
7 Staircase
8 Bathroom

1 Lageplan
2 Grundriss DG
3 Querschnitt
4 Grundriss OG
5 Grundriss EG
6 Pavillon mit Außenkamin
7 Treppenhaus
8 Badezimmer

PLUS-ENERGIEHAUS

1

The wooden house in Entlebuch Biosphere is based on the tradition of rural architecture. And as an energy producer, it moves with the times. The house slides into the slope and offers the main entrance to the middle floor at ground level. The connected room combines the kitchen, the dining area and a reading corner. From here one gets over a staircase down to the living room. This also provides access to the guest rooms on the lower floor, where up to ten visitors can be accommodated. Opposite the kitchen and hidden from the entrance, a narrow staircase leads up to the roof. This is where the living rooms of the landlords are arranged. The large roof is optically and statically an independent element. It stands on a massive staircase and lift core, a band of windows detaches the roof from the two lower floors and provides a view of the Entlebuch Biosphere all around. The solar tiles on the roof produce 43,800 kWh of electricity every year – 486 percent of what the house consumes. The surplus electricity is fed into the grid.

Architects: Scheitlin Syfrig Architekten
Completion: 2014
Location: Sörenberg, Switzerland
Gross floor area: 492 m^2
Number of bedrooms: 4
Main materials / building construction: wood / timber construction
Ecological aspects: solar panels on the roof, which produce 43,800 kWh electricity per year (486% of the consumption)

2

3

Architekten: Scheitlin Syfrig Architekten
Fertigstellung: 2014
Ort: Sörenberg, Schweiz
Bruttogeschossfläche: 492 m^2
Anzahl der Schlafzimmer: 4
Hauptmaterialien / Konstruktionsweise: Holz / Holzbau
Ökologische Aspekte: Solarpanels auf Dach, die 43.800 kWh Strom pro Jahr (486 % des Verbrauchs) produzieren

Das Holzhaus im Entlebuch lehnt sich in seiner Gestalt an die Tradition der ländlichen Bauweise an und geht auch als Energieerzeuger mit der Zeit. Das Haus schiebt sich in den Hang und bietet hangaufwärts den ebenerdigen Hauptzugang ins mittlere Geschoss. Der zusammenhängende Raum vereint die Küche, den Essbereich sowie eine Leseecke. Von hier gelangt man über eine Treppe hinunter zum Wohnzimmer. Dieses bietet zugleich die Erschließung der Gästezimmer im unteren Geschoss, wo bis zu zehn Besucher einquartiert werden können. Gegenüber der Küche und versteckt vom Eingang führt eine schmale Treppe hinauf ins Dach. Hier ordnen sich die Wohnräume der Hausherren an. Das große Dach ist optisch und statisch ein eigenständiges Element. Es steht auf einem massiven Treppen- und Liftkern, ein Fensterband löst das Dach von den beiden unteren Geschossen und gibt rundherum einen Blick ins Entlebuch frei. Die Solarziegel auf dem Dach produzieren jedes Jahr 43.800 kWh Strom – 486 Prozent dessen, was das Haus verbraucht. Der Stromüberschuss wird ins Netz eingespeist.

4

5

6

1 Exterior view from northwest
2 Exterior view from northeast
3 Exterior view from south with terrace
4 Attic
5 Middle floor interior with dining table
6 Middle floor interior

1 Außenansicht von Nordwesten
2 Außenansicht von Nordosten
3 Außenansicht von Süden mit Terrasse
4 Dachgeschoss
5 Innenraum Mittelgeschoss mit Esstisch
6 Innenraum Mittelgeschoss

1

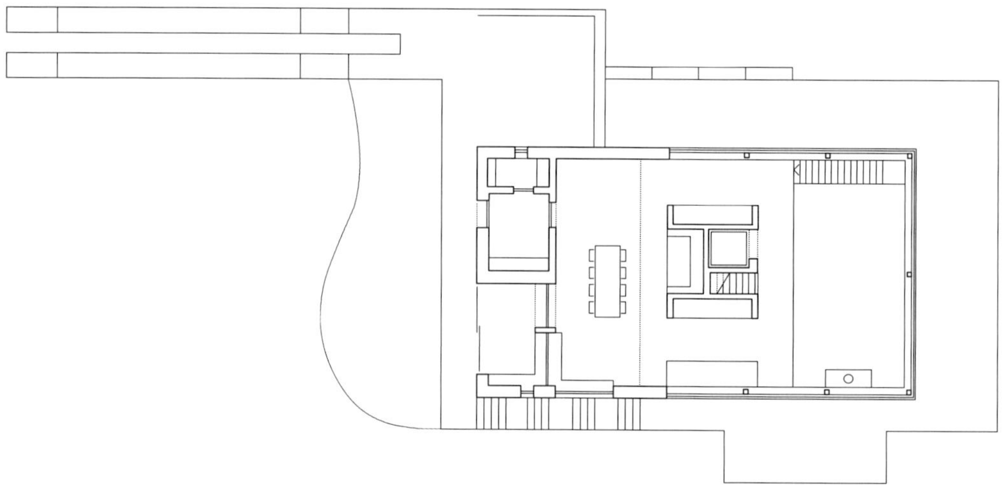

2

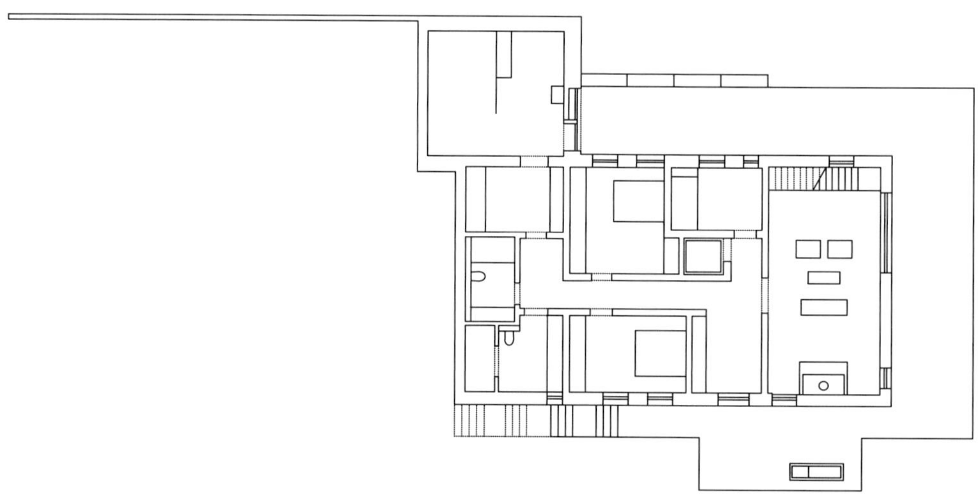

1 Ground floor plan
2 Basement plan
3 Longitudinal section from west
4 Longitudinal section from east
5 Energy consumption scheme

1 Grundriss EG
2 Grundriss UG
3 Längsschnitt Westseite
4 Längsschnitt Ostseite
5 Schema Energieverbrauch

3

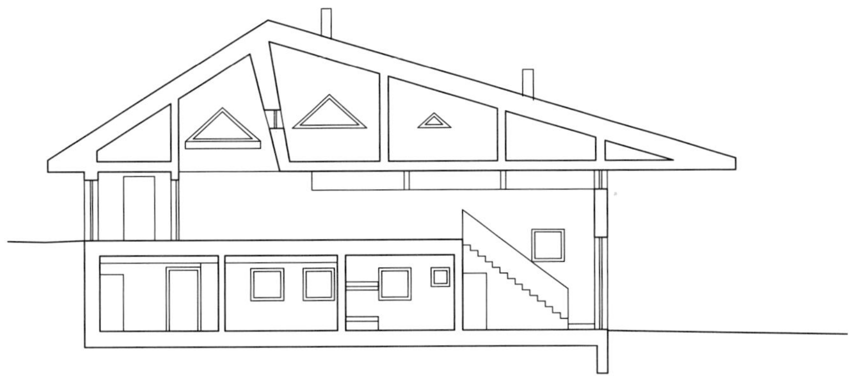

4

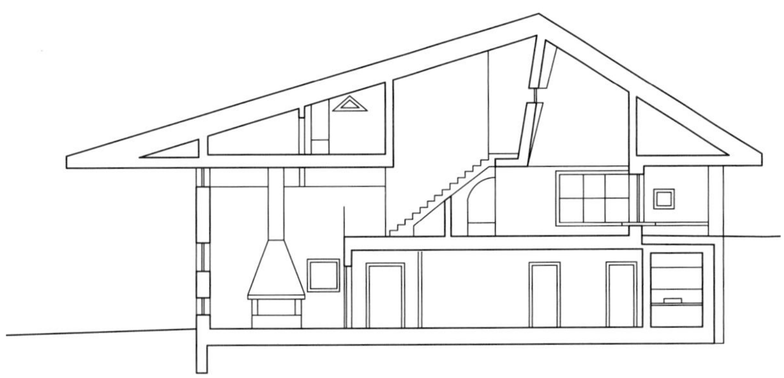

5

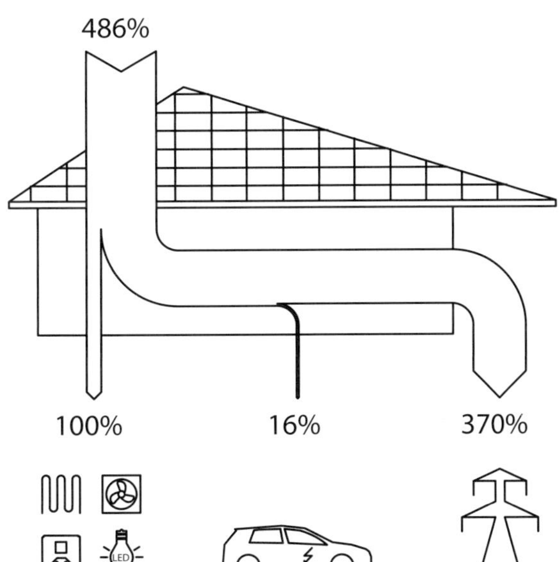

1

EFH NEU-ENDORF

1 Entrance area
2 Exterior view from west
3 Bathroom
4 Exterior view from east

1 Eingangsbereich
2 Außenansicht von Westen
3 Badezimmer
4 Außenansicht von Osten

2

Architects: GAUTSCHI LENZIN SCHENKER Architekten
Completion: 2013
Location: Neuendorf, Switzerland
Gross floor area: 250 m^2
Number of bedrooms: 3
Main materials / building construction: fair-faced concrete, lime sand brick with slurry plaster, brick with lime plaster, anhydrite and solid wood floor / solid construction
Ecological aspects: sustainable building materials

Architekten: GAUTSCHI LENZIN SCHENKER Architekten
Fertigstellung: 2013
Ort: Neuendorf, Schweiz
Bruttogeschossfläche: 250 m^2
Anzahl der Schlafzimmer: 3
Hauptmaterialien / Konstruktionsweise: Sichtbeton, Kalksandstein mit Schlämmputz, Backstein mit Kalkputz, Anhydrit- und Massivholzboden / Massivbauweise
Ökologische Aspekte: nachhaltige Baumaterialien

The residential building is located in a heterogeneous residential quarter in which no uniform stylistic language is used. The sculptural-looking building is composed of three different elements, the center of life is the heated two-story main body, the two outdoor spaces covered by the cantilevered roof complement this perfectly, especially in summer. A garage offers further comfort.

On the ground floor there is the open living and dining area as well as adjoining rooms. The rooms and the bathroom were accommodated on the upper floor. A generous, flowing spatial figure characterizes the inner circulation area. The composition develops in all dimensions from the projecting concrete forecourt, the garage with the two canopy areas to the two-story volume, which ends with the south-east façade.

The client's wish for a massive, robust house is met by the façade with slurry lime-sand brickwork. Canopies and paved outside areas are designed as raw in-situ concrete slabs.

Das Wohnhaus liegt in einem heterogenen Wohnquartier, in dem keine einheitliche Stilsprache verfolgt wird. Der skulptural anmutende Bau setzt sich aus drei verschiedenen Elementen zusammen. Lebensmittelpunkt ist der beheizte zweigeschossige Hauptkörper, die beiden von einem auskragenden Dach überdeckten Außenräume ergänzen diesen vor allem im Sommer optimal. Weiteren Komfort bietet eine Garage.

Im Erdgeschoss befinden sich der offene Wohn- und Essbereich sowie Nebenräume. Die Zimmer und das Bad wurden im Obergeschoss untergebracht. Eine großzügige, fließende Raumfigur prägt den inneren Zirkulationsbereich. Die Komposition entwickelt sich in allen Dimensionen vom ausladenden Betonvorplatz über die Garage mit den beiden Vordachbereichen bis hin zum doppelgeschossigen Volumen, welches mit der Südostfassade seinen Abschluss findet.

Dem Wunsch der Bauherrschaft nach einem massiven, robusten Haus trägt die Fassade mit geschlämmtem Kalksandsteinmauerwerk Rechnung. Vordächer und befestigte Außenbereiche sind mit rohen Ortbetonplatten ausgebildet.

3, 4

1

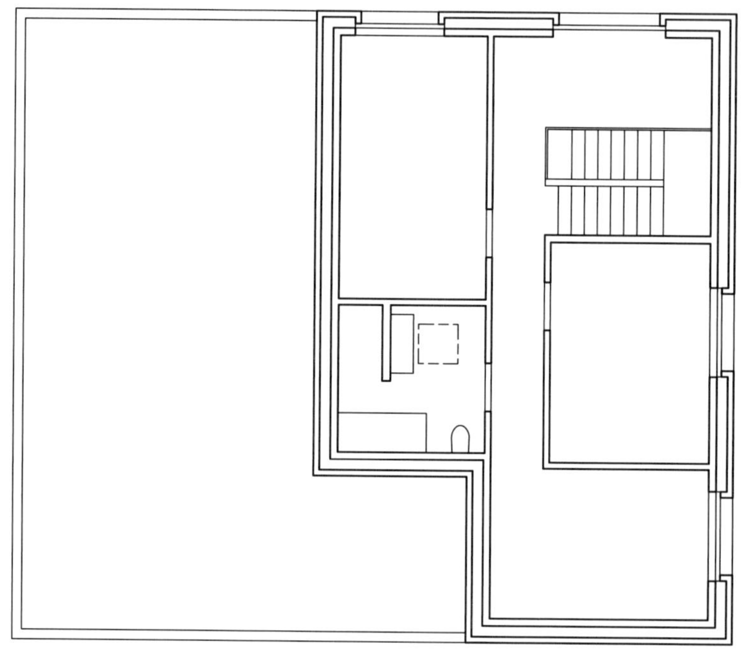

2

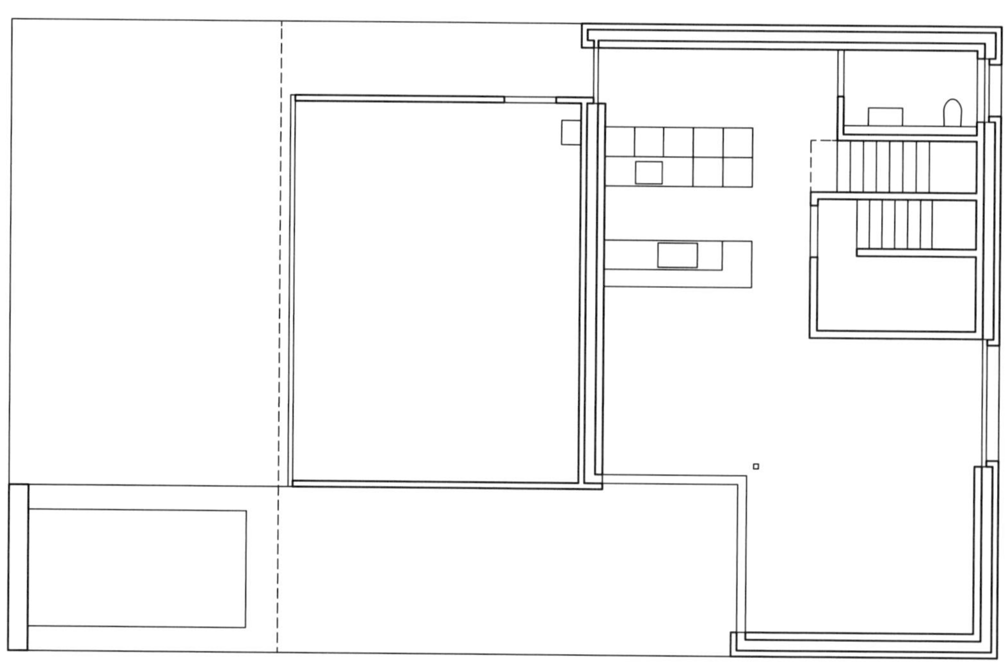

3

4

5

6

1 First floor plan
2 Ground floor plan
3 Living room
4 Exterior view from northwest
5 Stairs
6 Corridor first floor

1 Grundriss OG
2 Grundriss EG
3 Wohnraum
4 Außenansicht von Nordwesten
5 Treppe
6 Korridor OG

EFH RODERSDORF

The prefabricated timber house is situated on a hillside plot with a view over the hills of Alsace. The cubature of the detached house is the reflection of a skilful exploitation of the building regulations, with the interior being divided into split levels in such a way as to create four independent living levels.

The roof and the adjoining façades of the Rodersdorf single-family house are clad with a skin of copper titanium zinc, while the long sides are clad with an airy construction of wooden slats. The spatial structure is determined by a suspended wooden room shell, in which the upper floors are located, so that wood is also the determining material in the interior. The over-high space between shell and casing is the highlight of the house and at the same time its center.

Large window fronts as well as many smaller windows create bright, light-flooded rooms, open up the building to the outside and allow a view of the surrounding landscape.

1, 2

Architects: Berrel Berrel Kräutler
Completion: 2016
Location: Rodersdorf, Switzerland
Gross floor area: 240 m^2
Number of bedrooms: 2
Main materials / building construction: wood, copper titanium zinc / prefabricated timber construction

Architekten: Berrel Berrel Kräutler
Fertigstellung: 2016
Ort: Rodersdorf, Schweiz
Bruttogeschossfläche: 240 m^2
Anzahl der Schlafzimmer: 2
Hauptmaterialien / Konstruktionsweise: Holz, Kupfertitanzink / vorfabrizierte Holzkonstruktion

Das vorfabrizierte Holzhaus steht auf einer Hangparzelle mit Blick über die Hügel des Elsass. Die Kubatur des Einfamilienhauses ist das Abbild einer geschickten Ausnutzung der baugesetzlichen Vorgaben, wobei das Innere so in Split-Levels aufgeteilt ist, dass sich vier unabhängige Wohnebenen ergeben.

Das Dach und die angrenzenden Fassaden des Einfamilienhauses Rodersdorf sind mit einer Haut aus Kupfertitanzink, die Längsseiten dagegen mit einer luftigen Holzlattenkonstruktion eingekleidet. Die Raumstruktur ist bestimmt von einer eingehängten hölzernen Raumschale, in der sich die Obergeschosse befinden, sodass Holz auch im Inneren das bestimmende Material darstellt. Der überhohe Raum zwischen Schale und Hülle ist das Highlight des Hauses und zugleich sein Zentrum.

Große Fensterfronten sowie viele kleinere Fenster erzeugen helle, lichtdurchflutete Räume, öffnen das Gebäude nach außen und ermöglichen den Ausblick auf die umliegende Landschaft.

3

4

1 Exterior view from north and below
2 Lateral exterior view from south
3 Kitchen
4 Basement floor

1 Nordansicht von unten
2 Seitliche Außenansicht von Süden
3 Küche
4 Untergeschoss

1

2

1 Top floor
2 Over-high living space
3 Site plan
4 First floor plan
5 Ground floor plan
6 Section

1 Oberstes Geschoss
2 Überhoher Wohnraum
3 Lageplan
4 Grundriss OG
5 Grundriss EG
6 Schnitt

3

4

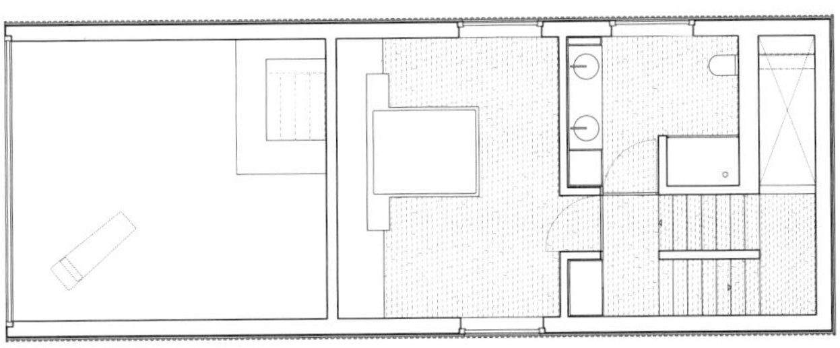

5

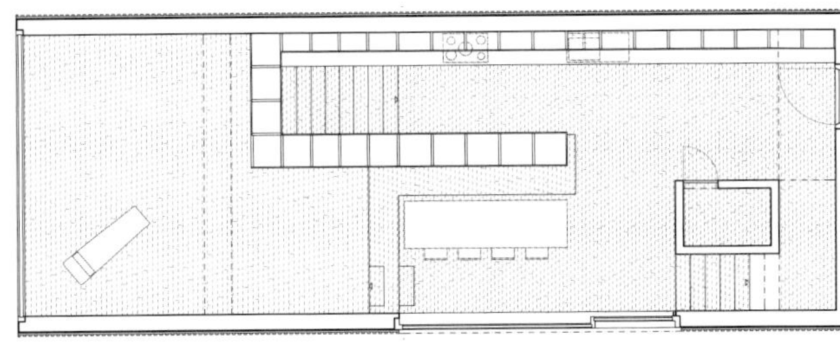

6

1

ZIGER-LOFT

1 Top floor forecourt
2 Exterior view from west
3 Exterior view from south
4 Detail handrail

1 Vorplatz DG
2 Außenansicht von Westen
3 Außenansicht von Süden
4 Handlaufdetail

2

Architects: BRIMO – Architektur und Immobilien
Completion: 2017
Location: Braunwald, Glarus Süd, Switzerland
Gross floor area: 222 m^2
Number of bedrooms: 2–3
Main materials / building construction: larch, spruce, glass, concrete / in-situ concrete, timber element construction spruce, steel supports
Ecological aspects: U-values 0.18 W/m^2K, natural materials

Architekten: BRIMO – Architektur und Immobilien
Fertigstellung: 2017
Ort: Braunwald, Glarus Süd, Schweiz
Bruttogeschossfläche: 222 m^2
Anzahl der Schlafzimmer: 2–3
Hauptmaterialien / Konstruktionsweise: Lärche, Fichte, Glas, Beton / Ortbeton, Holzelementbau Fichte, Stahlstützen
Ökologische Aspekte: U-Werte 0,18 W/m^2K, natürliche Materialien

The view of the valley as well as the mountain panorama and good sun exposure were decisive factors in the choice of the building location, but had to ensure local references and harmonious integration into the terrain.

Entering the round Ziglerloft on the ground floor, the mountains on the other side of the valley are directly in view. This idyll is complemented by the elegantly curved larch wood kitchen and the copper wood storage stove. Three glass doors lead directly to the outdoor spaces around the building.

The two upper floors can be reached via separate wooden staircases, which fan out into the center of the house. The handrails of the stairs, which are curved on both sides, are completed by a harp railing made of fine wooden slats. From the forecourts in the staircase bedrooms and bathrooms of the upper floors are accessible. They can be divided or connected with sliding doors as required. The slightly inclined exterior walls give a feeling of security inside the house; they follow the outer shape of the round building.

Die Aussicht ins Tal und auf das Bergpanorama sowie eine gute Besonnung waren entscheidende Faktoren bei der Wahl des Gebäudestandorts in Braunwald. Ebenso mussten aber lokale Bezüge sowie die harmonische Einpassung ins Gelände gewährleistet werden.

Betritt man das runde Haus im Erdgeschoss, so gleitet der Blick durch den hellen Raum unmittelbar auf die Berge der anderen Talseite. Dieses Idyll wird durch die elegant geschwungene Küche aus Lärchenholz sowie den kupfernen Holzspeicherofen ergänzt. Über drei Glastüren gelangt man direkt auf die Außenplätze um das Gebäude.

Die beiden Obergeschosse erreicht man jeweils über separate Holztreppen, welche fächerartig ins Zentrum des Hauses zulaufen. Die beidseitig geschwungenen Handläufe der Treppen werden von einem Harfengeländer aus feinen Holzlamellen komplettiert. Von den Vorplätzen im Treppenhaus sind Schlafzimmer und Baderäume der Obergeschosse erreichbar, diese können je nach Bedarf mit Schiebetüren unterschiedlich geteilt oder verbunden werden. Die leicht geneigten Außenwände vermitteln im Inneren des Hauses ein Gefühl von Geborgenheit; sie folgen der äußeren Form des runden Gebäudes.

3, 4

1

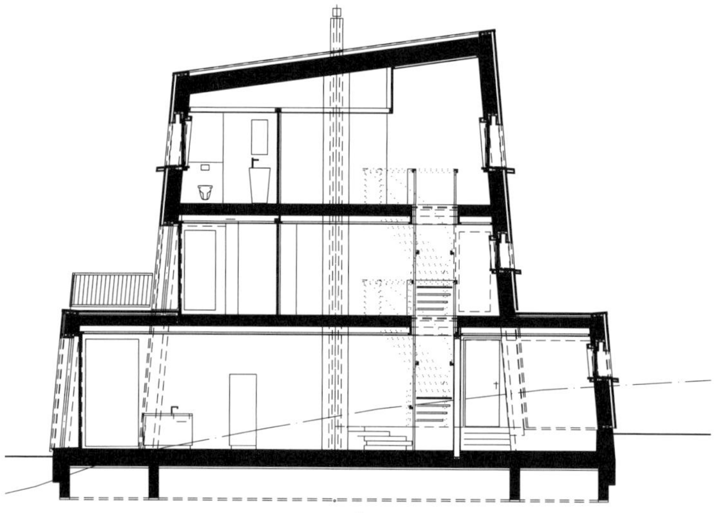

2

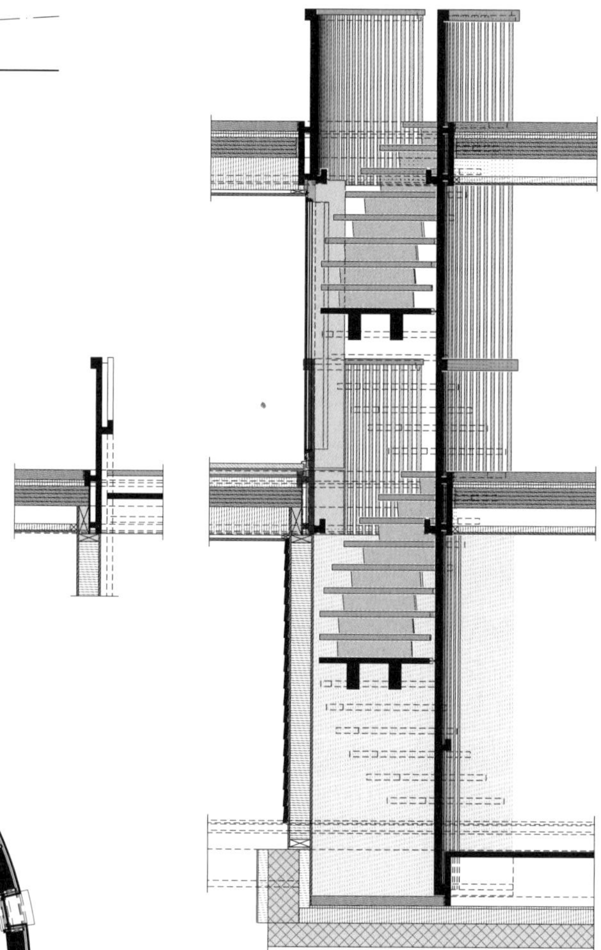

3

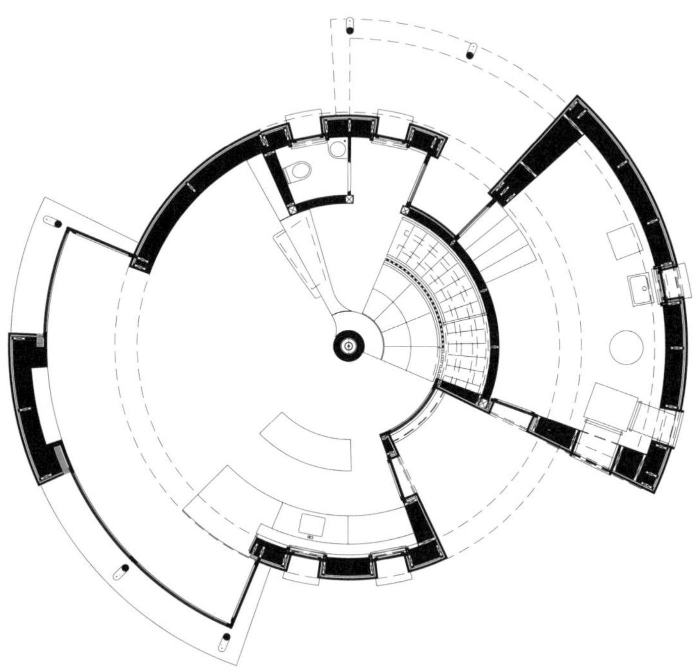

4

5

6

7

1 Section north-south
2 Cross section staircase
3 Ground floor plan
4 Basic stove
5 Project model
6 Stairs
7 Kitchen

1 Schnitt Nord-Süd
2 Querschnitt Treppenanlage
3 Grundriss EG
4 Grundofen
5 Projektmodell
6 Treppe
7 Küche

EFH BILDBÜNTEN

1

This new residential building is quietly restrained in its heterogeneous surroundings. The sculpturally structured wooden house in a soft black tone forms an outdoor ensemble with the two adjoining buildings in exposed concrete. The willow and the edge of the forest at the foot of the Freudenberg are spatially integrated into it. The living and dining room is directly related to this natural garden through the generous window opening. A single-flight staircase stretches from the living room to the open workroom on the upper floor, which in turn is connected to the living room via an air space. The rooms all have different proportions and precisely set views, which opens up spatial diversity and different worlds of experience for the compact house. The walls, the ceiling and the roof are made of solid multilayer panels of spruce wood, visible from the inside. The use of purely natural materials such as the lime mortar floor, the clay walls and the raw solid wood create a noticeable pleasant room climate.

Architects: Gredig Walser Architekten AG
Completion: 2014
Location: Bad Ragaz, Switzerland
Gross floor area: 340 m^2
Number of bedrooms: 4
Main materials / building construction: wood, lime, clay / element construction in wood

2

3

Architekten: Gredig Walser Architekten AG
Fertigstellung: 2014
Ort: Bad Ragaz, Schweiz
Bruttogeschossfläche: 340 m²
Anzahl der Schlafzimmer: 4
Hauptmaterialien / Konstruktionsweise: Holz, Kalk, Lehm / Elementbau in Holz

Das neue Wohnhaus hält sich in seinem heterogenen Umfeld leise zurück. Das plastisch gegliederte Holzhaus in einem weichen Schwarzton bildet mit den beiden Nebenbauten in Sichtbeton ein Außenraumensemble. Die Weide und der Waldsaum am Fuß des Freudenbergs werden darin räumlich eingebunden. Der Wohn- und Essraum steht durch die großzügige Fensteröffnung in direktem Bezug zu diesem Naturgarten. Über eine einläufige Treppe wird eine Raumfolge vom Wohnraum bis zum offenen Arbeitsraum im Obergeschoss aufgespannt, der wiederum über einen Luftraum mit dem Wohnraum verbunden ist. Die Zimmer weisen alle unterschiedliche Proportionen und präzise gesetzte Ausblicke auf, was dem kompakten Haus räumliche Vielfalt und unterschiedliche Erlebniswelten eröffnet. Die Wände, die Decke und das Dach sind aus massiven Mehrschichtplatten aus Fichtenholz gebaut, welche innen sichtbar sind. Die Verwendung von rein natürlichen Materialien wie der Kalkmörtelboden, die Lehmwände und das rohe Massivholz schaffen ein spürbar angenehmes Raumklima.

4

5

1 Southwest façade with mountain backdrop
2 Dining room and kitchen
3 Living room with lime mortar floor and clay wall
4 Living room with air space to the upper floor
5 Bedroom with balcony in front

1 Südwestfassade mit Bergkulisse
2 Esszimmer und Küche
3 Wohnraum mit Kalkmörtelboden und Lehmwand
4 Wohnraum mit Luftraum zum Obergeschoss
5 Schlafzimmer mit vorgelagertem Balkon

1

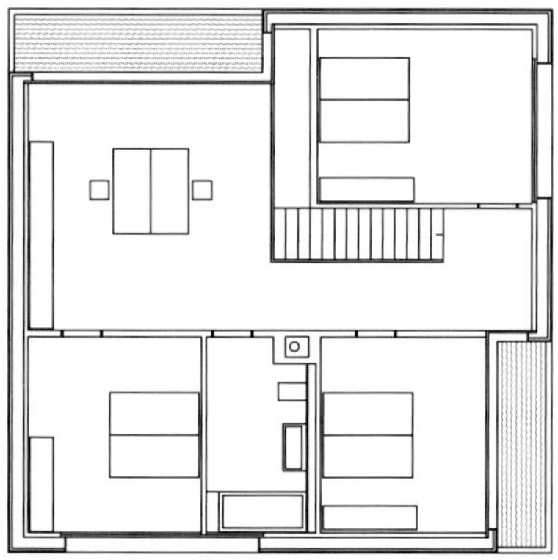

2

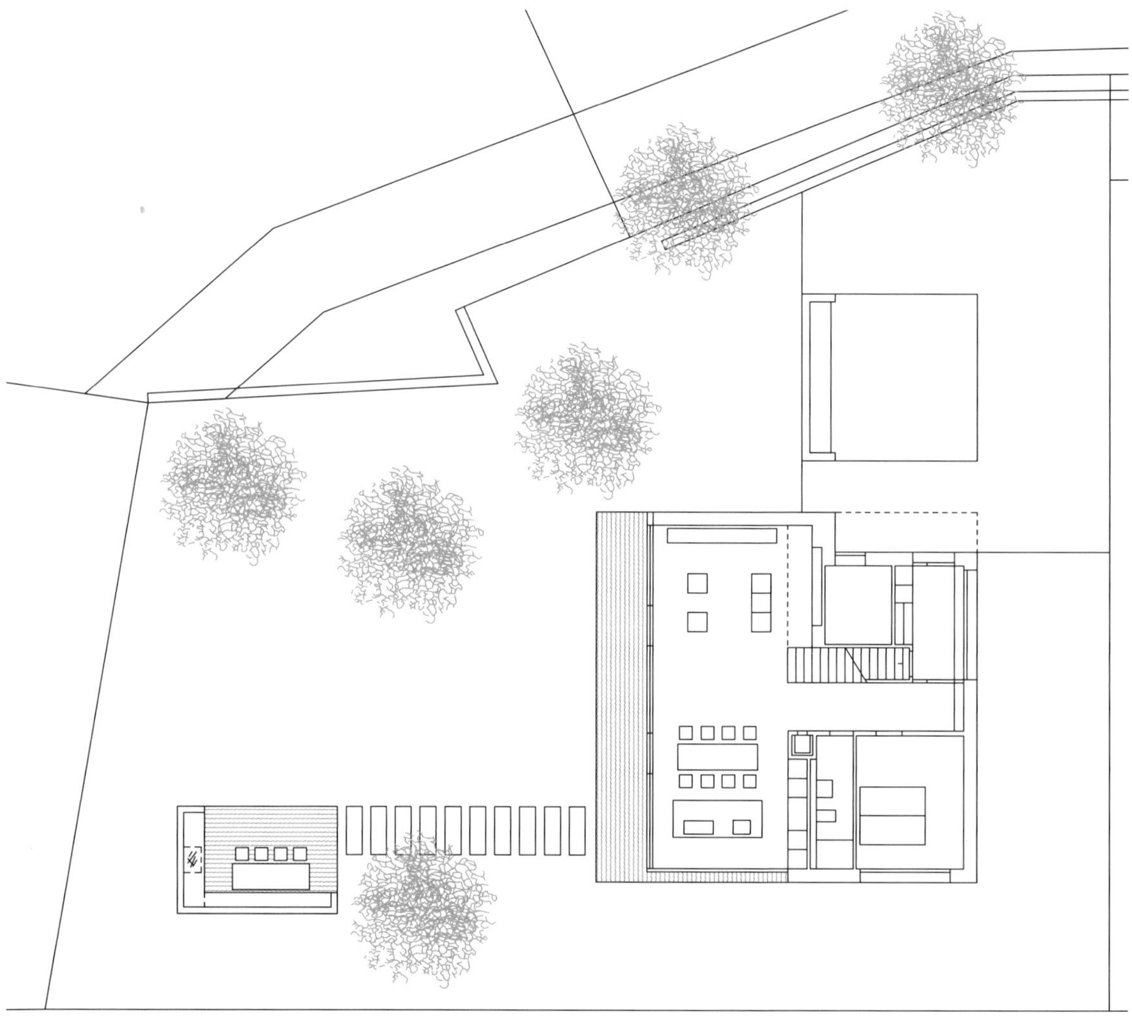

1 First floor plan
2 Ground floor plan
3 Longitudinal section
4 Site plan

1 Grundriss OG
2 Grundriss EG
3 Längsschnitt
4 Lageplan

3

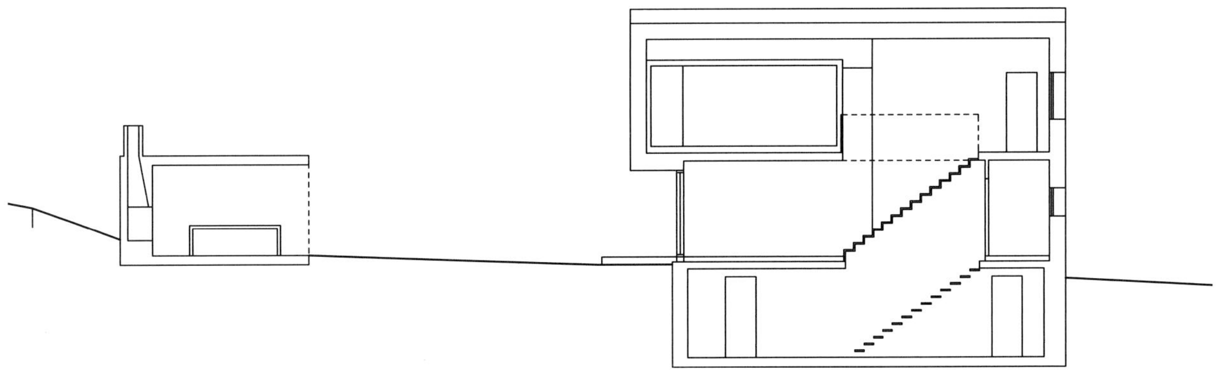

4

EFH EMBERGER

1

Architects: LP architektur
Completion: 2012
Location: Wagrain, Austria
Gross floor area: 280 m^2
Number of bedrooms: 4
Main materials / building construction: wood / timber frame construction with solid wood ceiling
Ecological aspects: district heating, solar plant

The new three-story residential building is positioned in the property in such a way that it takes into account the specified distances and establishes urban development references to the surroundings. The entrance is located on the east side of the building and is followed by a generously, covered forecourt. The entrance is subtle and can be read as a building recess. Via the spatial interface of the cloakroom area, the ground floor plan develops as a one-room concept towards the west and is zoned into sub-areas which experience different qualities through their external references. A simple wooden façade combined with concrete dominates the appearance of the building.

2

Der Neubau des dreigeschossigen Wohnhauses ist so im Grundstück positioniert, dass er die vorgegebenen Abstände berücksichtigt und städtebauliche Bezüge zur Umgebung herstellt. Über die an der Ostseite situierte Zufahrt mit anschließender großzügiger, überdachter Vorzone erreicht man den Eingang, der subtil – als Gebäudeeinschnitt lesbar – in Erscheinung tritt. Über die räumliche Schnittstelle des Garderobenbereichs entwickelt sich der Erdgeschossgrundriss als Ein-Raum-Konzept nach Westen hin und zoniert sich in Teilbereiche, die über ihre Außenbezüge unterschiedliche Qualitäten erfahren. Eine einfache Holzfassade in Kombination mit Beton prägt das Erscheinungsbild des Hauses.

3

Architekten: LP architektur
Fertigstellung: 2012
Ort: Wagrain, Österreich
Bruttogeschossfläche: 280 m²
Anzahl der Schlafzimmer: 4
Hauptmaterialien / Konstruktionsweise: Holz / Holzriegelbau mit Massivholzdecke
Ökologische Aspekte: Fernwärme, Solaranlage

1 Exterior view from east
2 Exterior view from north
3 Exterior view from west
4 Exterior view from south
5 Living space

1 Außenansicht von Osten
2 Außenansicht von Norden
3 Außenansicht von Westen
4 Außenansicht von Süden
5 Wohnraum

4, 5

1

2

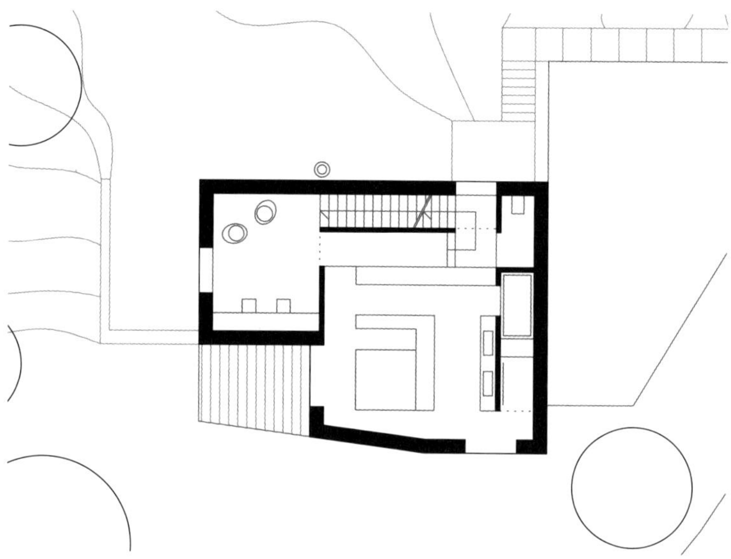

3

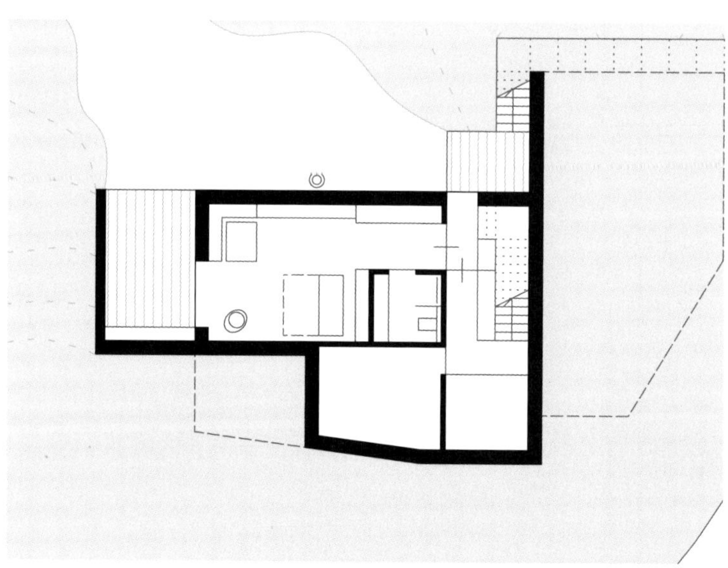

4

5

1 Site plan
2 First floor plan
3 Basement floor plan
4 Dining room
5 Entrance

1 Lageplan
2 Grundriss OG
3 Grundriss UG
4 Esszimmer
5 Hauseingang

MAISON MONT-SUR-ROLLE

1

A house combined with a small guesthouse, a strongly sloping terrain, a panorama view and limiting communal building regulations determined the structure and form of the Maison Mont-sur-Rolle. The property, which is situated on the Rolle hills, has a wonderful view on the Lake Geneva and the Alps towards the south. The building is organized around the integrated kitchen, dining and living area, which forms the building's core. The two glass fronts of the southern façade reflect two levels with a difference in height that is analogous to the sloping terrain. While the upper floor is dedicated to dining, enjoyment and receiving guests, the lower level accommodates the bedrooms and family living room. The different heights are also reflected in the living room steps. Since the communal building regulations required slanted roofs with projecting canopies, the project was developed around that theme. The three roof areas are aligned according to the three preferred views, while the large roof overhangs protect the two terraces.

Architects: Pierre-Alain Dupraz Architecte
Completion: 2014
Location: Mont-sur-Rolle, Switzerland
Gross floor area: 130 m^2
Number of bedrooms: 3
Main materials / building construction: anodized aluminum panels / timber frame construction
Ecological aspects: pellet heating

2

3

214

Architekten: Pierre-Alain Dupraz Architecte
Fertigstellung: 2014
Ort: Mont-sur-Rolle, Schweiz
Bruttogeschossfläche: 130 m^2
Anzahl der Schlafzimmer: 3
Hauptmaterialien / Konstruktionsweise: eloxierte Aluminiumplatten / Holzrahmenbau
Ökologische Aspekte: Pelletheizung

Der Wunsch nach einem Haus mit einem kleinen Gästehaus, das stark geneigte Gelände, ein Panoramablick und einschränkende kommunale Bauvorschriften bestimmten Form und Struktur vom Maison Mont-sur-Rolle. Das Grundstück auf den Hügeln von Rolle hat nach Süden eine wunderbare Aussicht auf den Genfer See und die Alpen. Das Gebäude ist um den integrierten Küchen-, Ess- und Wohnbereich organisiert, der als Kern des Gebäudes dient. Die beiden Glasfronten der Südfassade zeigen zwei Ebenen mit einem Höhenunterschied, der dem geneigten Gelände entspricht. Während das Obergeschoss dem Essen, Genießen und dem Empfang von Gästen gewidmet ist, beherbergt die untere Ebene die Schlafzimmer und das Familienwohnzimmer. Die unterschiedlichen Höhen zeigen sich auch in den Stufen des Wohnzimmers. Da die kommunalen Bauvorschriften Schrägdächer mit Vordach verlangen, wurde das Projekt um dieses Thema herum entwickelt. Die drei Dachflächen sind entsprechend der drei bevorzugten Ausblicke ausgerichtet, während die großen Dachüberstände die beiden Terrassen schützen.

4

5

1 Exterior view in the evening
2 Living area and kitchen
3 Street view
4 Street view with Alps and Lake Geneva
5 Dining and living area

1 Außenansicht am Abend
2 Wohnzimmer und Küche
3 Straßenansicht
4 Straßenansicht mit Alpen und Genfer See
5 Ess- und Wohnbereich

1

2

1 View outside
2 Garden view
3 Longitudinal elevation
4 Roof structure
5 Ground floor plan
6 Site plan

1 Ausblick
2 Gartenansicht
3 Aufriss Längsseite
4 Dachkonstruktion
5 Grundriss EG
6 Lageplan

3

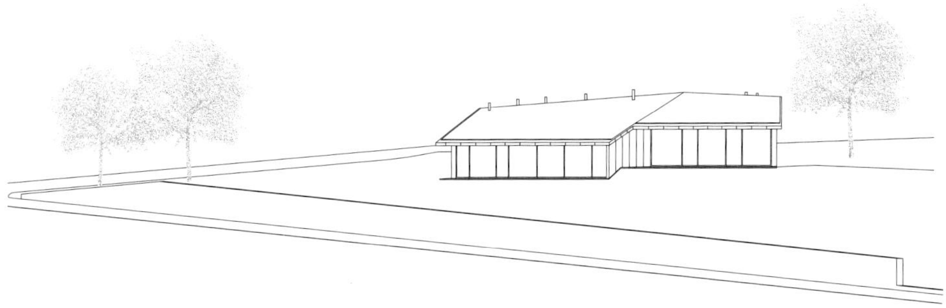

4

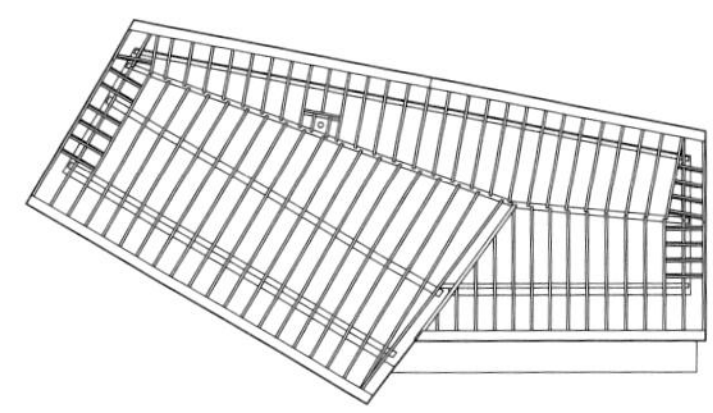

5

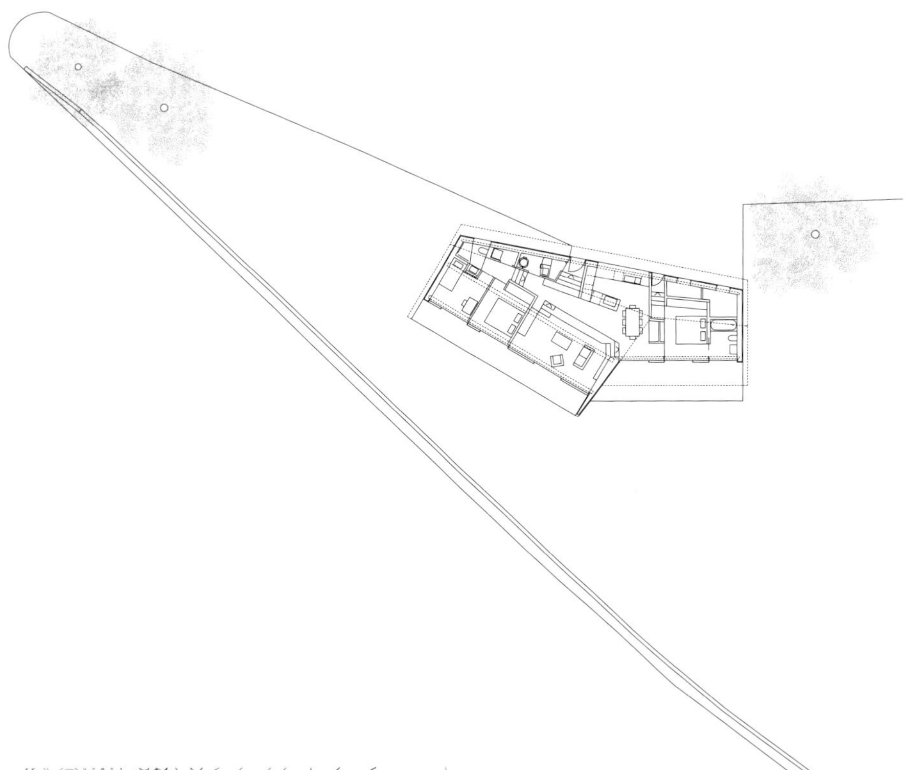

6

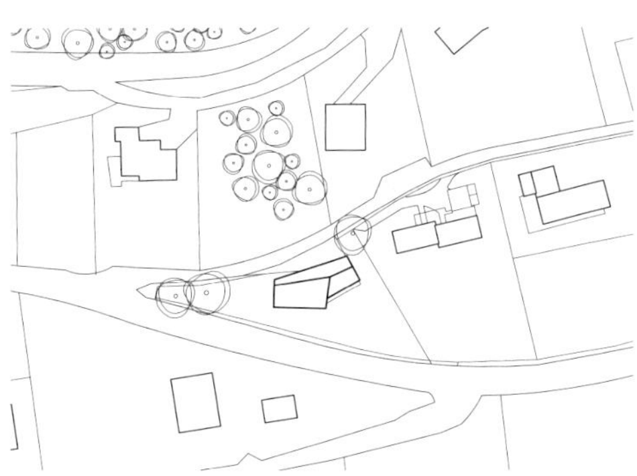

GRANDEZZA & WEITBLICK

1

Architects: Husistein & Partner AG
Completion: 2013
Location: Rombach, Switzerland
Gross floor area: 199 m^2
Number of bedrooms: 3
Main materials / building construction: wood, rock wool, wooden elements / timber construction on base in solid construction
Ecological aspects: Minergie-A, air-to-water heat pump with photovoltaic

The white single-story building seems to float elegantly above the slope. The single-family house in Rombach is supported only by the barely perceptible plinth, a remnant of a house from the 1950s, and a row of slender steel pillars. Perforated, offset façade elements enclose the white cuboid with a fine ornamentation. Together with the wide, slender roof and the terrace on the slope, which offers a wide view of the valley, they reinterpret the architectural language of the 1950s and 1960s. Inside, the roof's layers of beams stretched in different directions are visible. The supporting structure, spans and direction of support characterize the rooms, which are entirely in white. The compact building core in mustard yellow and Bordeaux contrasts the spatial continuum of the main living area.

2

218

3

Elegant scheint der weiße eingeschossige Baukörper über dem Hang zu schweben. Das Einfamilienhaus in Rombach stützt sich nur auf dem kaum wahrnehmbaren Sockel, einem Überbleibsel eines Hauses aus den 1950er-Jahren, und einer Reihe schlanker Stahlpfeiler ab. Gelochte, gegeneinander versetzte Fassadenelemente umfassen den weißen Quader mit einem feinen Ornament. Sie interpretieren zusammen mit dem weit ausladenden, schlanken Dach und der hangseitigen Terrasse, die den weiten Blick ins Tal freigibt, die Architektursprache der 1950er- und 1960er-Jahre neu. Im Innern sind die in unterschiedliche Richtungen gespannten Balkenlagen des Daches sichtbar. Tragwerk, Spannweiten und Tragrichtung prägen die ganz in Weiß gehaltenen Räume. Der kompakte Gebäudekern in Senfgelb und Bordeaux kontrastiert das Raumkontinuum des Hauptwohnteils.

4

Architekten: Husistein & Partner AG
Fertigstellung: 2013
Ort: Rombach, Schweiz
Bruttogeschossfläche: 199 m^2
Anzahl der Schlafzimmer: 3
Hauptmaterialien / Konstruktionsweise: Holz, Steinwolle, Holzelemente / Holzkonstruktion auf Sockel in Massivbauweise
Ökologische Aspekte: Minergie-A, Luft-Wasser-Wärmepumpe mit Photovoltaik

1 Dining area with view towards the living room
2 Living room
3 Exterior view from the garden
4 Exterior view from the entrance
5 Skylight in the building core
6 Bathroom

1 Essbereich mit Blick Richtung Wohnzimmer
2 Wohnzimmer
3 Außenansicht vom Garten
4 Außenansicht von der Einfahrt
5 Oberlicht im Gebäudekern
6 Bad

5

6

1

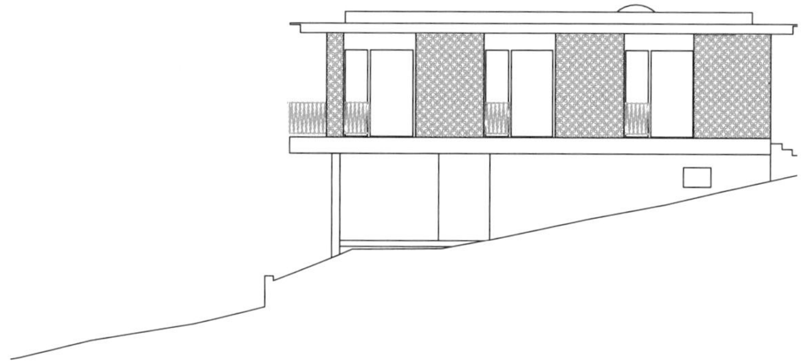

2

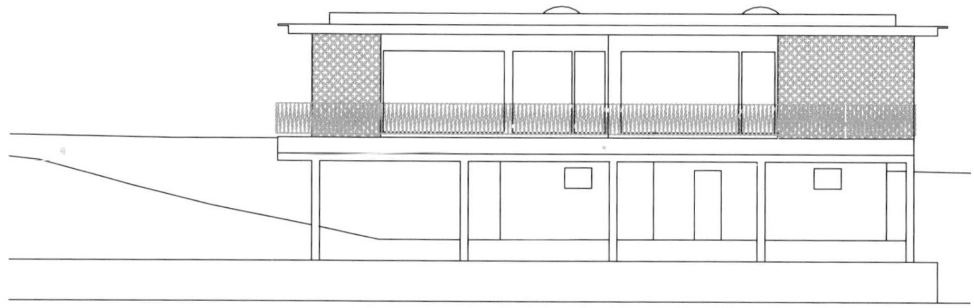

3

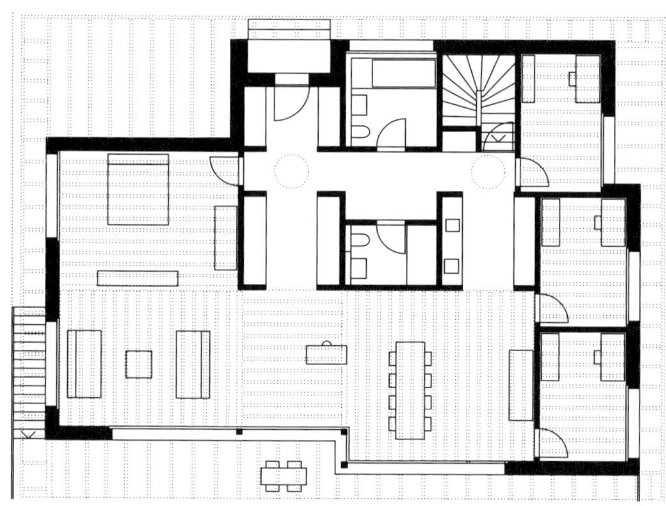

4

5

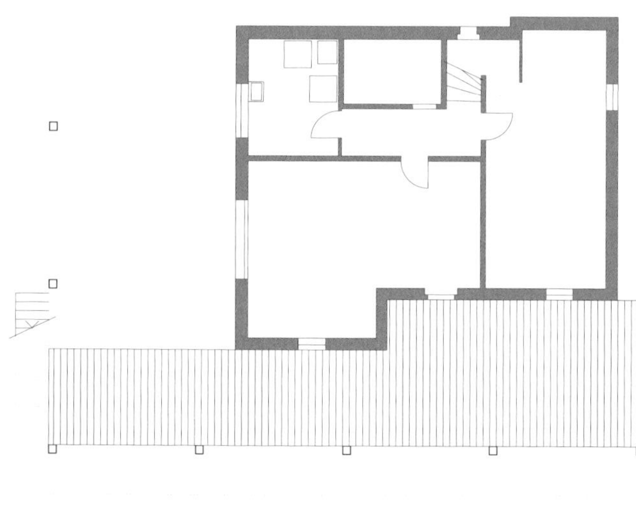

6

7

8

1 East elevation
2 South elevation
3 Floor plan living floor
4 Site plan
5 Floor plan garden floor
6 View from the living room
7 View of the building core
8 Living space

1 Ansicht Ostseite
2 Ansicht Südseite
3 Grundriss Wohngeschoss
4 Lageplan
5 Grundriss Gartengeschoss
6 Aussicht vom Wohnzimmer
7 Blick auf Gebäudekern
8 Wohnraum

SONNEN-HAUS

1

COMMOD HOUSE BSL Sun House consists of two modules in timber frame construction, which are stretched out in an L-shape. The house was manufactured in the factory and was placed on screw foundations on the building site in only 1.5 hours. The sheltered sun terrace offers a view as far as Koralpe. A well thought-out and optimized room layout creates space and at the same time allows for openness, which spans the living area as the light-flooded center of the house and the focal point between the two bedrooms. The sun light can reach every corner of the house and makes the Sun House an energy place, which nevertheless shields itself from the slope. A special highlight is the panorama window in the shape of an orthogonal trapezoid. Inside, natural materials predominate, such as the real wood oak flooring and the oiled spruce beams that span the high gable area. The wood creates a very pleasant and healthy room climate. All used materials are recyclable and can be dismantled.

Architects: COMMOD-HAUS GmbH
Completion: 2019
Location: near Graz, Styria, Austria
Gross floor area: 80 m^2
Number of bedrooms: 2
Main materials / building construction: wood / timber frame construction
Ecological aspects: natural and recyclable materials, cellulose insulation, wood-based materials

2

3

Architekten: COMMOD-HAUS GmbH
Fertigstellung: 2019
Ort: bei Graz, Steiermark, Österreich
Bruttogeschossfläche: 80 m^2
Anzahl der Schlafzimmer: 2
Hauptmaterialien / Konstruktionsweise: Holz / Holzriegelbauweise
Ökologische Aspekte: natürliche und recycelbare Materialien, Zellulosedämmung, Holzwerkstoffe

COMMOD HOUSE BSL Sonnenhaus besteht aus zwei Modulen in Holzriegelkonstruktion, die in L-Form aufgespannt sind. Das Haus wurde im Werk gefertigt und in nur 1,5 Stunden auf dem Bauplatz auf Schraubfundamenten versetzt. Die geschützt gelegene Sonnenterrasse bietet einen Ausblick bis hin zur Koralpe. Eine durchdachte und optimierte Raumaufteilung schafft Platz und lässt gleichzeitig Offenheit zu, die den Wohnbereich als lichtdurchflutetes Zentrum des Hauses und Mittelpunkt zwischen den beiden Schlafräumen aufspannt. Die Sonnenstrahlen erreichen jede Ecke des Hauses und machen das Sonnenhaus zu einem Energieort, der sich dennoch zum Hangrücken hin schützend abschirmt. Ein besonderes Highlight ist das Aussichtsfenster in Form eines orthogonalen Trapezoids. Im Inneren überwiegen natürliche Materialien wie das Eichendielenparkett aus Echtholz und die geölten Fichtenholzträger, die den hohen Giebelbereich aufspannen. Das Holz sorgt für ein sehr angenehmes und gesundes Raumklima. Alle eingesetzten Materialien sind recycel- und rückbaubar.

4

5

6

1 Exterior view from west
2 Exterior view with sun terrace
3 Exterior view with modern interpreted window shutter
4 Carport with photovoltaic panels and storage room
5 Entrance area canopy with platform
6 Interior with white oiled spruce wood beams

1 Außenansicht von Westen
2 Außenansicht mit Sonnenterrasse
3 Außenansicht mit modern interpretiertem Fensterladen
4 Carport mit Photovoltaikpaneelen und Abstellraum
5 Eingangsbereichüberdachung mit Podest
6 Innenraum mit weiß geölten Fichtenholzträgern

1

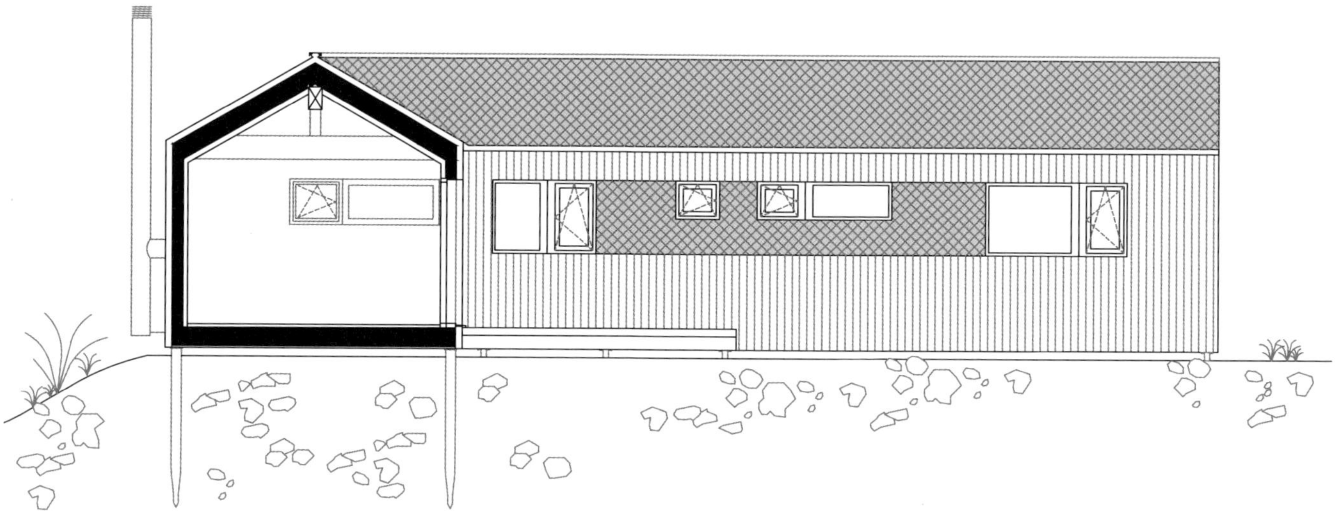

2

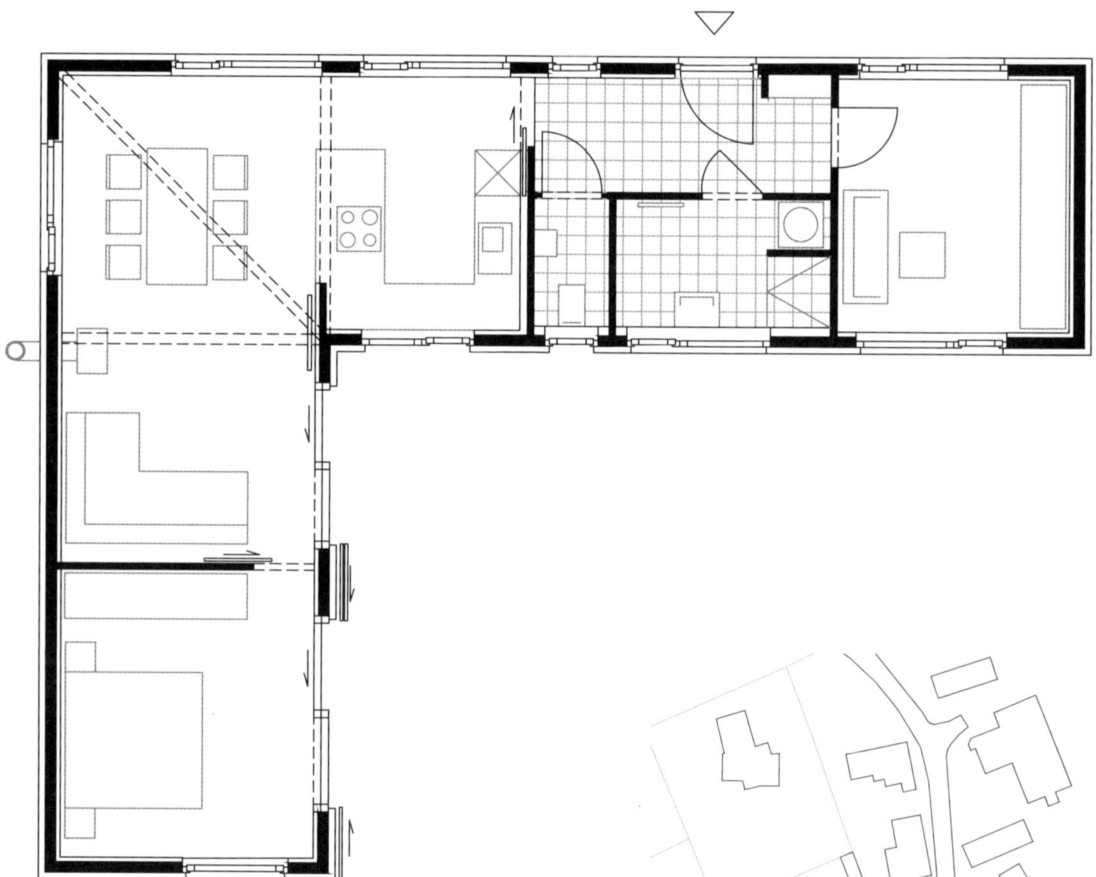

3

5

4

1 Section
2 Ground floor plan
3 Site plan
4 Bedroom with real wood oak flooring
5 Detail of the window in the shape of an orthogonal trapezoid

1 Schnitt
2 Grundriss
3 Lageplan
4 Schlafzimmer mit Eichendielenparkett aus Echtholz
5 Detail des Fensters in Form eines orthogonalen Trapezoids

HAUS P

1

The conical plot of land, measuring around 500 square meters, is situated on the ridge of a lake municipality in Zurich. The dimensions of the structure result from the tapering shape of the building plot, which is located at an intersection. The single-family house comprises two full floors with attic, as well as a basement with underground parking. The architecture is direct and accurate; the protruding and receding floors of the single-shell concrete construction are stacked on top of each other.

The heavy structure lends a presence to the site and is in dialogue with a mighty pine tree bordering the house on the slope. The window openings are precisely placed in the individual rooms and create views of the lake and the distance. A sculptural staircase opens up the densely organized floors. A puristically designed garden room encloses the compact structure, transforms the interior into the exterior and creates a high degree of homely intimacy with a hedge surrounding the property.

Architects: spillmann echsle architekten
Completion: 2010
Location: Erlenbach, Zurich, Switzerland
Gross floor area: 283 m^2
Number of bedrooms: 4
Main materials / building construction: lightened exposed concrete / exposed concrete construction single-shell
Ecological aspects: Minergie, controlled ventilation, geothermal probe

2

Architekten: spillmann echsle architekten
Fertigstellung: 2010
Ort: Erlenbach, Zürich, Schweiz
Bruttogeschossfläche: 283 m²
Anzahl der Schlafzimmer: 4
Hauptmaterialien / Konstruktionsweise: aufgehellter Sichtbeton / Sichtbetonbau einschalig
Ökologische Aspekte: Minergie, kontrollierte Lüftung, Erdsonde

Das konische und rund 500 Quadratmeter messende Grundstück liegt am Bergrücken einer Zürcher Seegemeinde. Die Abmessungen des Baukörpers ergeben sich aus der sich verjüngenden Form der Bauparzelle, die an einer Kreuzung liegt. Das Einfamilienhaus umfasst zwei Vollgeschosse mit Attika sowie ein Untergeschoss mit Tiefgarage. Die Architektur ist direkt und präzise; die vor- und rückspringenden Geschosse der einschaligen Betonkonstruktion sind aufeinander gestapelt.

Der schwere Baukörper verleiht dem Ort eine Präsenz und steht in Dialog mit einer mächtigen, hangseitig an das Haus grenzenden Föhre. Die Fensteröffnungen sind in den einzelnen Räumen präzis gesetzt und schaffen Ausblicke auf den See und in die Ferne. Eine skulpturale Treppe erschließt die dicht organisierten Geschosse. Ein puristisch ausgestalteter Gartenraum umfasst den kompakten Baukörper, transformiert den Innen- in den Außenraum und schafft, mit einer das Grundstück umschließenden Hecke, eine hohe wohnliche Intimität.

3

4

1 View from the terrace of the attic
2 Entrance side with pine
3 Garden terrace
4 Exterior view

1 Ausblick von der Terrasse der Attika
2 Eingangsseite mit Föhre
3 Gartenterrasse
4 Außenansicht

1

1 Living room
2 Second floor plan
3 Site plan
4 First floor plan
5 Ground floor plan
6 Longitudinal section
7 Basement floor plan
8 Cross section

1 Wohnzimmer
2 Grundriss 2. OG
3 Lageplan
4 Grundriss 1. OG
5 Grundriss EG
6 Längsschnitt
7 Grundriss UG
8 Querschnitt

2

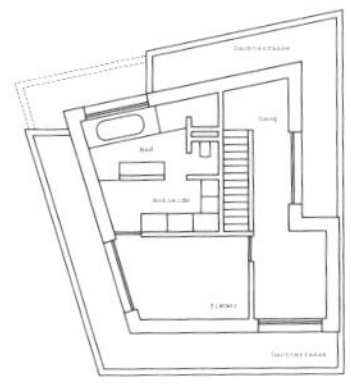

3

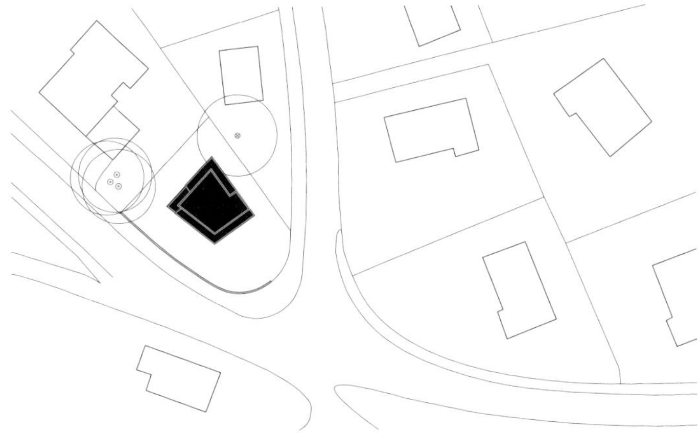

4

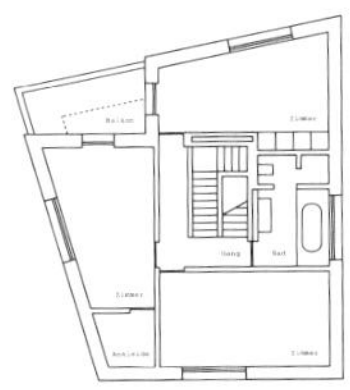

5

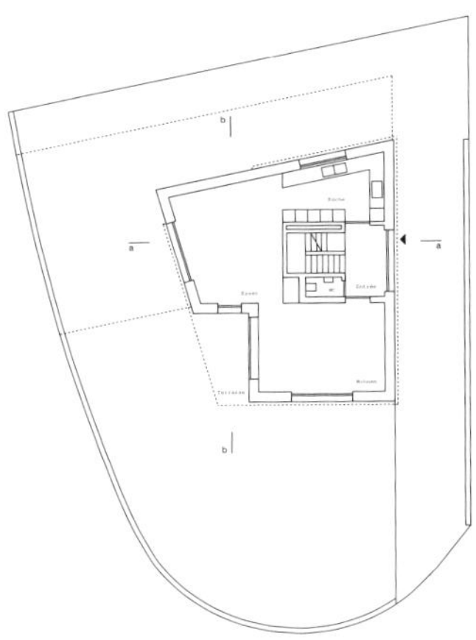

6

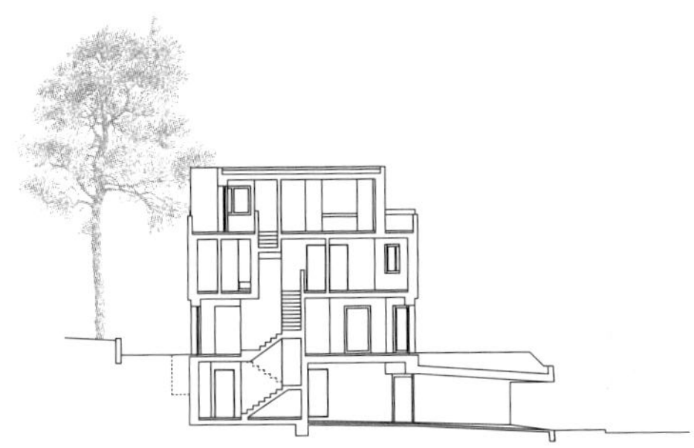

7

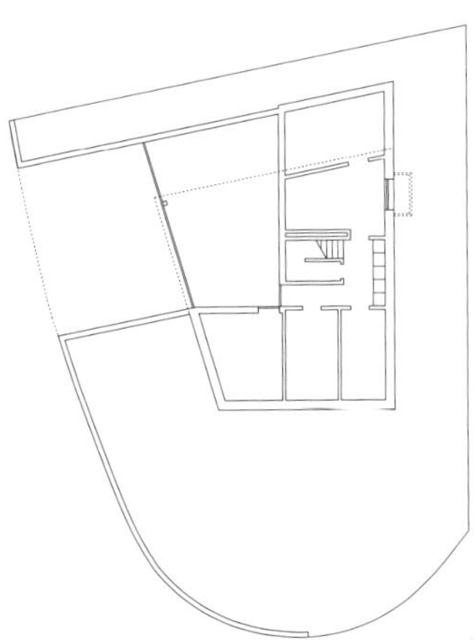

8

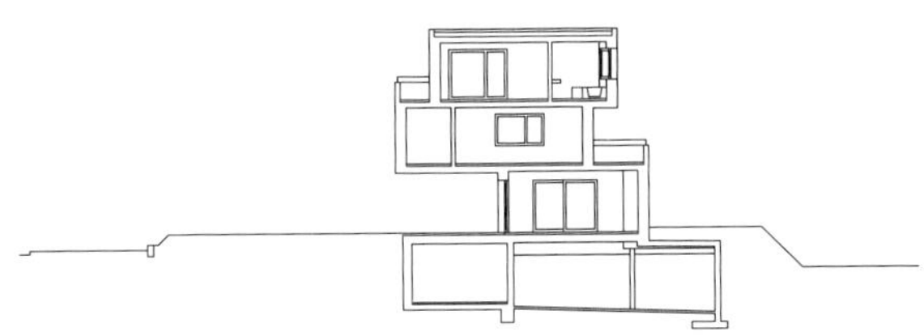

BADEHAUS

1

Architects: COMMOD-HAUS GmbH
Completion: 2019
Location: near Eisenstadt, Austria
Gross floor area: 69 m²
Number of bedrooms: 2
Main materials / building construction: wood / timber frame construction
Ecological aspects: natural and recyclable materials, cellulose insulation, wood-based materials

The Bathhouse is an ensemble of different shades of white – from the geometrically blended wooden façade, which captures the most diverse light scenarios, to the custom-made interior. Vertical slats in front of the windows provide privacy and shade, giving the house a cool aura and cooling for the residents during the hot summer months. The only non-white design element is the dining table and the matching bench. The seating group picks up on the slant that runs through the entire house from the entrance and opens up the living area to direct the residents and their view directly out to the lake. The Bathhouse consists of a central living area from where the two bedrooms, separated by sliding doors, are accessed. When the sliding elements are opened, the living room merges smoothly into the adjacent rooms. The play of light and shadow on the façade creates a completely different picture during the day and depending on the weather conditions.

2

Das Badehaus ist ein Ensemble aus verschiedenen Weiß-Schattierungen – von der geometrisch geschnittenen Holzfassade, die unterschiedlichste Lichtszenarien einfängt, bis zum Interieur nach Maß. Vertikale Lamellen vor den Fenstern bilden Sichtschutz und Beschattung, was dem Haus eine kühle Aura verleiht und den Bewohnern während der heißen Sommermonate Abkühlung verschafft. Die einzigen nicht weißen Designelemente sind der Esstisch und die dazugehörige Sitzbank. Die Sitzgruppe greift die Schräge auf, die sich vom Eingang durch das ganze Haus zieht und den Wohnraum öffnet, um die Bewohner und deren Blick direkt hinaus zum See zu leiten. Das Badehaus besteht aus einem zentralen Wohnbereich, von dem aus die beiden Schlafräume, abgetrennt durch Schiebetüren, erschlossen werden. Bei Öffnung der Schiebeelemente geht der Wohnraum fließend in die angrenzenden Räume über. Das Spiel von Licht und Schatten auf der Fassade erzeugt tagsüber und je nach Witterung ein immer völlig anderes Bild.

3

4

Architekten: COMMOD-HAUS GmbH
Fertigstellung: 2019
Ort: bei Eisenstadt, Österreich
Bruttogeschossfläche: 69 m^2
Anzahl der Schlafzimmer: 2
Hauptmaterialien / Konstruktionsweise: Holz / Holzriegelbauweise
Ökologische Aspekte: natürliche und recycelbare Materialien, Zellulosedämmung, Holzwerkstoffe

1 Exterior view from north with vertical slats in front of the windows
2 Exterior view from south
3 Exterior view of the wings
4 View of sliding elements in the living area
5 Bathroom with custom-made interior
6 Exterior view with exciting play of light and shadow
7 Detail of the handmade façade

1 Außenansicht von Norden mit vertikalen Lamellen vor den Fenstern
2 Außenansicht von Süden
3 Außenansicht der Flügel
4 Sicht auf Schiebeelemente im Wohnraum
5 Bad mit Interieur nach Maß
6 Außenansicht mit spannendem Licht- und Schattenspiel
7 Detail der in Handarbeit gefertigten Fassade

5,6

7

1

2

1 Dining table in gray oiled oak with custom-made stainless steel legs
2 Central living area with 270-degree kitchen
3 View from north
4 Site plan
5 View from south
6 Section
7 Ground floor plan

1 Esstisch in Eiche grau geölt mit maßgefertigten Edelstahlbeinen
2 Zentraler Wohnbereich mit 270-Grad Küche
3 Ansicht Nordseite
4 Lageplan
5 Ansicht Südseite
6 Schnitt
7 Grundriss

3

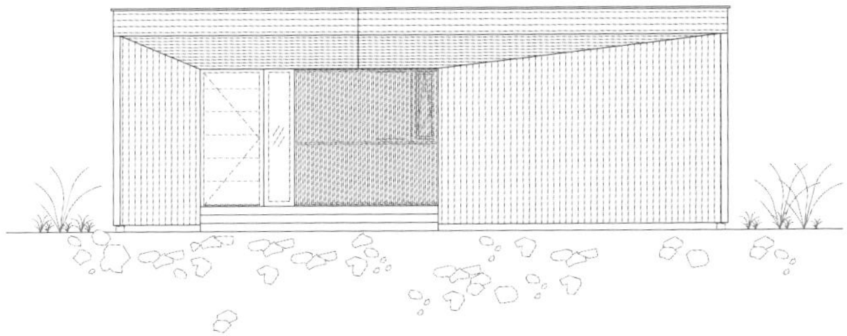

4

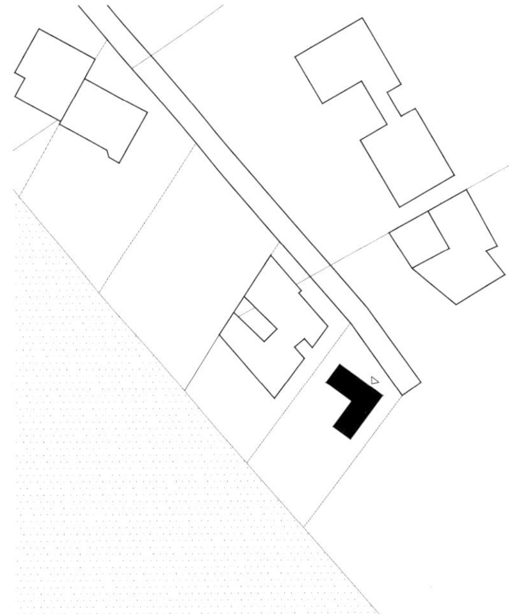

5

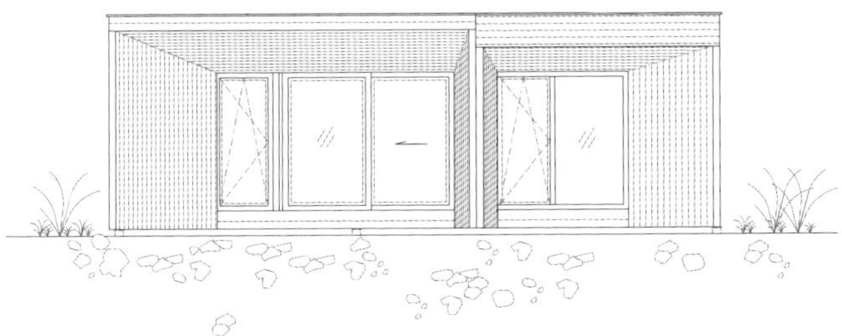

6

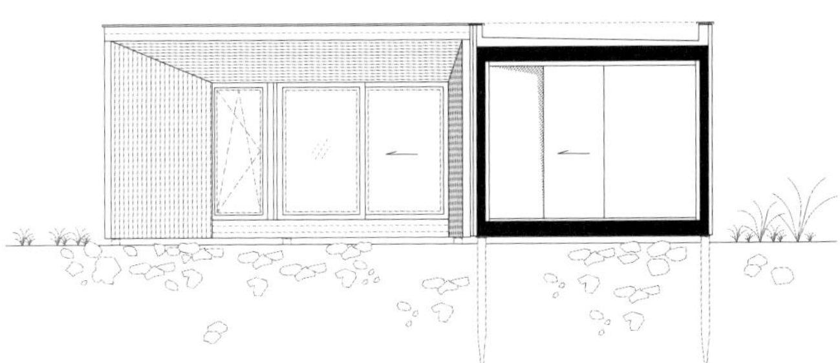

7

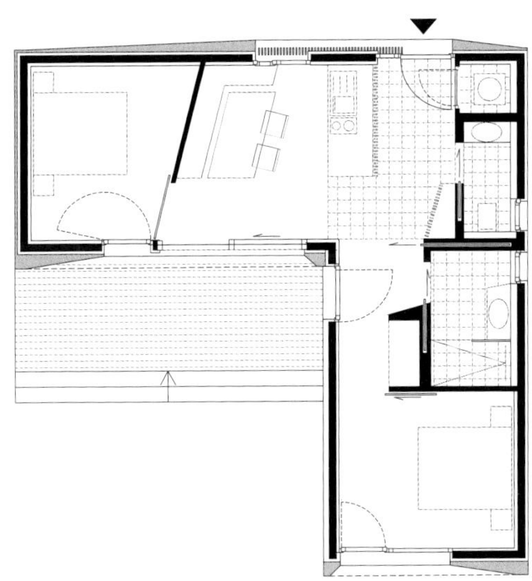

EFH FLURLINGEN

1

Topography, view, noise emission and development characterize the building and shape its design. It is understood as part of the landscape, therefore it should be gently overgrown by the meadows and vines on the slope and become one with nature. The non-linear front façade separates the living and dining areas from the private rooms. The entrance floor has various utility rooms. The living and cooking area and other rooms on the living floor are accessed via a sculptural staircase. An urban terrace at the main façade with a view over the Rhine to the Alps and a nature-related area behind the building interweaves house and surroundings. The architects opted for a load-bearing fair-faced concrete envelope with a steel support grid, which allows flexible floor plan handling according to life phases. Linear courtyard-side wet cells allow numerous floor plan variations on the valley side. Thanks to a reduced range of materials – matt white paint, oiled oak wood and black chalkboard – the interior design creates a neutral stage that is sunlit depending on the time of day.

Architects: Dost Architektur
Completion: 2014
Location: Flurlingen, Switzerland
Gross floor area: 200 m^2
Number of bedrooms: 2
Main materials / building construction: exposed concrete / solid construction
Ecological aspects: earth probe, flat roof integrated photovoltaic system, rainwater tank

2

3

Architekten: Dost Architektur
Fertigstellung: 2014
Ort: Flurlingen, Schweiz
Bruttogeschossfläche: 200 m²
Anzahl der Schlafzimmer: 2
Hauptmaterialien / Konstruktionsweise: Sichtbeton / Massivbau
Ökologische Aspekte: Erdsonde, flachdachintegrierte Photovoltaikanlage, Regenwassertank

Topografie, Aussicht, Lärmemissionen und die Erschließung bedingen das Gebäude und prägen seine Gestaltung. Der Baukörper wird als Teil der Landschaft verstanden, folglich soll er von den Wiesen und Reben des Hanges sanft überwachsen und mit der Natur eins werden. Durch die nicht linear verlaufende Frontfassade werden Wohn- und Essbereich von den persönlichen Räumen getrennt. Das Eingangsgeschoss verfügt über verschiedene Nutzräume wie Garagen, Hobbyraum, Heimkino und Weinkeller. Wohn- und Kochbereich sowie weitere Zimmer befinden sich im Wohngeschoss und werden über ein skulpturales Treppenvolumen erschlossen. Eine urbane Terrasse an der Hauptfassade mit Sicht über den Rhein bis in die Alpen und ein naturbezogener Bereich hinter dem Gebäude verweben das Haus mit seiner Umgebung. Die Architekten setzten auf eine tragende Sichtbetongebäudehülle mit Stahlstützenraster, die eine nach Lebensphase flexible Handhabung des Grundrisses zulässt. Lineare hofseitige Nasszellen lassen talseitig zahlreiche Grundrissvarianten in der Raumschicht zu. Die Innenarchitektur schafft dank reduzierter Materialpalette – mattweißer Anstrich, geöltes Eichenholz und schwarze Wandtafel – eine neutrale Bühne, die je nach Tageszeit besonnt wird.

4

5

6

1 Western façade
2 Kitchen closed
3 Kitchen open
4 Front yard
5 South façade
6 Dining room

1 Westfassade
2 Küche geschlossen
3 Küche geöffnet
4 Vorplatz
5 Südfassade
6 Esszimmer

1

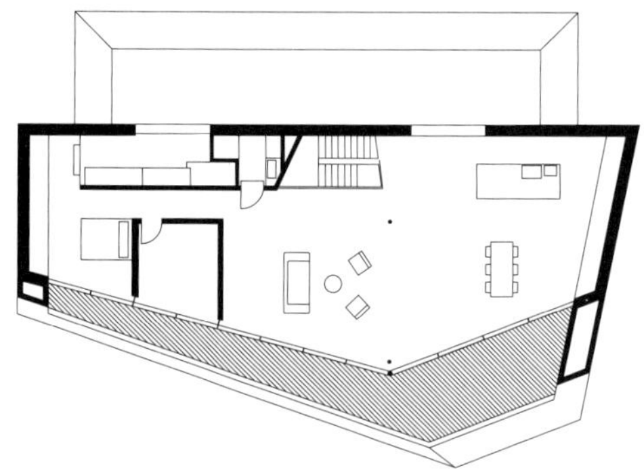

2

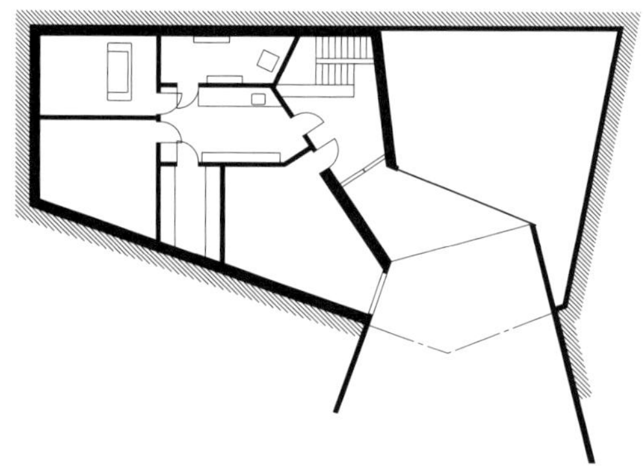

3

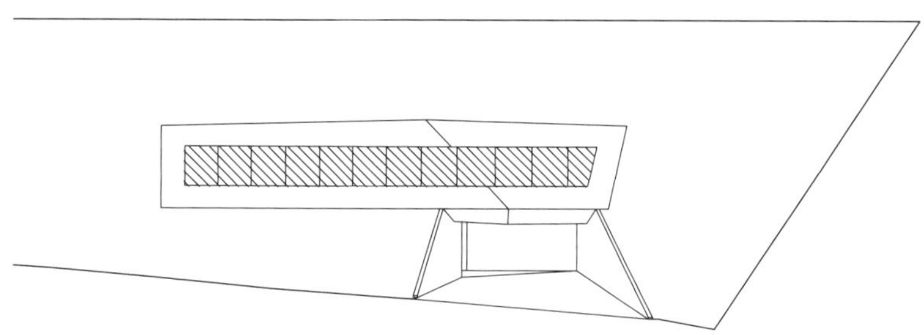

4

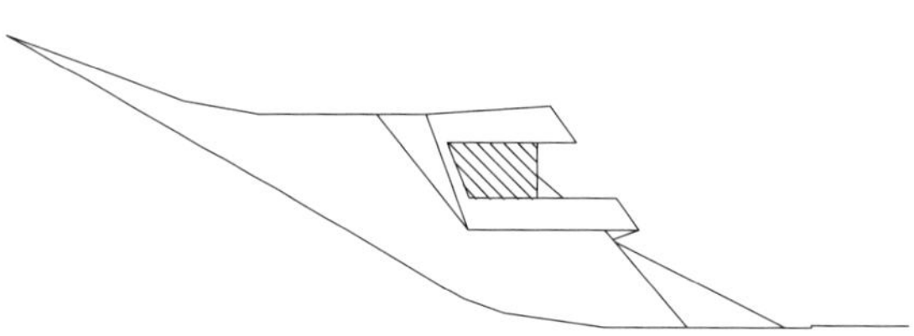

5

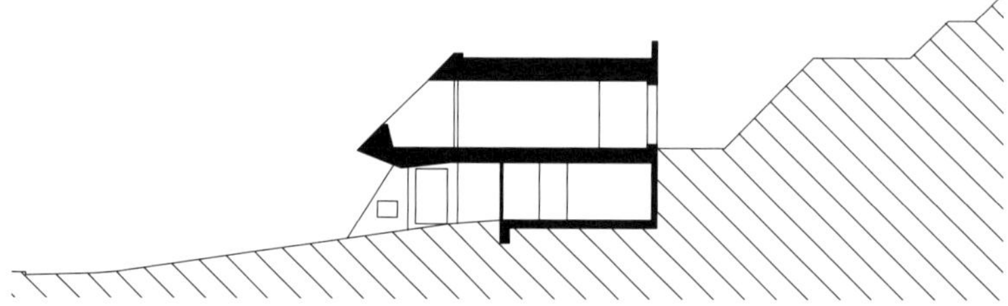

6

7

8

9

1 First floor plan
2 Ground floor plan
3 West elevation
4 North elevation
5 Cross section
6 Living area with lighting
7 Bathroom
8 Court terrace
9 Closed kitchen as chalkboard

1 Grundriss OG
2 Grundriss EG
3 Aufriss Westseite
4 Aufriss Nordseite
5 Querschnitt
6 Wohnbereich mit Beleuchtung
7 Badezimmer
8 Hofterrasse
9 Geschlossene Küche als Kreidetafel

1

NEU-STIFT 1

1 Stairs with highlighted treads
2 Exterior view from the garden
3 Living room with bright and pleasant lighting
4 Lounge terrace

1 Treppe mit hervorgehobenen Stufen
2 Außenansicht vom Garten
3 Wohnraum mit heller und angenehmer Beleuchtung
4 Lounge-Terrasse

2

Architects: Atelier Architekt MOOSMANN
Completion: 2014
Location: Vienna, Austria
Gross floor area: 180 m^2
Number of bedrooms: 3
Main materials / building construction: terrace made of siberian larch / timber construction
Ecological aspects: passive house, triple glazing, bio pool with regeneration biotope, hot water with solar collectors, renewable resource wood

The house Neustift 1 is situated on a hillside property in an exposed position and thus has a unique view over the surrounding vineyards. In the basement of the three-story building is the main living room, which is built into the slope on three sides, but offers a fully glazed view front. The other two floors have bathrooms and are otherwise freely configurable; due to the absence of partitions and supports there are no limits. Along the entire western front side, a supply zone was built in for each floor, with cloakroom, toilet, building services and kitchen, which is accompanied on the opposite side by a large mirror front, which provides a more generous feeling of space. In order to minimize the construction costs, the building is made up of simple cubatures, which are almost completely enclosed by a pergola construction, which, lushly planted with climbing plants, also forms an optimal privacy screen. In front of the basement there is a large, bricked swimming pool with additional regeneration biotope, supplemented by a 25-square-meter terrace. The varied exterior design is also continued on the ground floor, where a lounge terrace extends the living area.

Architekten: Atelier Architekt MOOSMANN
Fertigstellung: 2014
Ort: Wien, Österreich
Bruttogeschossfläche: 180 m^2
Anzahl der Schlafzimmer: 3
Hauptmaterialien / Konstruktionsweise: Terrasse aus sibirischer Lärche / Holzbau
Ökologische Aspekte: Passivhaus, Dreifachverglasung, Bio-Pool mit Regenerationsbiotop, Warmwasser mit Solarkollektoren, nachwachsender Rohstoff Holz

Das Haus Neustift 1 liegt, in exponierter Lage, auf einem Hanggrundstück und verschafft sich so eine einmalige Aussicht über die umliegenden Weinberge. Im Kellergeschoss des dreistöckigen Gebäudes befindet sich der Hauptwohnraum. Dieser ist an drei Seiten in den Hang hineingebaut, bietet aber eine voll verglaste Aussichtsfront. Die beiden anderen Etagen verfügen über Badezimmer und sind ansonsten frei gestaltbar, durch das Fehlen von Zwischenwänden und Stützen sind hierbei keine Grenzen gesetzt. Entlang der gesamten westlichen Stirnseite wurde für jede Etage eine Versorgungszone mit Garderobe, Toilette, Haustechnik und Küche eingebaut, welche auf der gegenüberliegenden Seite von einer großen Spiegelfront begleitet wird, die für ein großzügigeres Raumgefühl sorgt. Um die Baukosten zu minimieren, bilden möglichst einfache Kubaturen das Gebäude. Diese werden durch eine Pergola-Konstruktion fast völlig umschlossen, welche, üppig begrünt mit Schlingpflanzen, zudem einen optimalen Sichtschutz bildet. Dem Untergeschoss vorgelagert liegt ein großer, gemauerter Swimmingpool mit zusätzlichem Regenerationsbiotop, ergänzt durch eine 25 Quadratmeter große Terrasse. Die vielfältige Außenraumgestaltung wird auch im Erdgeschoss fortgeführt, wo eine Lounge-Terrasse das Wohnareal erweitert.

3, 4

1

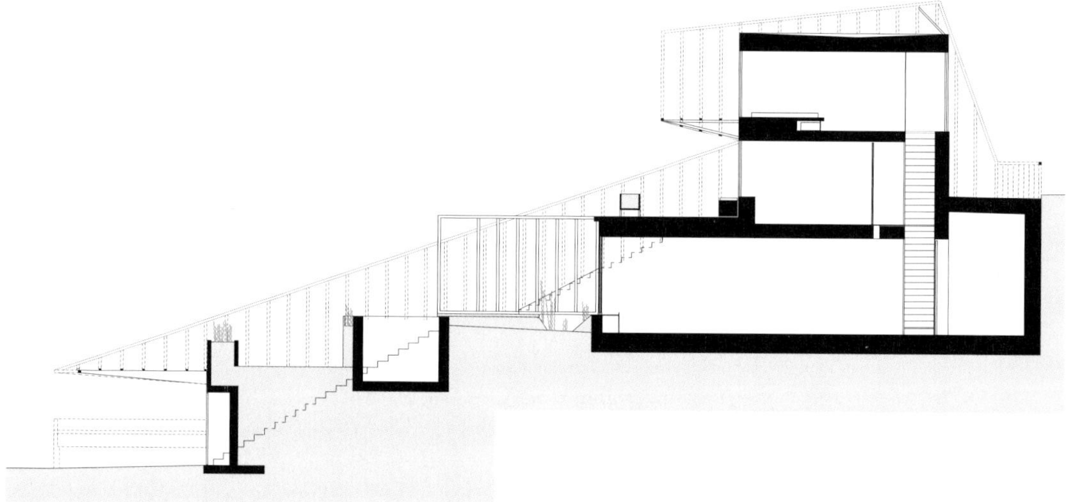

2

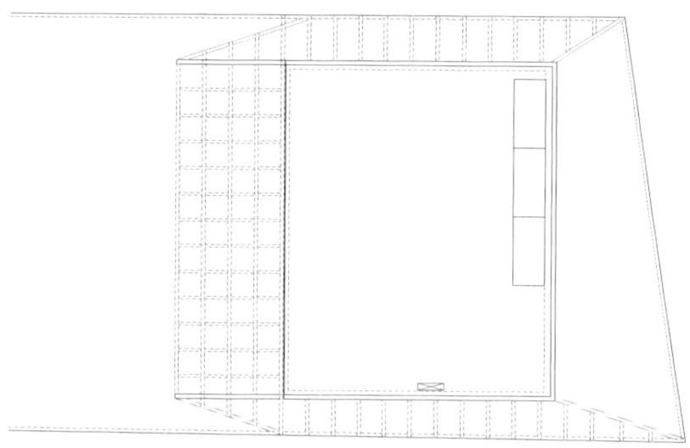

3

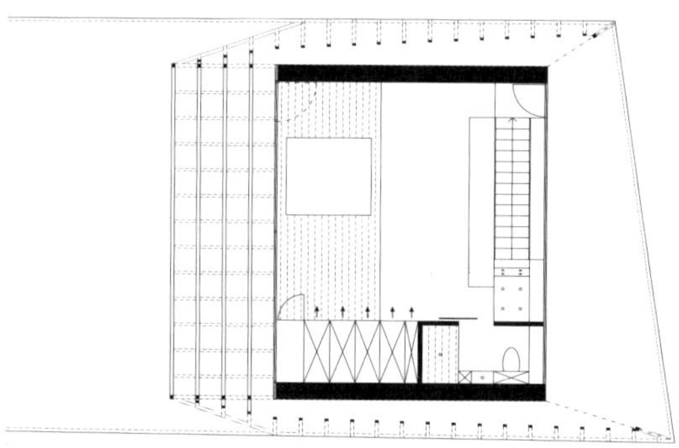

4

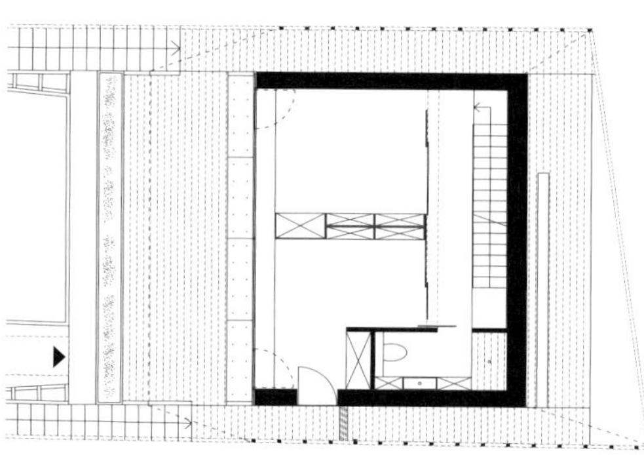

5

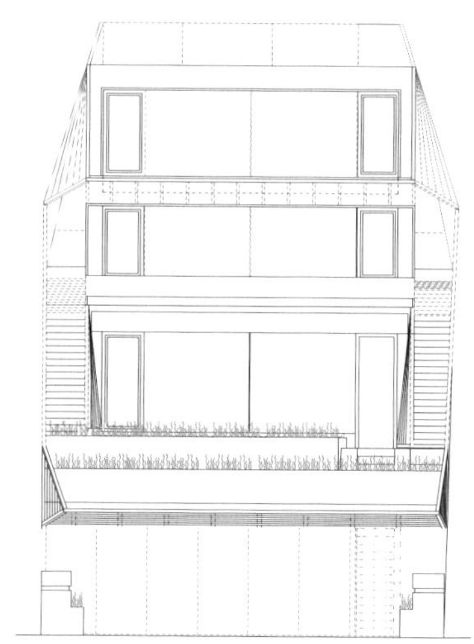

6

7

8

1 Cross section
2 First floor plan
3 Ground floor plan
4 Basement floor plan
5 North elevation
6 Living room with view of the vineyards of Vienna
7 Master bedroom with large mirrored wall
8 Living room as a loft with stairs to the ground floor

1 Querschnitt
2 Grundriss OG
3 Grundriss EG
4 Grundriss UG
5 Aufriss Nordseite
6 Wohnraum mit Blick auf die Weinberge Wiens
7 Hauptschlafzimmer mit großer Spiegelwand
8 Wohnraum als Loft mit Treppe zum Erdgeschoss

EFH HALLAU

1

The plot is situated on the edge of the characteristic Hallau vineyard landscape. The classic roof shape as well as the orientation of the ridge are influenced by the quarter, while the volume is oriented towards the course of the sun and the view.

The polygonal building geometry, executed in black glazed concrete, evokes associations with a crystal, especially a wine crystal. The terrain nestles around the building and covers a large part of the built volume, which thus recedes in relation to the imposing surroundings.

The white interior with its integrated glass façade connects and separates the light-flooded living and garden areas at the same time.

Architects: Dost Architektur
Completion: 2016/17
Location: Hallau, Switzerland
Gross floor area: 175 m^2
Number of bedrooms: 3
Main materials / building construction: black glazed concrete / exposed concrete solid construction
Ecological aspects: photovoltaic system integrated in the roof

2

3

Architekten: Dost Architektur
Fertigstellung: 2016/17
Ort: Hallau, Schweiz
Bruttogeschossfläche: 175 m²
Anzahl der Schlafzimmer: 3
Hauptmaterialien / Konstruktionsweise: schwarz lasierter Beton / Sichtbetonmassivbau
Ökologische Aspekte: im Dach integrierte Photovoltaikanlage

Die Parzelle liegt am Rande der charakteristischen Reblandschaft von Hallau. Die klassische Dachform sowie die Ausrichtung des Firstes sind vom Quartier geprägt, während sich das Volumen in seiner Ausrichtung an Sonnenverlauf und Aussicht orientiert.

Die polygonale Gebäudegeometrie, in schwarz lasiertem Beton ausgeführt, weckt Assoziationen an einen Kristall, insbesondere an einen Weinkristall. Das Terrain schmiegt sich um das Gebäude und bedeckt einen Großteil des gebauten Volumens, welches sich so gegenüber der imposanten Umgebung zurücknimmt.

Das weiße Innere mit eingebundener Glasfassade verbindet und trennt zugleich die lichtdurchfluteten Wohn- und Gartenräume.

4

5

1 South façade
2 Living space with a view
3 East façade
4 Corridor
5 Exterior view detail

1 Südfassade
2 Wohnraum mit Weitsicht
3 Ostfassade
4 Korridor
5 Detail Außenansicht

1

2

1 Living room with kitchen
2 Exterior view from the garden
3 Section
4 Ground floor plan
5 South façade
6 Basement floor plan
7 Garage floor plan

1 Wohnraum mit Küche
2 Außenansicht vom Garten
3 Schnitt
4 Grundriss EG
5 Südfassade
6 Grundriss UG
7 Grundriss Garage

3

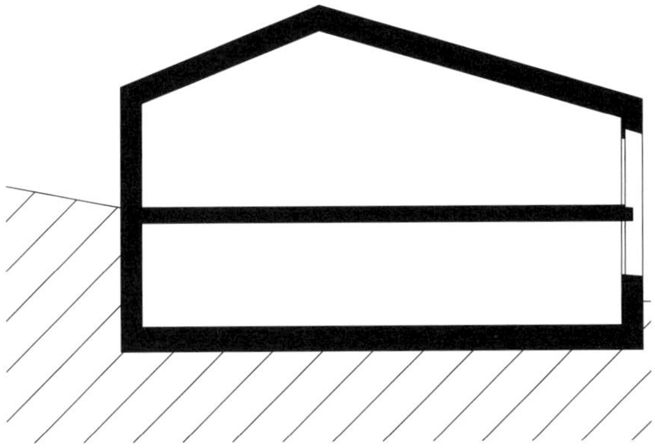

4

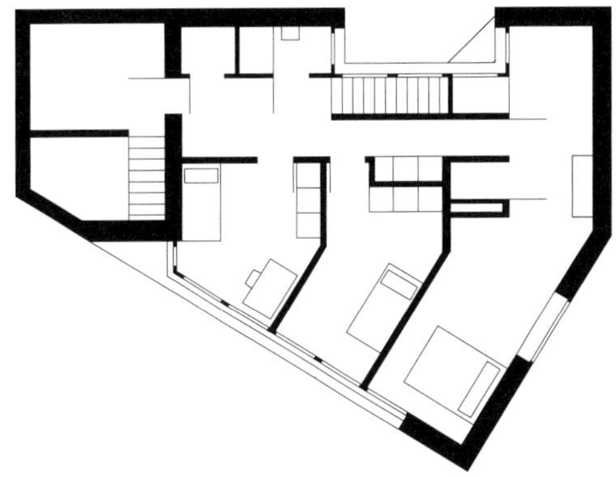

5

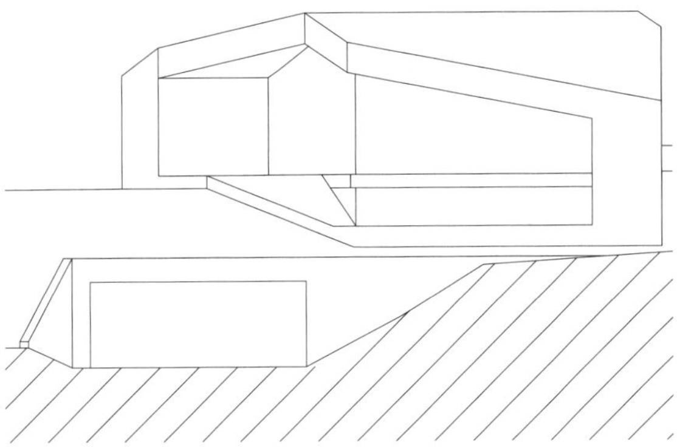

6

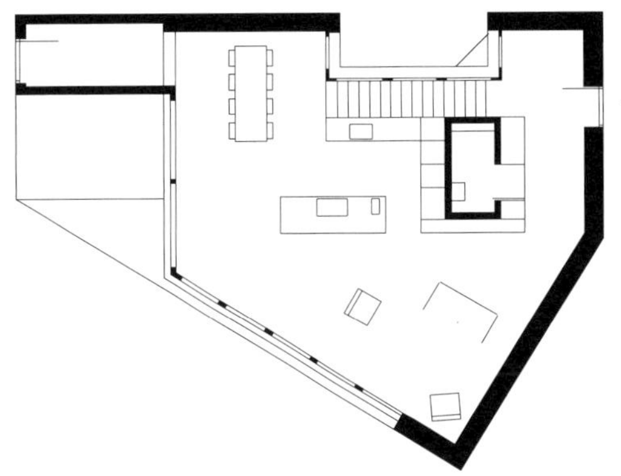

7

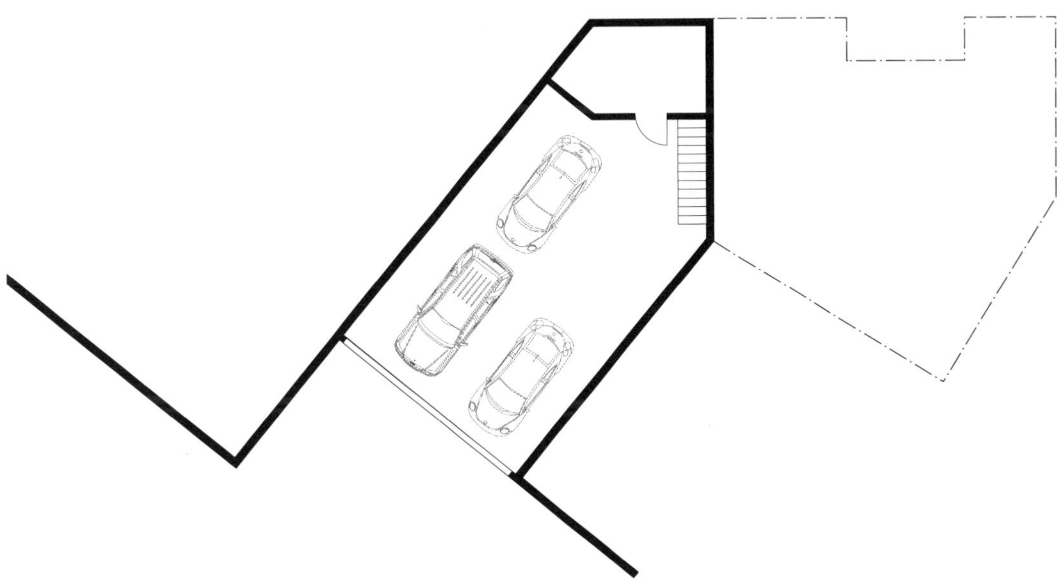

HAUS LOBAU 2

1

The two-story House Lobau 2 captivates with its resource-conserving and environmentally friendly construction, as well as with its natural appearance, which allows the building to merge completely with the surrounding landscape. The light-colored wooden slat façade, in dialogue with the generously proportioned window fronts in the southern section of the building, conveys a pleasant atmosphere with extensive views of the surrounding landscape. Inside, all wooden walls are coated with clay plaster. Main floor and guest apartment offer a friendly, bright ambience at any time of day. The two terraces on the upper and ground floor and the surrounding garden extend the living space, especially in summer. Additionally, the accessible flat roof with integrated raised garden bed invites to relax and regenerate.

Architects: Atelier Architekt MOOSMANN
Completion: 2018
Location: Vienna, Austria
Gross floor area: 162 m^2
Number of bedrooms: 1
Main materials / building construction: wood (CLT elements, diamond nut, oak, silver fir), stone tiles / timber construction
Ecological aspects: green roof, heat pump, solar gains via south-facing window areas, wooden walls inside coated with clay plaster, ground source heat pump

2

Architekten: Atelier Architekt MOOSMANN
Fertigstellung: 2018
Ort: Wien, Österreich
Bruttogeschossfläche: 162 m^2
Anzahl der Schlafzimmer: 1
Hauptmaterialien / Konstruktionsweise: Holz (BSP-Elemente, Diamantnuss, Eiche, Weißtanne), Steinfliesen / Holzbau
Ökologische Aspekte: Gründach, Wärmepumpe, solare Gewinne über südseitige Fensterflächen, innen Holzwände mit Lehmputz beschichtet, Erdwärmepumpe

Das zweigeschossige Haus Lobau 2 besticht ebenso mit seiner ressourcenschonenden und umweltfreundlichen Bauweise wie mit einer natürlichen Optik, die das Gebäude ganz mit der umliegenden Landschaft verschmelzen lässt. Die helle Holzlattenfassade vermittelt, im Dialog mit den großzügig angelegten Fensterfronten im südlichen Abschnitt des Gebäudes, eine angenehme Atmosphäre mit ausgiebigen Blickbezügen in die umgebene Landschaft. Im Inneren sind sämtlichen Holzwände mit Lehmputz beschichtet. Hauptgeschoss und Gästewohnung bieten zu jeder Tageszeit ein freundliches, helles Ambiente. Die beiden Terrassen im Ober- und Erdgeschoss und der umliegende Garten erweitern, vor allem im Sommer, den Wohnraum. Zusätzlich lädt das begehbare Flachdach mit integriertem Hochbeet zum Erholen und Entspannen ein.

3

4

5

1 Exterior view from south
2 Entrance
3 Outdoor terrace with glass railing
4 Exterior view from north
5 Outdoor terrace upper floor

1 Außenansicht von Süden
2 Eingang
3 Außenterrasse mit Glasgeländer
4 Außenansicht von Norden
5 Außenterrasse Obergeschoss

1

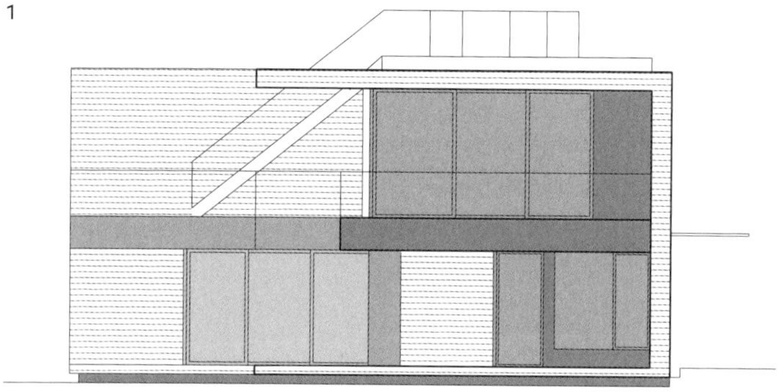

2

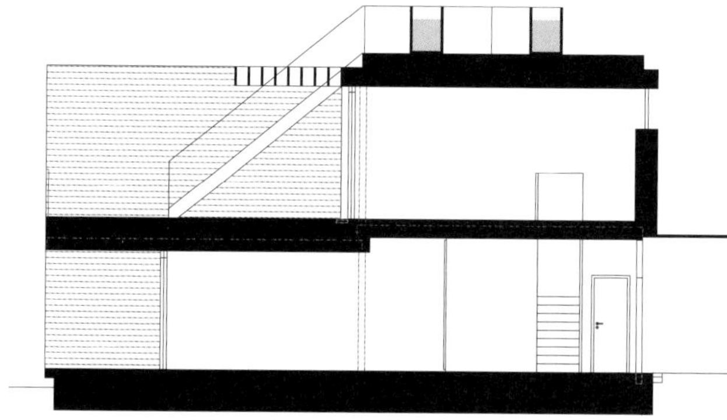

3

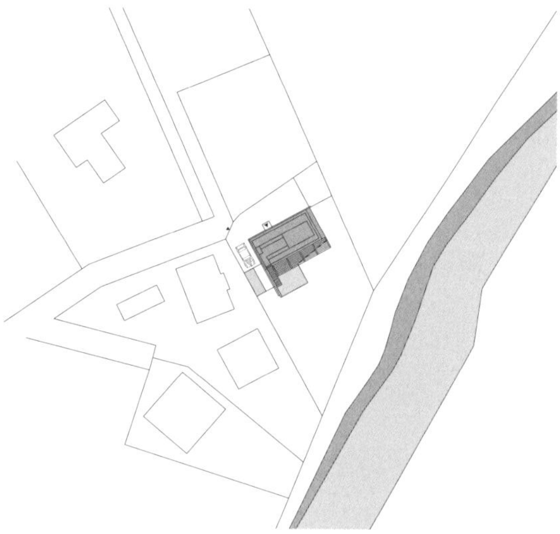

4

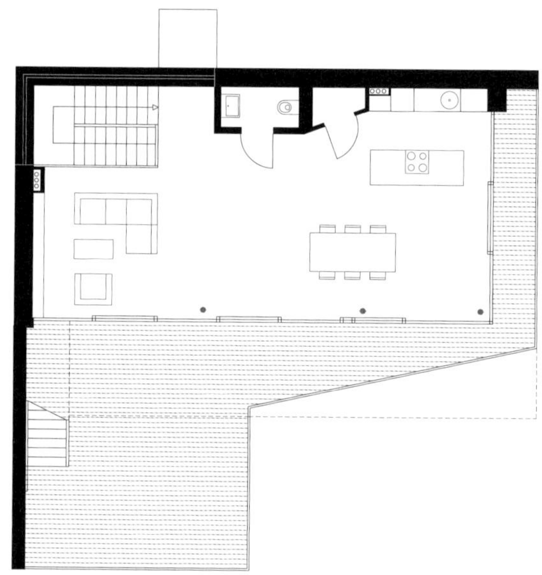

5

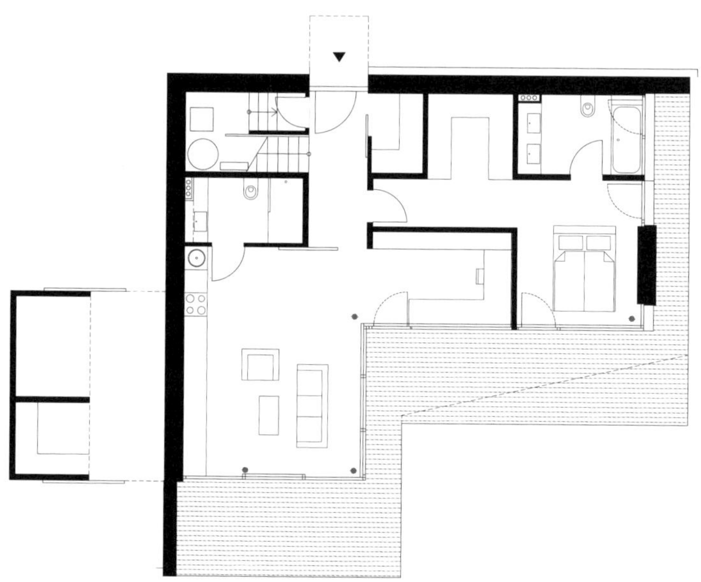

6

7

1 East elevation
2 Cross section
3 Site plan
4 First floor plan
5 Ground floor plan
6 Guest area and office space
7 Kitchen, living and dining room

1 Aufriss Ostseite
2 Querschnitt
3 Lageplan
4 Grundriss OG
5 Grundriss EG
6 Gästebereich und Büroraum
7 Küche, Wohn- und Esszimmer

ELLI

1

The ELLI project is a prototype for individual, inner-city redensification. The five-story residential tower with its minimal floor space of 50 square meters and an airy terrace above the city's rooftops stands on a former commercial courtyard area.

Concrete elements prefabricated using optimized production techniques form the structure and shape the architectural expression of the single-family house both outside and inside. The building is characterized by its spaciousness and the rough beauty of the silky shining exposed concrete. Wide curtains in different shades of red set contrasting accents to the brut concrete. The basement storys extend over the entire area of the former industrial courtyard. Here, the first basement level houses a column-free studio room with 273 square meters and striking circular skylights – a place of retreat and concentration. An underground car park was built on the lower basement floor.

Architects: Holzer Kobler Architekturen
Interior architects: zweikant architekturen
Completion: 2017
Location: Zurich, Switzerland
Gross floor area: 1,060 m^2
Number of bedrooms: 3
Main materials/building construction: concrete, steel, glass / precast concrete
Ecological aspects: thermal insulation, redensification

2

3

Architekten: Holzer Kobler Architekturen
Innenarchitekten: zweikant architekturen
Fertigstellung: 2017
Ort: Zürich, Schweiz
Bruttogeschossfläche: 1.060 m²
Anzahl der Schlafzimmer: 3
Hauptmaterialien / Konstruktionsweise: Beton, Stahl, Glas / Betonfertigbau
Ökologische Aspekte: Wärmedämmung, Nachverdichtung

Das Projekt ELLI ist ein Prototyp für individuelle, innerstädtische Nachverdichtung. Der fünfgeschossige Wohnturm mit seiner minimalen Grundfläche von 50 Quadratmetern und einer luftigen Terrasse über den Dächern der Stadt steht auf einer ehemals gewerblich genutzten Hoffläche.

Unter optimierten Produktionstechniken vorgefertigte Betonelemente bilden die Struktur und prägen den architektonischen Ausdruck des Einfamilienhauses sowohl im Äußeren als auch im Innern. Das Gebäude zeichnet sich durch seine räumliche Großzügigkeit und die raue Schönheit des seidenglänzenden Sichtbetons aus. Breite Vorhänge aus unterschiedlichen Rottönen setzen kontrastierende Akzente zum Beton brut. Die Untergeschosse erstrecken sich über die gesamte Fläche des ehemaligen Gewerbehofs. Hier befindet sich im ersten Untergeschoss ein stützenfreier Atelierraum mit 273 Quadratmetern und markanten kreisförmigen Oberlichtern – ein Ort des Rückzugs und der Konzentration. Im zweiten Untergeschoss wurde eine Tiefgarage realisiert.

4

5

1 Atelier
2 Living room
3 Kitchen
4 View of the courtyard
5 Staircase

1 Atelier
2 Wohnzimmer
3 Küche
4 Innenhofansicht
5 Treppenhaus

1

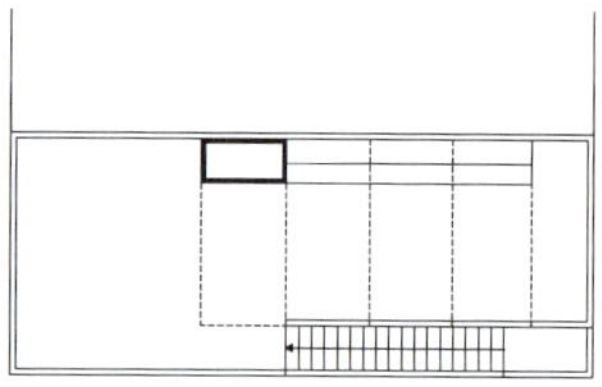

2

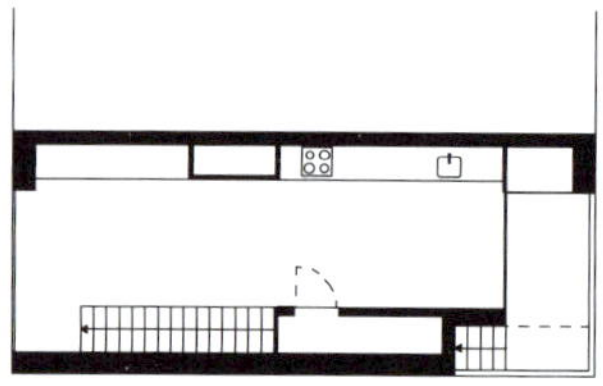

3

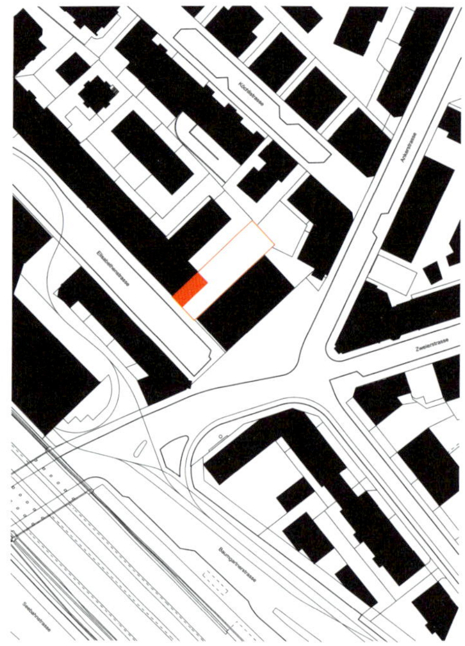

4

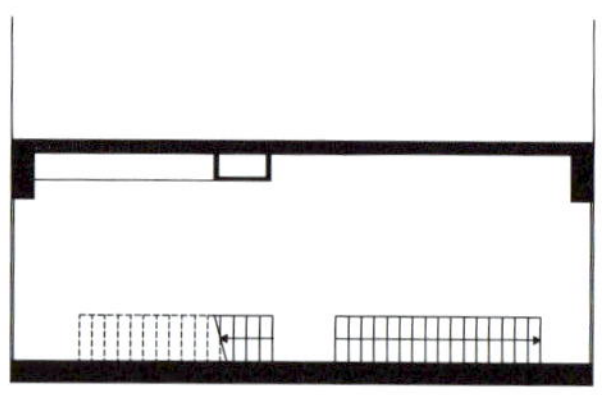

5

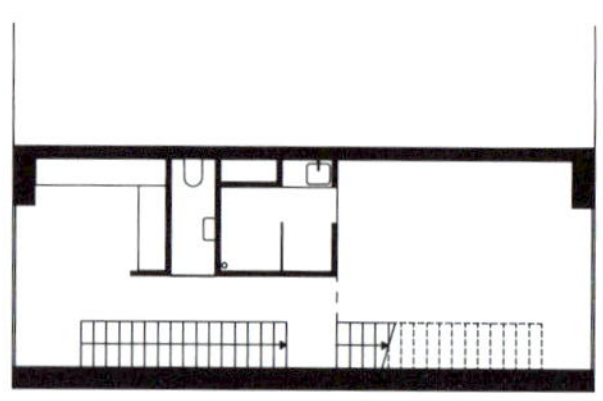

6

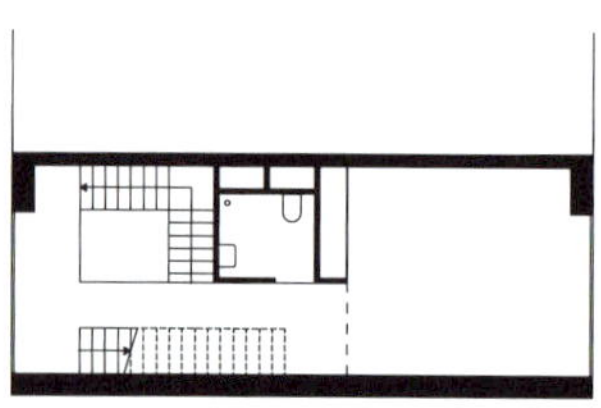

7

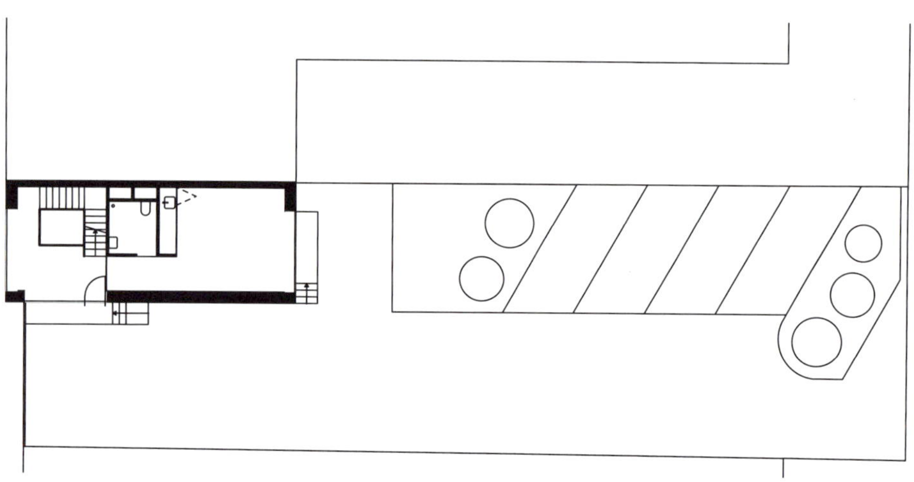

8

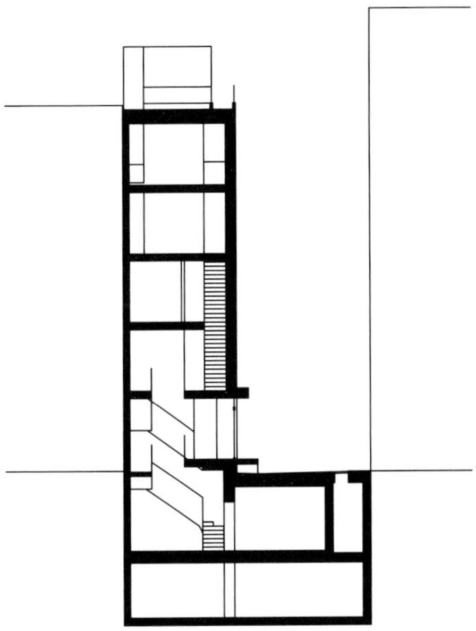

9

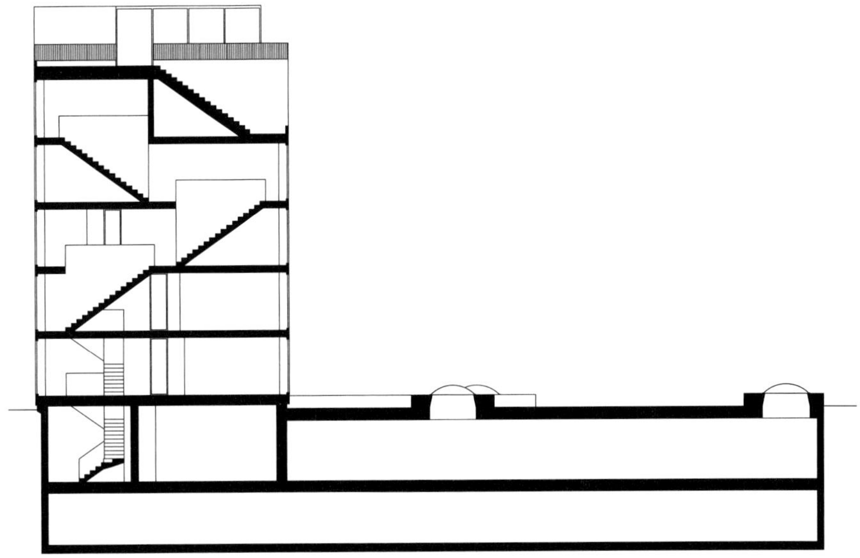

10, 11

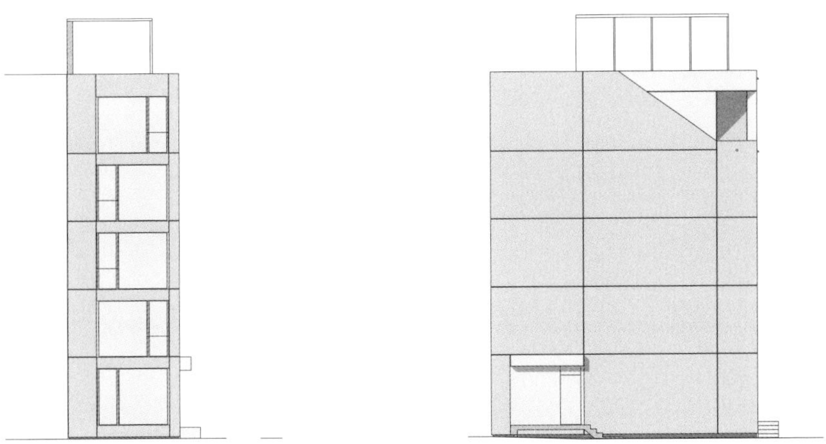

12

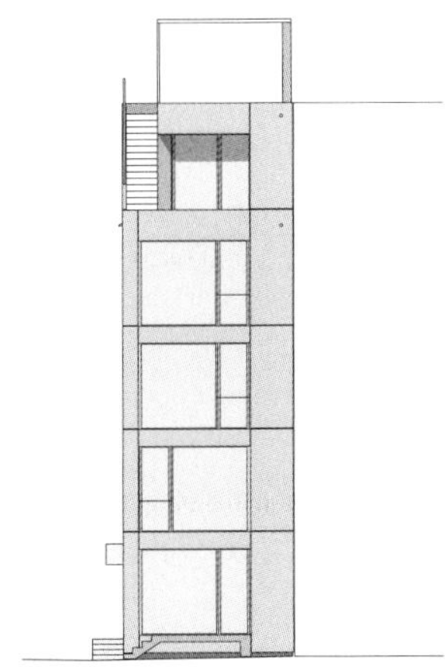

1 Terrace floor plan
2 Fourth floor plan
3 Site plan
4 Third floor plan
5 Second floor plan
6 First floor plan
7 Ground floor plan
8 Cross section
9 Longitudinal section
10 South elevation
11 East elevation
12 North elevation

1 Grundriss Terrasse
2 Grundriss 4. OG
3 Lageplan
4 Grundriss 3. OG
5 Grundriss 2. OG
6 Grundriss 1. OG
7 Grundriss EG
8 Querschnitt
9 Längsschnitt
10 Aufriss Südseite
11 Aufriss Ostseite
12 Aufriss Nordseite

HAUS SCHNIFIS

1

Architects: ma-ma Werkraum für Baukunst, Martin Mackowitz
Completion: 2019
Location: Walgau, Vorarlberg, Austria
Gross floor area: 139 m^2
Number of bedrooms: 3
Main materials / building construction: copper, lime plaster, wood / solid construction
Ecological aspects: Lehmo woodstove, component activation with solar thermal energy

The Schnifis House is centrally located in the Walgau. This region is characterized by agricultural buildings and has acted as a source of inspiration for the new construction. This is particularly reflected in the clear, simple volume, the solid plinth with lime plaster, the open horizontal battens to the west, the simple sliding doors and the central kitchen. The ground floor is cut into the slope and designed in a massive construction method with component activation. On top of it there is a wooden building with a gable roof in copper roofing. Appropriate floor plans play with density and generosity. The upper floor has a west terrace and an open gable with gallery, compact rooms are lined up in the east. The handling of tradition and innovation and the use of sensible building materials serve as a basis for a contemporary relationship to agriculture, landscape and ultimately towards a sustainable culture of living.

2

3

Das Haus Schnifis liegt zentral im Walgau. Diese Region ist geprägt von landwirtschaftlichen Gebäuden und war Inspirationsquelle für den Neubau. Das macht sich vor allem im klaren schlichten Volumen, dem massiven Sockel mit Kalkputz, der offenen Horizontallattung im Westen, den einfachen Schiebetüren und der zentralen Küche bemerkbar. Das Erdgeschoss ist in den Hang eingeschnitten und in einer massiven Bauweise mit Bauteilaktivierung ausgeführt. Darauf steht ein Holzbau mit einem Satteldach in Kupfereindeckung. Angemessene Grundrisse spielen mit Dichte und Großzügigkeit. Das Obergeschoss hat eine Westterrasse und einen offenen Giebel mit Galerie, im Osten reihen sich kompakte Räume. Der Umgang mit Tradition und Innovation und das Verwenden von sinnvollen Baustoffen dient als Grundlage für einen zeitgemäßen Bezug zu Landwirtschaft, Landschaft und schlussendlich zu einer nachhaltigen Lebenskultur.

4

Architekten: ma-ma Werkraum für Baukunst, Martin Mackowitz
Fertigstellung: 2019
Ort: Walgau, Vorarlberg, Österreich
Bruttogeschossfläche: 139 m^2
Anzahl der Schlafzimmer: 3
Hauptmaterialien / Konstruktionsweise: Kupfer, Kalkputz, Holz / Massivbauweise
Ökologische Aspekte: Lehmo Holzofen, Bauteilaktivierung mit Solarthermie

1 Exterior view from northwest
2 Living room
3 Exterior view from northeast
4 Dining room
5 Bathroom
6 Bedroom
7 Kitchen

1 Außenansicht von Nordwesten
2 Wohnzimmer
3 Außenansicht von Nordosten
4 Esszimmer
5 Badezimmer
6 Schlafzimmer
7 Küche

5, 6, 7

1

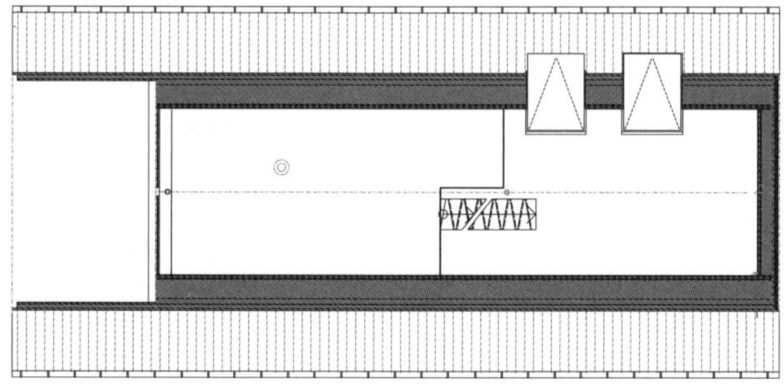

2

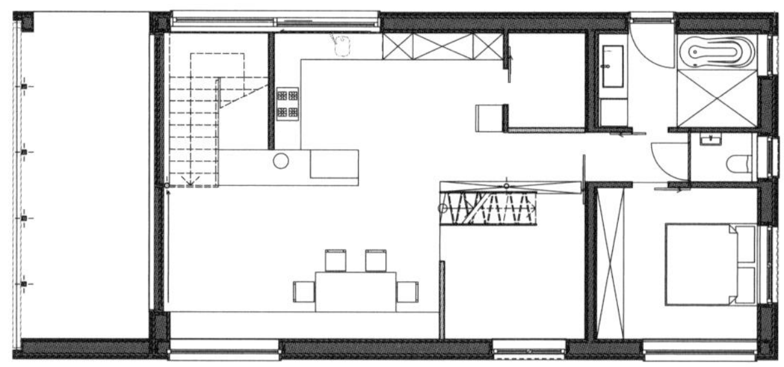

3

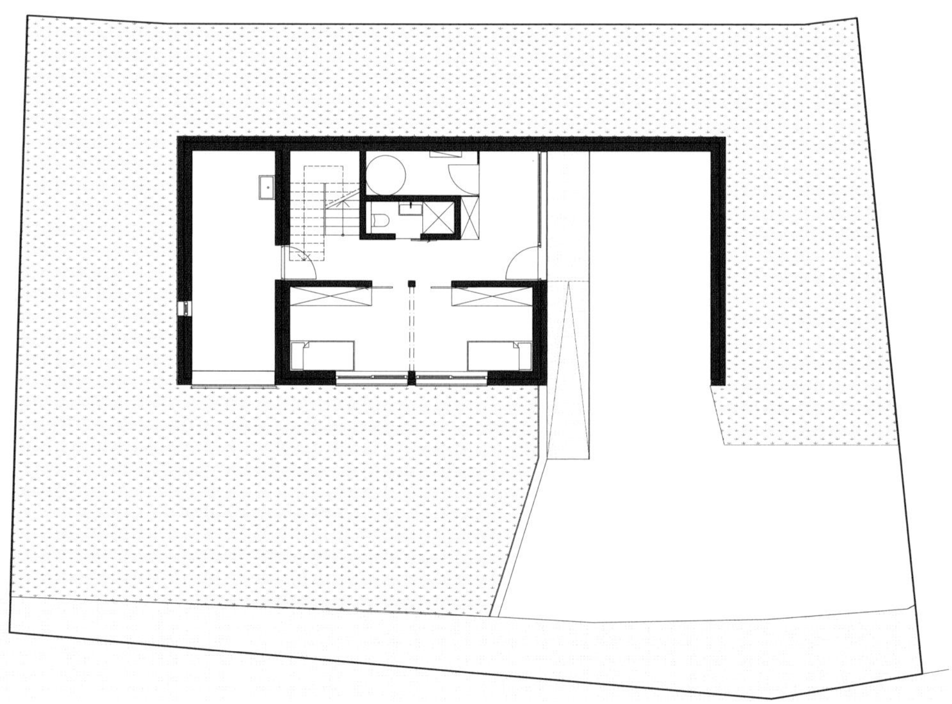

4

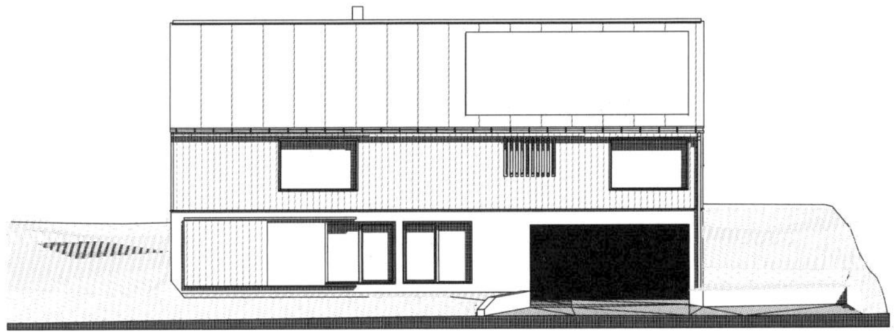

5

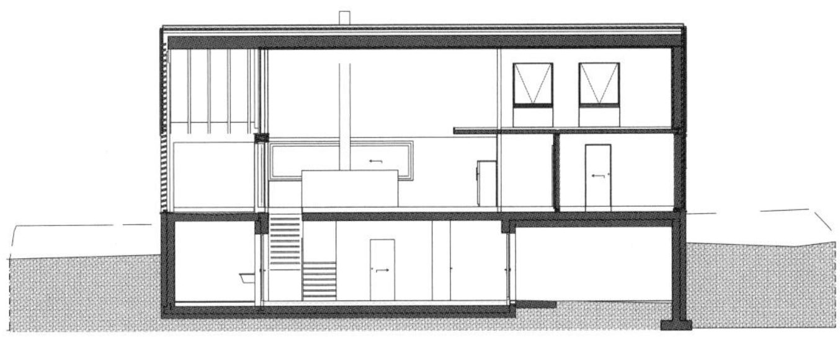

6

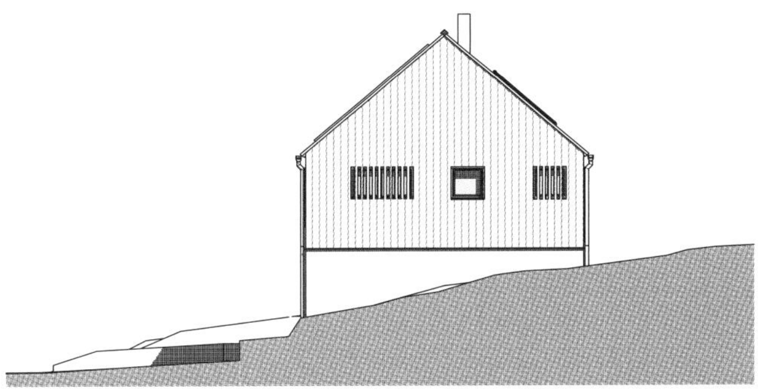

7

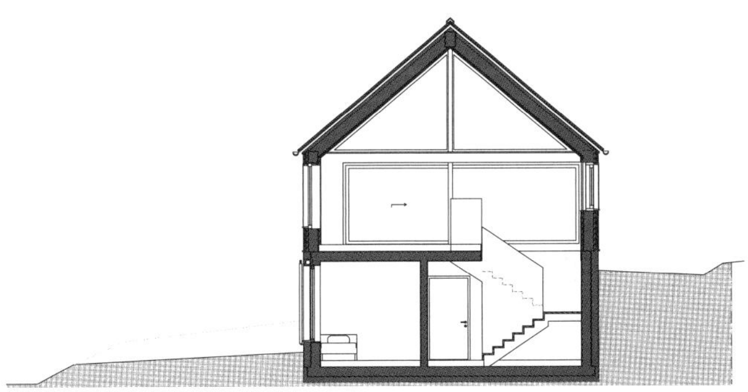

1 Second floor plan
2 First floor plan
3 Ground floor plan
4 Southwest elevation
5 Longitudinal section
6 Southeast elevation
7 Cross section

1 Grundriss 2. OG
2 Grundriss 1. OG
3 Grundriss EG
4 Aufriss Südwestseite
5 Längsschnitt
6 Aufriss Südostseite
7 Querschnitt

EFH EGOLZWIL

The detached house is partly built into the slope and integrates into the steep topography. It has a garage as well as a spacious terrace, which as a projecting element also covers the entrance area.

On the ground floor are the entrance area and additional adjoining rooms, but the actual center of life is on the first floor, where the living, dining and sleeping areas are concentrated.

The upper floor consists of two connected volumes, each of which is closed with a transverse gable roof. The northern volume is offset upwards by a mezzanine floor and contains the bedrooms, while the southern part of the floor serves as living and dining area. The rooms are placed as closed bodies in the floor plan, creating a flowing space in between with visual references between the individual open areas. They are both high due to the gabled roofs and bright due to the many windows.

1, 2

Architects: dolmus Architekten
Completion: 2013
Location: Egolzwil, Switzerland
Gross floor area: 320 m^2
Number of bedrooms: 4
Main materials / building construction: wood, sanded subfloor, textured plaster / solid construction

Architekten: dolmus Architekten
Fertigstellung: 2013
Ort: Egolzwil, Schweiz
Bruttogeschossfläche: 320 m^2
Anzahl der Schlafzimmer: 4
Hauptmaterialien / Konstruktionsweise: Holz, geschliffener Unterlagsboden, Strukturputz / Massivbau

Das Einfamilienhaus ist teilweise in den Hang gebaut und integriert sich in die steile Topografie. Es verfügt über eine Garage und eine großzügige Terrasse, die als auskragendes Element auch den Eingangsbereich überdacht.

Im Erdgeschoss befinden sich der Eingangsbereich und zusätzliche Nebenräume. Der eigentliche Lebensmittelpunkt befindet sich jedoch im ersten Stock, in welchem sich Wohn-, Ess- und Schlafbereich konzentrieren.

Dabei besteht das Obergeschoss aus zwei aneinander gefügten Volumen, die jeweils mit einem querliegenden Satteldach abgeschlossen werden. Das nördliche Volumen ist um ein Halbgeschoss nach oben versetzt und beinhaltet die Schlafräume, der südliche Teil des Geschosses dient als Wohn- und Essbereich. Die Zimmer sind als abgeschlossene Körper im Grundriss platziert. Dazwischen entsteht ein fließender Zwischenraum mit Blickbezügen zwischen den einzelnen offenen Bereichen. Durch die Satteldächer konnten hohe, durch die vielen Fenster helle Räume geschaffen werden.

3

4

1 South façade
2 West façade
3 Terrace
4 Playroom

1 Südfassade
2 Westfassade
3 Terrasse
4 Spielzimmer

1

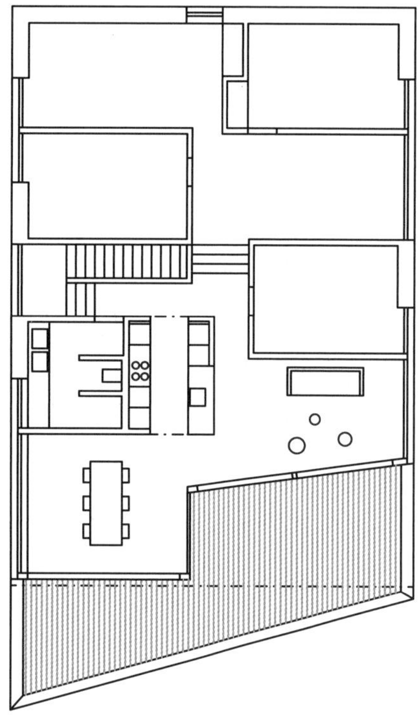

2

3

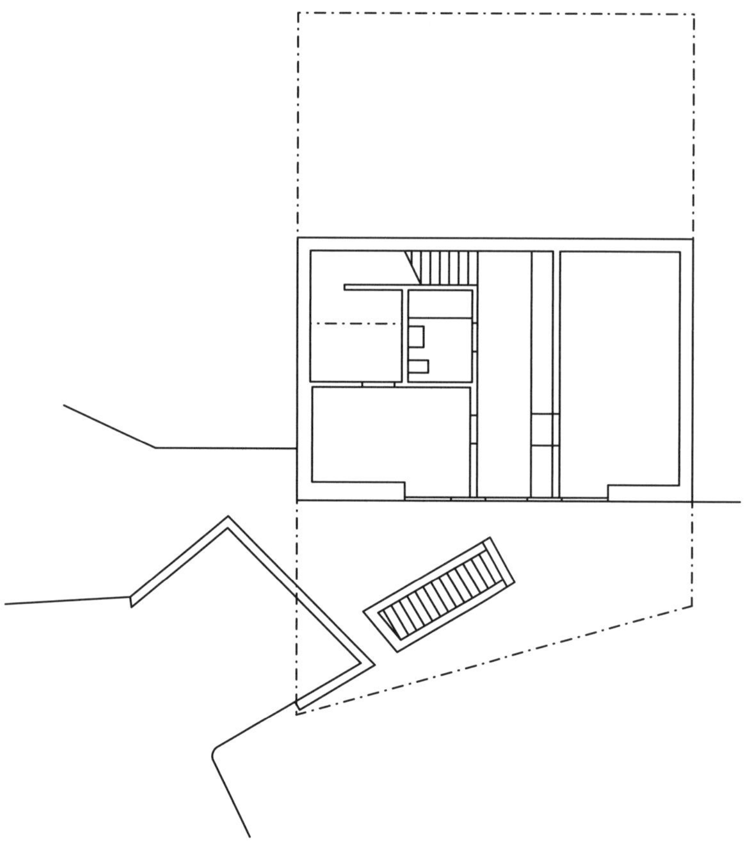

4

5

6

1 First floor plan
2 Exploration sketch
3 Ground floor plan
4 Terrace from outside
5 East façade
6 Living room

1 Grundriss OG
2 Explorationsskizze
3 Grundriss EG
4 Terrasse von außen
5 Ostfassade
6 Wohnzimmer

1

HÄUSER AM WASSER

1 Exterior view House North, entrance area
2 Exterior view House South, garden
3 Exterior view from the water with surroundings
4 Exterior view from the water

1 Außenansicht Haus Nord, Eingangsbereich
2 Außenansicht Haus Süd, Garten
3 Außenansicht vom Wasser mit Umgebung
4 Außenansicht vom Wasser

2

Architects: Architekt Jürgen Radatz
Completion: 2016
Location: Vienna, Austria
Gross floor area: 183.30 m² each house
Number of bedrooms: 5
Main materials / building construction: wood, concrete, glass / timber frame construction, solid wood ceilings, concrete cellar
Ecological aspects: timber frame construction, solid wood ceilings, cellulose insulation, clay plaster

Architekten: Architekt Jürgen Radatz
Fertigstellung: 2016
Ort: Wien, Österreich
Bruttogeschossfläche: 183,30 m² je Haus
Anzahl der Schlafzimmer: 5
Hauptmaterialien / Konstruktionsweise: Holz, Beton, Glas / Holzriegelbau mit Massivholzdecken und Betonkeller
Ökologische Aspekte: Holzriegelbau, Massivholzdecken, Zellulosedämmung, Lehmputz

The two coupled allotment garden houses and their garden courtyards form the ensemble on the promenade of the Lower Old Danube. The northern house accommodates a compact two-room apartment on the ground floor and a studio on the upper floor. Both floors open – room-high glazed – to the garden courtyard or the Old Danube. In the southern house, the split-level concept allows for an open space continuum: from the 2.30-meter-high kitchen area, the high air space of the dining area and seating steps mediate to the living room of 3.60 meters in height. The bedroom directly below – half buried in the ground – is accordingly pleasantly adapted. Floor-to-ceiling glazing makes the basement a bright and attractive retreat, not only for particularly hot days. Within the limited construction height and restrictions, efficient built-in furniture and space-economical optimizations achieve an astonishingly generous interior space. Red cedar characterizes the façades and terraces of the houses built in timber frame construction with solid wood ceilings. Their surface structure is taken up by the outer walls and shed roofs made of shuttered concrete, the latter providing sheltered seating. The interior walls were plastered with clay, a central water-to-water heat pump heats and cools the houses via the floors. The comfort ventilation system continuously renews the indoor air.

Die beiden gekuppelten Kleingartenwohnhäuser bilden mit ihren vorgelagerten Gartenhöfen das Ensemble an der Uferpromenade der Unteren Alten Donau. Das nördliche Haus beherbergt im Erdgeschoss eine kompakte Zweizimmerwohnung und im Obergeschoss ein Studio. Beide Stockwerke öffnen sich – raumhoch verglast – zum Gartenhof oder zur Alten Donau. Beim südlichen Haus ermöglicht die Split-Level-Konzeption ein offenes Raumkontinuum: Vom 2,30 Meter hohen Küchenbereich vermitteln der hohe Luftraum des Essbereichs und Sitzstufen zum Wohnraum mit 3,60 Meter Höhe. Das Schlafzimmer direkt darunter – halb ins Erdreich eingegraben – ist entsprechend angenehm konditioniert. Bodengleiche Verglasungen machen das Untergeschoss nicht nur an besonders heißen Tagen zu einem hellen und attraktiven Rückzugsort. Innerhalb der begrenzten Bauhöhe und Beschränkungen erreichen effiziente Einbaumöbel und raumökonomische Optimierungen ein erstaunlich großzügiges räumliches Angebot. Rotzeder prägt Fassaden und Terrassen der in Holzriegelbauweise mit Massivholzdecken errichteten Häuser. Ihre Oberflächenstruktur nimmt den schalreinen Beton der Außenmauern und Flugdächer auf. Letztere bieten geschützte Sitzplätze. Die Innenwände wurden mit Lehm verputzt. Eine zentrale Wasser-Wasser-Wärmepumpe heizt und kühlt die Häuser über die Fußböden. Die Komfortlüftung erneuert stetig die Raumluft.

3, 4

1

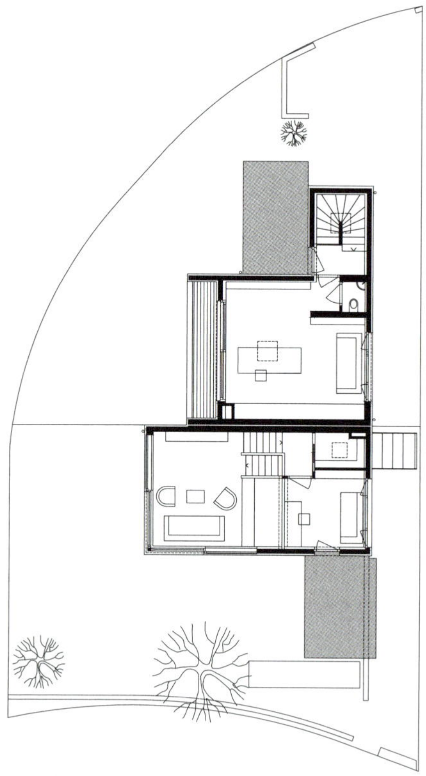

2

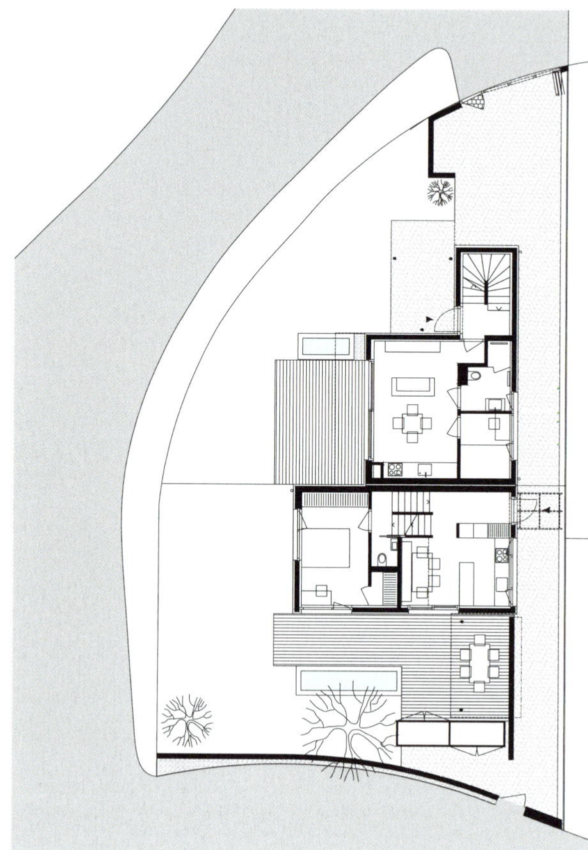

3

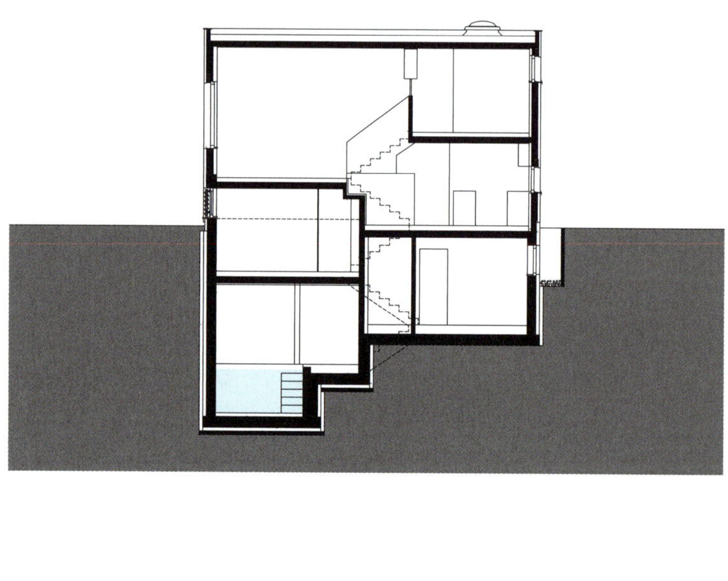

4

5

6

7

1 First floor plan
2 Ground floor plan
3 Section House South
4 Interior gallery House South
5 Study House North
6 Pool in the basement
7 Dining place and kitchen House South

1 Grundriss OG
2 Grundriss EG
3 Schnitt Haus Süd
4 Innenraumgalerie Haus Süd
5 Arbeitszimmer Haus Nord
6 Pool im Untergeschoss
7 Essplatz und Küche Haus Süd

WOHNEN IM DORF

1

Over a period of 150 years, the listed town house has undergone a number of expansions of use. The deconstruction and gentle renovation of the building brings back to life the basic idea of the courtyard-like structure and the inherent qualities of the historically shaped site. The concept for the residential building is based on the typology of a courtyard. The coherent construction weaves itself stringently into the historical context.

The extension building is a consistent unit. Its concrete spatial sculpture – dark on the outside, light on the inside – forms a protective shell throughout the building. The striking façade made of wooden elements was developed in cooperation with regional craftsmen. The oil-painted wooden slats, burnt with dark pigments, clad the building in a deep black shell. The stained three-layer panels of the interior fittings are also a design draft of the architect and were specially manufactured for this residential building.

Architects: Tom Munz Architekt
Completion: 2018
Location: Thal, Switzerland
Gross floor area: 386 m^2
Number of bedrooms: 3
Main materials / building construction: concrete, wood, metal / hybrid construction
Ecological aspects: timber construction, recycled concrete

2

3

266

Architekten: Tom Munz Architekt
Fertigstellung: 2018
Ort: Thal, Schweiz
Bruttogeschossfläche: 386 m^2
Anzahl der Schlafzimmer: 3
Hauptmaterialien / Konstruktionsweise: Beton, Holz, Metall / Hybridbauweise
Ökologische Aspekte: Holzbauweise, Recyclingbeton

Rund um das denkmalgeschützte Bürgerhaus haben sich während rund 150 Jahren etliche Nutzungserweiterungen vollzogen. Die Rückbauten und sanfte Sanierung des Gebäudes machen die Grundidee des hofartigen Gefüges und die inhärenten Qualitäten des historisch geprägten Ortes wieder erlebbar. Das Konzept für das Wohnhaus orientiert sich an der Typologie einer Hofanlage. Die schlüssige Konstruktion webt sich stringent in den historischen Kontext.

Der Erweiterungsbau zeigt sich als konsequente Einheit. Seine Raumskulptur aus Beton bildet – außen dunkel, innen hell – eine schützende Hülle um das ganze Haus. Zusammen mit regionalen Handwerkern wurde die markante Fassade aus Holzelementbau erarbeitet. Die ölbemalten, mit dunklen Pigmenten verbrannten Holzlatten kleiden den Baukörper in eine sattschwarze Hülle. Auch die gebeizten Dreischichtplatten im Innenaùsbau sind ein Designentwurf des Architekten und wurden speziell für das Wohnhaus gefertigt.

4

5

1 Courtyard view at dusk
2 Kitchen and living area
3 View from southeast
4 Exposed concrete in the interior
5 View from north

1 Hofansicht bei Dämmerung
2 Küche und Wohnbereich
3 Ansicht Südostseite
4 Sichtbeton im Innenraum
5 Ansicht Nordseite

1

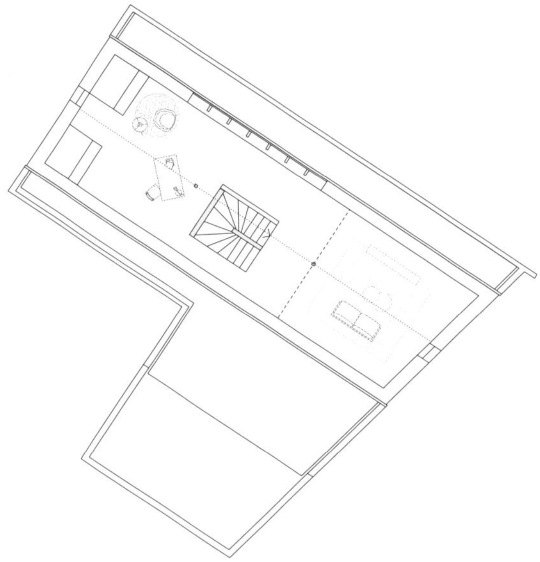

2

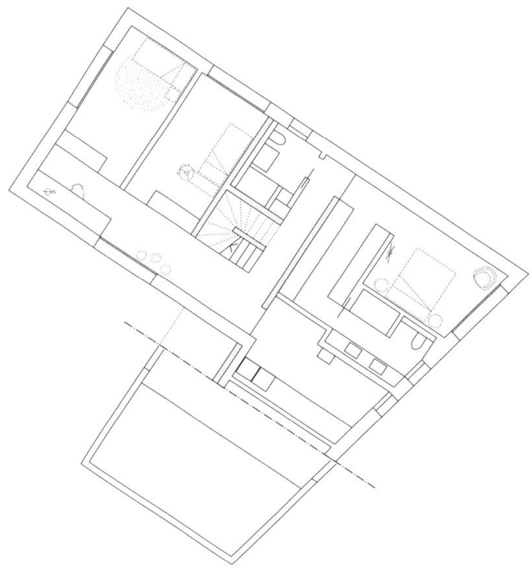

3

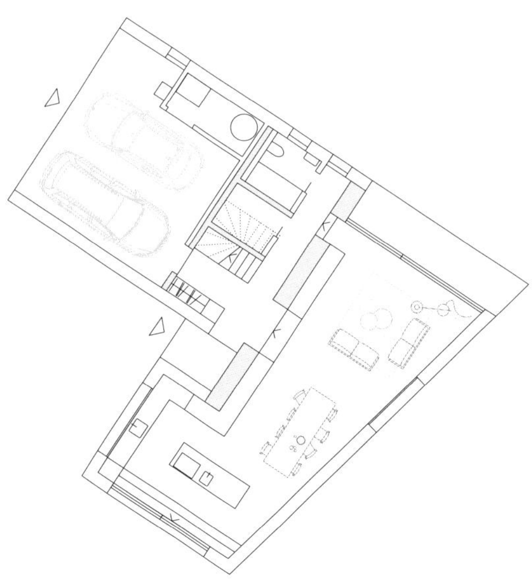

4

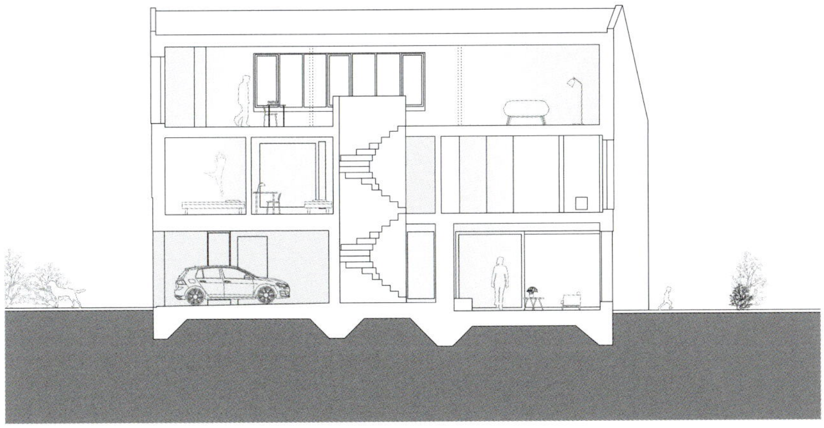

5

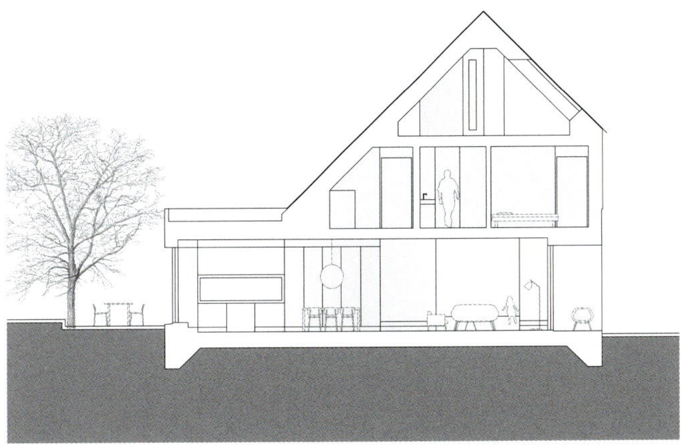

6

1 Top floor plan
2 First floor plan
3 Ground floor plan
4 Longitudinal section
5 Cross section
6 Site plan

1 Grundriss DG
2 Grundriss OG
3 Grundriss EG
4 Längsschnitt
5 Querschnitt
6 Lageplan

CORPUS ATER

1

Architects: WAAX Architekten
Completion: 2017
Location: Oedt, Traun, Austria
Gross floor area: 248 m^2
Number of bedrooms: 2
Main materials / building construction: wood / timber frame construction
Ecological aspects: timber frame construction, brine-water heat pump (deep drilling), preparation for the installation of a photovoltaic system

The small "Black Construction" (corpus ater) was built in the mid-1950s in a domed style and was gradually extended with annexes, huts and canopies. As a result of the building project, the old stock was completely renovated and enlarged by a south-facing extension. This respects the usual house forms, but reinterprets them in construction and materiality. The new building is characterized above all by the black façade made of vertical wooden slats and the striking gable roof. The two differently sloped concrete surfaces facing the garage and the entrance also characterize the appearance. On the garden side, the glass surfaces and the inner courtyard, which is bordered by the old building, dominate. The two-story living area can be opened towards the garden with two large sliding doors. The roof terrace can be reached via a gallery illuminated by skylights. On the façade facing the street, the wooden slats are pulled over the windows.

2

Das kleine Haus „Schwarzbau“ (corpus ater) wurde Mitte der 1950er-Jahre in gekuppelter Bauweise errichtet und schrittweise mit Anbauten, Hütten und Vordächern erweitert. Durch das Bauvorhaben wurde der Altbestand komplett renoviert und um einen Richtung Süden orientierten Zubau erweitert. Dieser respektiert die üblichen Hausformen, interpretiert sie aber in Konstruktion und Materialität neu. Der Neubau wird vor allem durch die schwarze Fassade aus vertikalen Holzlatten und dem markanten Satteldach charakterisiert. Auch die zwei unterschiedlich schräg geneigten Betonflächen zur Garage und zum Eingang prägen die Erscheinung. Gartenseitig dominieren die Glasflächen und der durch den Altbestand begrenzte Innenhof. Der zweigeschossige Wohnbereich kann mit zwei großen Schiebetüren Richtung Garten geöffnet werden. Über eine mit Dachflächenfenstern belichtete Galerie gelangt man auf die Dachterrasse. An der zur Straße gewandten Fassade wird die Holzlattung über die Fenster gezogen.

3

Architekten: WAAX Architekten
Fertigstellung: 2017
Ort: Oedt, Traun, Österreich
Bruttogeschossfläche: 248 m^2
Anzahl der Schlafzimmer: 2
Hauptmaterialien / Konstruktionsweise: Holz / Holzriegelbau
Ökologische Aspekte: Holzriegelbauweise, Sole-Wasser-Wärmepumpe (Tiefenbohrung), Vorbereitung für die Einrichtung einer photovoltaischen Anlage

1 Exterior view from the street
2 Exterior view of the courtyard
3 Detail of the courtyard
4 Detail of street view
5 Street-side window covered with façade

1 Außenansicht von der Straße
2 Außenansicht vom Hof
3 Detail Hofansicht
4 Ausschnitt Straßenansicht
5 Straßenseitiges, mit Fassade überspanntes Fenster

4, 5

1

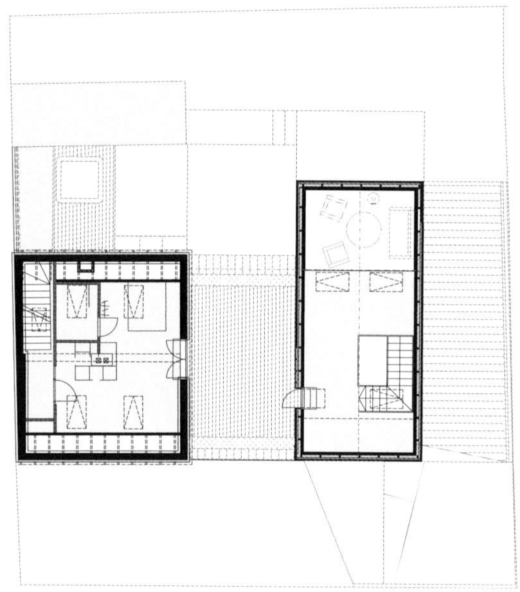

2

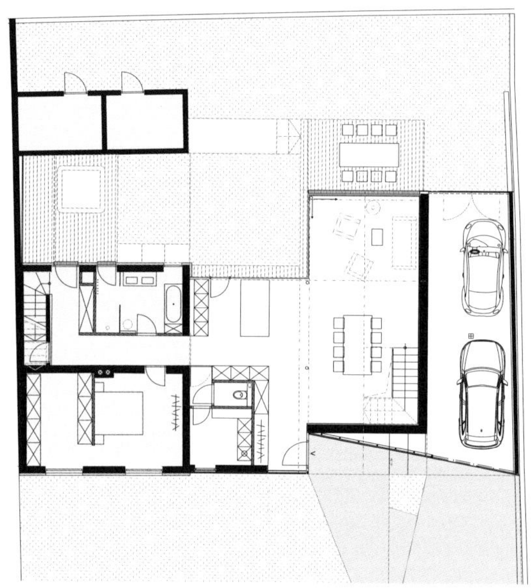

3

4

5

6

1 First floor plan
2 Ground floor plan
3 Exterior view from west
4 Entrance
5 Gallery
6 Old staircase

1 Grundriss OG
2 Grundriss EG
3 Westansicht
4 Eingang
5 Galerie
6 Alte Stiege

1

BOOTS-HAUS

1 Exterior view from southeast
2 Exterior view from east
3 Exterior view from north

1 Außenansicht von Südosten
2 Außenansicht von Osten
3 Außenansicht von Norden

2

Architects: Marazzi + Paul Architekten / Rychener Zeltner Architekten
Completion: 2015
Location: Hilterfingen, Switzerland
Gross floor area: 50 m^2
Number of bedrooms: 1
Main materials / building construction: spruce, slate shingle roof / element construction, timber construction
Ecological aspects: sustainable building material

Characteristic of the Boathouse is its minimalist geometry, emphasized by the classic gable roof and the clear building form. Conceptually, the design language is accentuated by the façade skin, which creates a flush transition between the walls covered with wooden shingles and the roof covered with slate shingles. When the shutters, also covered with shingles, are shut the house appears closed, but when they are opened the residents are offered an idyllic view of the lake and the mountain panorama. The wood theme has been implemented as consistently in the interior as it has been on the façade. The living area is characterized by warm wood tones, which radiate a particularly pleasant atmosphere.

Architekten: Marazzi + Paul Architekten / Rychener Zeltner Architekten
Fertigstellung: 2015
Ort: Hilterfingen, Schweiz
Bruttogeschossfläche: 50 m^2
Anzahl der Schlafzimmer: 1
Hauptmaterialien / Konstruktionsweise: Fichte, Schieferschindeldach / Elementbauweise, Holzbau
Ökologische Aspekte: nachhaltiges Baumaterial

Charakteristisch für das Bootshaus ist die minimalistisch gehaltene Geometrie, betont durch das klassische Satteldach und die klare Gebäudeform. Konzeptionell erfolgt eine Akzentuierung der Formensprache durch die Fassadenhaut, mit der ein bündiger Übergang zwischen den mit Holzschindeln besetzten Wänden und dem mit Schieferschindeln belegten Dach entsteht. Bleiben die, ebenfalls mit Schindeln besetzten, Fensterläden zugeklappt, wirkt das Haus geschlossen, werden sie jedoch geöffnet, bietet sich den Bewohnern ein idyllischer Ausblick auf das See- und Bergpanorama. Das Thema Holz wurde im Innenraum so konsequent wie an der Fassade umgesetzt. Der Wohnbereich ist geprägt von warmen Holztönen, die eine besonders angenehme Atmosphäre ausstrahlen.

3

1

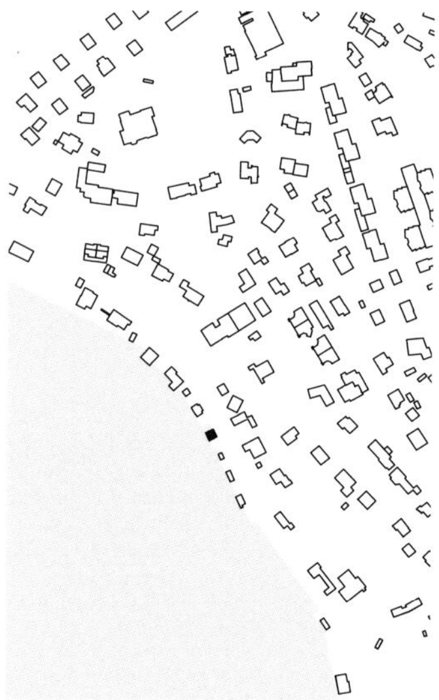

2

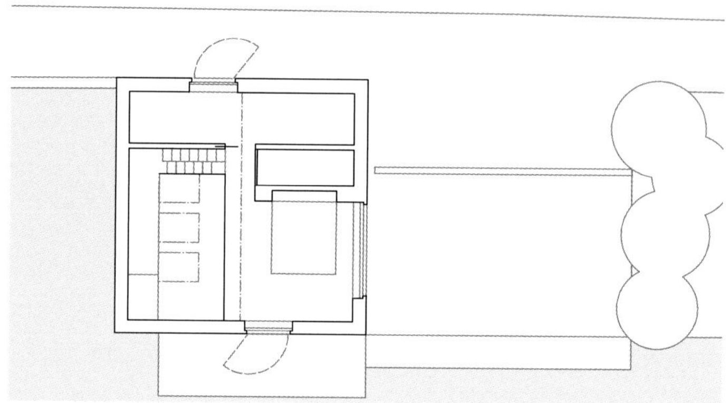

3

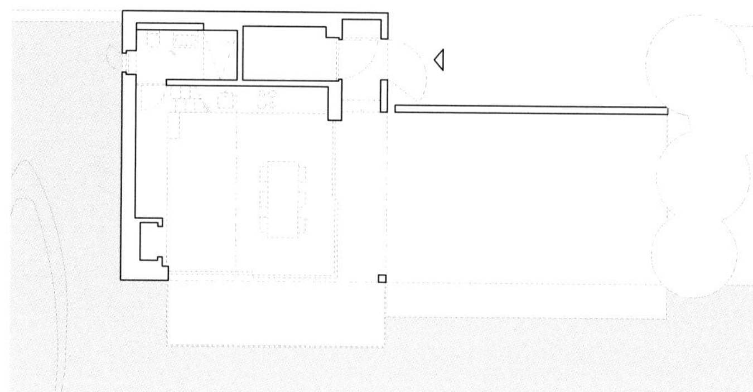

4

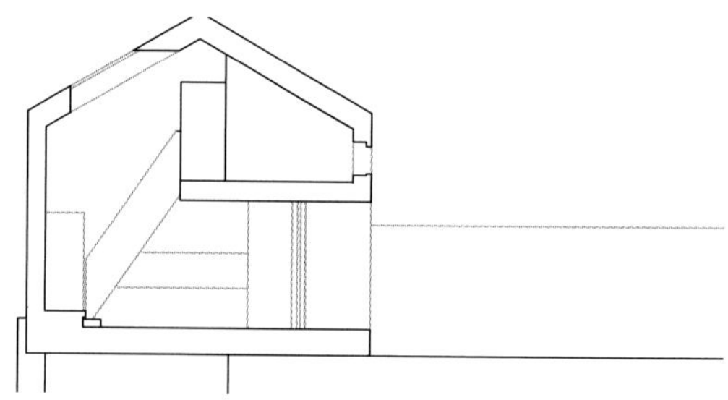

1 Site plan
2 First floor plan
3 Ground floor plan
4 Section
5 View of Lake Thun
6 Exterior view from southwest

1 Lageplan
2 Grundriss OG
3 Grundriss EG
4 Gebäudeschnitt
5 Blick auf den Thunersee
6 Außenansicht von Südwesten

5

6

HAUS D

1

Four small tower houses are grouped around a common center and become one building. The four structures, which are relatively homogeneous on the outside, have their own unique character on the inside according to their different functions. Thus, the wet rooms are located in the so-called water tower, the staircase in the stairwell. In the two further volumes there are several bedrooms as well as a study and a media room. The house becomes a village: On the ground floor, the small houses form an open space for communication and community. On the upper floor, a bridge connects the individual houses and their rooms, allowing retreat and concentration. The high tower house leads to the terrace. The building creates an ambiguous play with scale and with interior and exterior, which is reflected in the choice of materials. Heights and depths, width and narrowness and the resulting views and plays of light determine the character and atmospheres of the house.

Architects: feld72 Architekten
Completion: 2017
Location: Kaltern, South Tyrol
Gross floor area: 185 m^2
Number of bedrooms: 3
Main materials / building construction: plaster, wood / solid construction
Ecological aspects: ClimateHouse class A, lowest energy building

2

3

Architekten: feld72 Architekten
Fertigstellung: 2017
Ort: Kaltern, Südtirol
Bruttogeschossfläche: 185 m^2
Anzahl der Schlafzimmer: 3
Hauptmaterialien / Konstruktionsweise: Putz, Holz / Massivbauweise
Ökologische Aspekte: KlimaHaus Klasse A, Niedrigstenergiegebäude

Vier kleine Turmhäuser gruppieren sich um eine gemeinsame Mitte und werden zu einem Gebäude. Die vier Baukörper, die nach außen relativ homogen sind, haben nach innen entsprechend ihrer unterschiedlichen Funktionen einen ganz eigenen Charakter. So befinden sich die Nassräume im sogenannten Wasserturm, die Treppe im Treppenhaus. Die beiden weiteren Volumina nehmen mehrere Schlafzimmer sowie einen Arbeitsraum und einen Medienraum auf. Das Haus wird zum Dorf. Im Erdgeschoss bilden die kleinen Häuser einen offenen Platz für Kommunikation und Gemeinschaft. Im oberen Geschoss verbindet eine Brücke die einzelnen Häuser und deren Zimmer, die Rückzug und Konzentration ermöglichen. Das hohe Turmhaus führt zur Terrasse. Das Gebäude schafft ein mehrdeutiges Spiel mit dem Maßstab und mit Innen und Außen, was sich in der Materialwahl widerspiegelt. Höhen und Tiefen, Weite und Enge und daraus resultierende Ausblicke und Lichtspiele bestimmen Charakter und Atmosphären des Hauses.

4

5

6

7

1 Exterior view from north
2 Study room on the ground floor
3 Interior view
4 Living space on the ground floor
5 Bedroom
6 Exterior view from south
7 View into the living room

1 Außenansicht von Norden
2 Arbeitszimmer im EG
3 Innenansicht
4 Wohnraum im EG
5 Schlafzimmer
6 Außenansicht von Süden
7 Blick in den Wohnraum

1

2

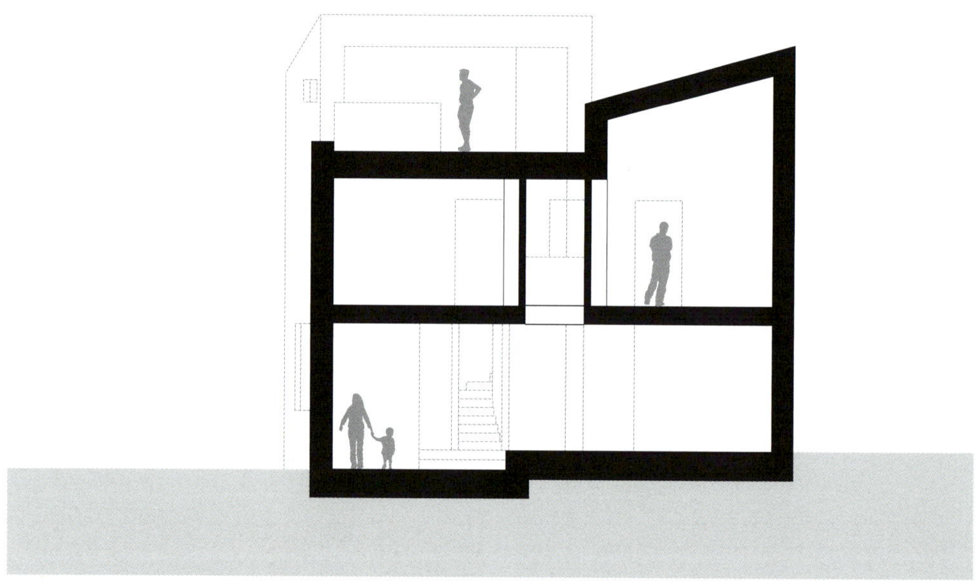

1 Site plan
2 Section
3 Top floor plan
4 First floor plan
5 Ground floor plan

1 Lageplan
2 Schnitt
3 Grundriss DG
4 Grundriss OG
5 Grundriss EG

3

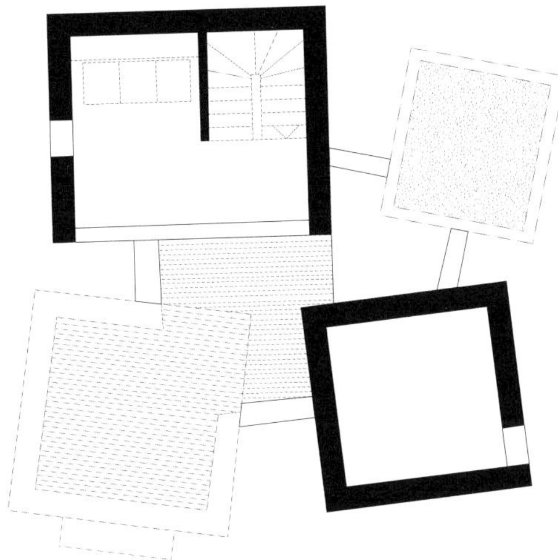

4

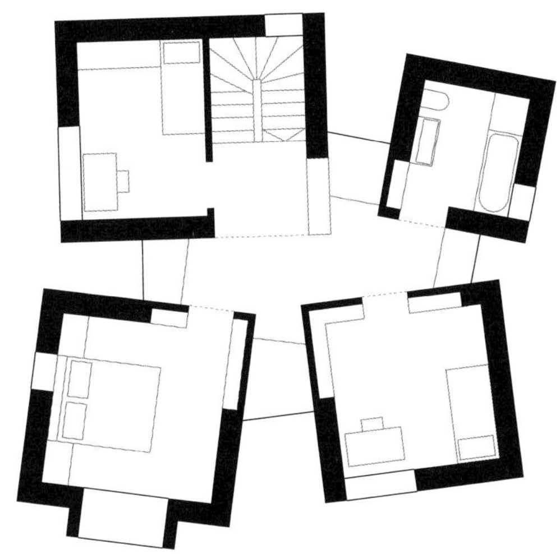

5

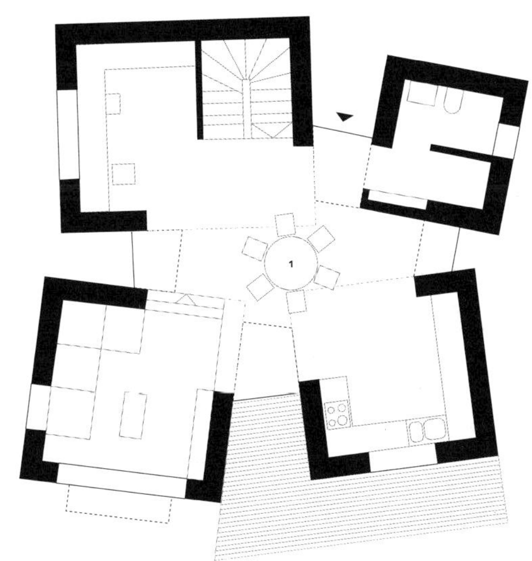

1

HAUS H IN Ü

1 Bathroom with view to the inner courtyard
2 Exterior view from southeast
3 The sunlit patio

1 Bad mit Blick zum Innenhof
2 Außenansicht von Südosten
3 Sonnenbeschienener Terrassenhof

2

Architects: architektur.terminal hackl und klammer
Completion: 2016
Location: Übersaxen, Voralberg, Austria
Gross floor area: 321 m^2
Number of bedrooms: 1
Main materials / building construction: concrete, wood, glass / mixed construction concrete and wood
Ecological aspects: air heat pump, use of passive solar energy, use of ecological materials

Architekten: architektur.terminal hackl und klammer
Fertigstellung: 2016
Ort: Übersaxen, Voralberg, Österreich
Bruttogeschossfläche: 321 m^2
Anzahl der Schlafzimmer: 1
Hauptmaterialien / Konstruktionsweise: Beton, Holz, Glas / Mischbauweise Beton und Holz
Ökologische Aspekte: Luftwärmepumpe, Nutzung passiver Sonnenenergie, Verwendung ökologischer Materialien

A two-story, two-sided cantilevered structure has been developed in its design from the requirements of the space allocation plan. In the base floor are the weather-protected entrance and adjoining rooms. From here, a single-flight staircase leads to the light-flooded living, dining and cooking area arranged around a terrace courtyard. Also on the upper floor are the bedroom with dressing room, bathroom and sauna with patio. All living rooms offer an impressive panorama from the Rätikon to the Swiss Alpstein massif. The base floor was constructed in concrete. The upper floor is a timber construction and the interior is completely covered with wood, supplemented by a high-quality lime filler.

Ein zweigeschossiger, zweiseitig auskragender Baukörper ist in seiner Formgebung aus den Anforderungen des Raumprogrammes entwickelt worden. Im Sockelgeschoss befinden sich der witterungsgeschützte Eingang sowie Nebenräume. Von hier gelangt man über eine einläufige Treppe in den lichtdurchfluteten und um einen Terrassenhof angeordneten Wohn-, Ess- und Kochbereich. Ebenfalls im Obergeschoss befinden sich das Schlafzimmer mit Ankleide, Bad und Sauna mit Innenhof. Von allen Wohnräumen bietet sich das imposante Panorama vom Rätikon bis zum schweizerischen Alpsteinmassiv. Das Sockelgeschoss wurde in Beton ausgeführt. Das Obergeschoss ist eine Holzkonstruktion und innen zur Gänze mit Holz bekleidet, ergänzt durch eine hochwertige Kalkspachtelung.

3

1

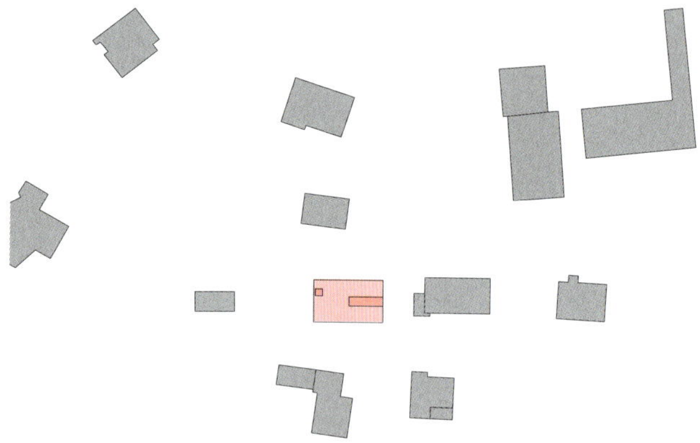

2

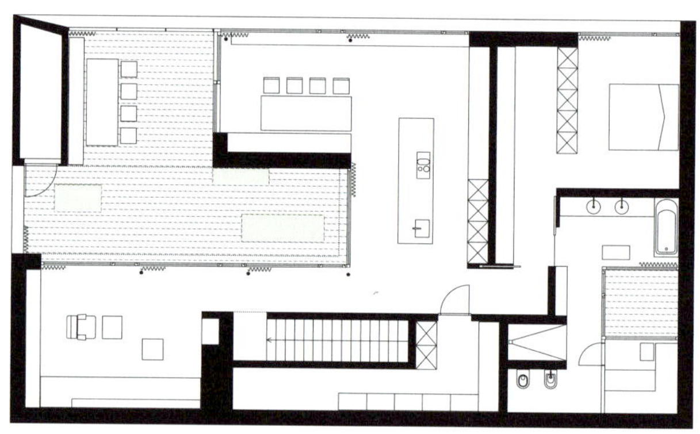

3

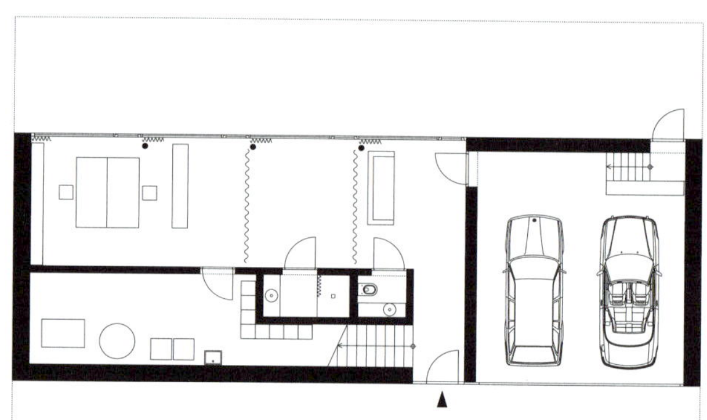

4

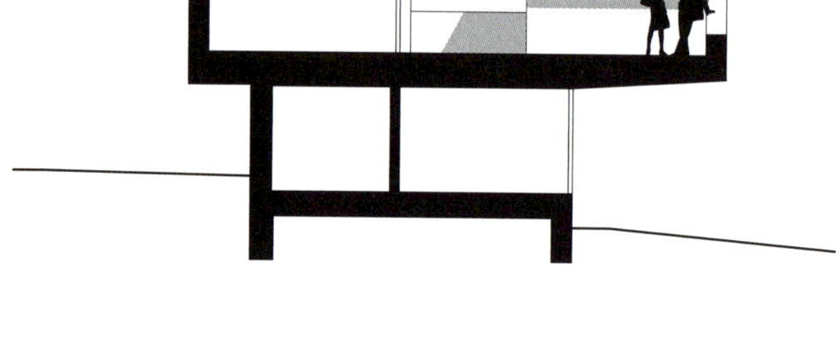

HAUS H IN Ü

5

6

1 Site plan
2 First floor plan
3 Ground floor plan
4 Section
5 Kitchen and dining area
6 Living room with view of the terrace courtyard

1 Lageplan
2 Grundriss OG
3 Grundriss EG
4 Schnitt
5 Küche und Essplatz
6 Wohnzimmer mit Blick auf den Terrassenhof

HAUS AM HÖRMANNWEG

The house is situated on a slope at the edge of the historic village center and follows the local building tradition. The project captivates by its clarity of form and space, and in synthesis with a consistently determined, uniform choice of materials. The use of high-quality regional materials gives the building a great added value: the plaster surfaces with dolomite and porphyry aggregates, in combination with larch wood, refer to the surrounding building typology. Exactly placed openings allow for specific views and create a reference to the surrounding village and mountain landscape. The entrance underlines the location along the path and makes the exterior space tangible. Visual and communication references in the interior enable the building to be fully perceived in its entire length, width and height. The reduction to the essentials is also reflected in the entire materiality: smoothed plaster surfaces of clay and lime with sand aggregates of dolomite and porphyry, polished concrete screeds with dolomite aggregates, wooden elements made of local larch wood.

1, 2

Architects: Architekt Daniel Ellecosta
Completion: 2012
Location: Truden im Naturpark, South Tyrol
Gross floor area: 250 m^2
Number of bedrooms: 3
Main materials / building construction: lime plaster, clay plaster and sanded screeds, each with dolomite and porphyry aggregate, larch / solid construction
Ecological aspects: ecological, sustainable choice of materials

Architekten: Architekt Daniel Ellecosta
Fertigstellung: 2017
Ort: Truden im Naturpark, Südtirol
Bruttogeschossfläche: 250 m^2
Anzahl der Schlafzimmer: 3
Hauptmaterialien / Konstruktionsweise: Kalkputz, Lehmputz und geschliffene Estriche, jeweils mit Dolomit und Porphyrzuschlag, Lärche / Massivbauweise
Ökologische Aspekte: ökologische, nachhaltige Materialwahl

Das Wohnhaus befindet sich in Hanglage am Rande des historischen Dorfkerns und schließt sich der örtlichen Bautradition an. Das Projekt besticht durch seine Klarheit in Form und Raum, in Synthese mit einer konsequent bestimmten, einheitlichen Materialwahl. Die Verwendung von hochwertigen regionalen Materialien verleiht dem Gebäude einen großen Mehrwert: die Putzoberflächen mit Dolomit- und Porphyrzuschlägen in Kombination mit Lärchenholz nehmen Bezug zur umliegenden Bautypologie. Genau platzierte Öffnungen ermöglichen gezielte Ausblicke und stellen den Bezug zur umgebenden Dorf- und Berglandschaft her. Das Eingangselement unterstreicht die Lage am Weg und konkretisiert erfassbar den Außenraum. Sicht- und Kommunikationsbezüge im Innenraum ermöglichen, das Gebäude in seiner gesamten Länge, Breite und Höhe vollständig zu erfassen. Die Reduktion auf das Wesentliche spiegelt sich auch hier in der gesamten Materialität wider: geglättete Putzoberflächen aus Lehm und Kalk mit Sandzuschlägen aus Dolomit und Porphyr, geschliffene Betonestriche mit Dolomitzuschlägen, Holzelemente aus lokalem Lärchenholz.

3

4

1 Exterior view from southeast
2 Exterior view from northeast
3 Exterior view from west
4 Exterior view from northwest

1 Außenansicht von Südosten
2 Außenansicht von Nordosten
3 Außenansicht von Westen
4 Außenansicht von Nordwesten

1

2

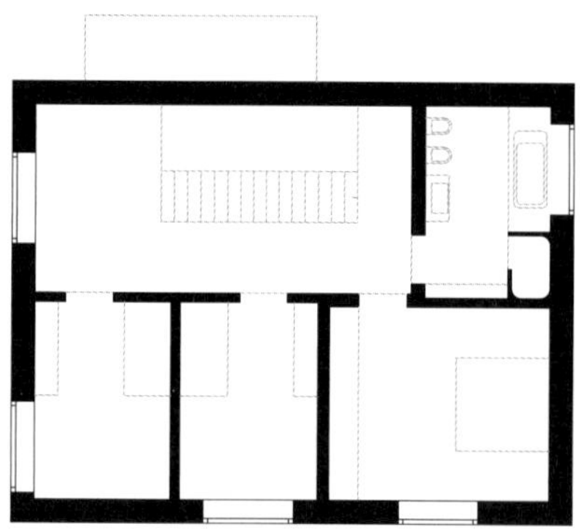

3

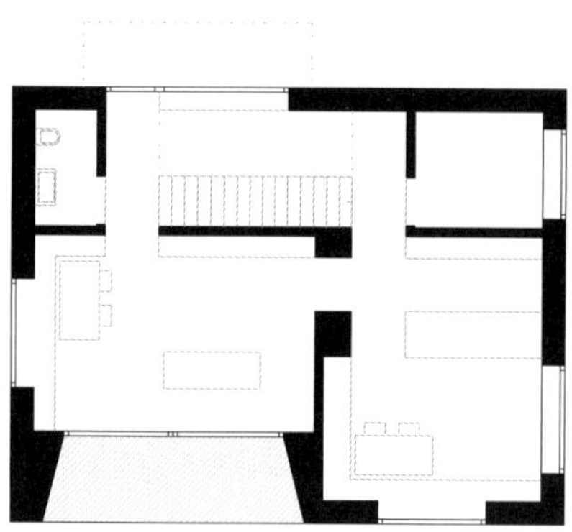

4

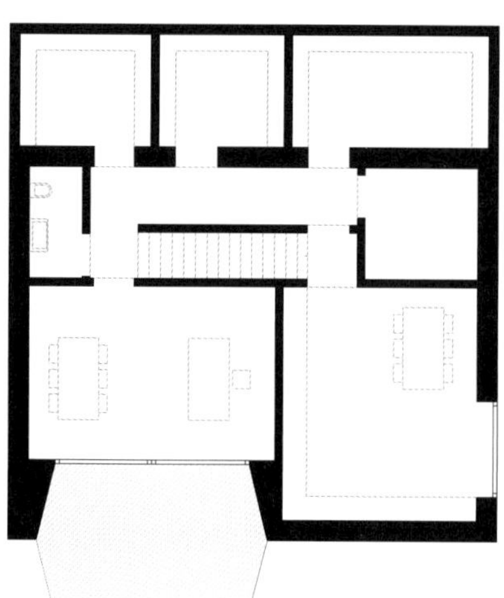

5

6

7

8

1 Site plan
2 First floor plan
3 Ground floor plan
4 Basement floor plan
5 Entrance area
6 Living room with oven and view into the kitchen
7 Exterior view from southeast
8 Living room with dining area and view outside

1 Lageplan
2 Grundriss OG
3 Grundriss EG
4 Grundriss UG
5 Eingangsbereich
6 Wohnzimmer mit Ofen und Blick in die Küche
7 Außenansicht von Südosten
8 Wohnzimmer mit Essbereich und Ausblick nach draußen

PETITE MAISON

1

Traditionally in the more rural parts of Switzerland the younger generation usually built a small dwelling for the parents next to the main farm. Here it is the other way round: a small house for the youngest of the family, setup in the garden of the parents' home. On a confined plot of land a compact house was build on a square footprint which, nonetheless, offers expressive volumes through the shape of its roof and incorporation of a canopy on the south-facing façade.

The entrance area of the Petite Maison Les Evouettes doubles as a carport, and as a covered summer terrace, to which a black tarpaulin can be attached to guard against the side wind. On the ground floor daytime activities concentrate. The kitchen and dining area are in contact with the garden via the glazed corner, while the lounge benefits from a raised ceiling. On the first floor the bedroom offers a great view and a sliding partition allows the office area to be converted into a guestroom.

Architects: Bonnard Woeffray architectes
Completion: 2016
Location: Les Evouettes, Port-Valais, Switzerland
Gross floor area: 140 m^2
Number of bedrooms: 2
Main materials / building construction: aluminum, linoleum, wood, metal / timber frame construction on a concrete slab
Ecological aspects: use of wood

2

3

Architekten: Bonnard Woeffray architectes
Fertigstellung: 2016
Ort: Les Evouettes, Port-Valais, Schweiz
Bruttogeschossfläche: 140 m^2
Anzahl der Schlafzimmer: 2
Hauptmaterialien / Konstruktionsweise: Aluminium, Linoleum, Holz, Metall / Holzfachwerk auf einer Betonplatte
Ökologische Aspekte: Nutzung von Holz

In den ländlicheren Teilen der Schweiz baute die jüngere Generation traditionell eine kleine Wohnung für die Eltern neben dem Haupthof. Hier ist es genau umgekehrt: Im Garten des Elternhauses wurde ein kleines Haus für die Jüngsten der Familie errichtet. Auf einem begrenzten Grundstück entstand das kompakte Haus auf einer quadratischen Grundfläche. Durch die Dachform und die Einbeziehung eines Vordaches an der Südfassade bietet es ausdrucksstarke Volumen.

Der Eingangsbereich der Petite Maison Les Evouettes dient als Carport und gleichzeitig als überdachte Sommerterrasse, an der eine schwarze Plane zum Schutz gegen den Seitenwind befestigt werden kann. Im Erdgeschoss konzentrieren sich die Tagesaktivitäten. Die Küche und der Essbereich haben über die verglaste Ecke des Gebäudes Kontakt zum Garten, während der Aufenthaltsraum von einer erhöhten Decke profitiert. Im ersten Stock bietet das Schlafzimmer eine großartige Aussicht. Eine Schiebewand ermöglicht es, den Bürobereich in ein Gästezimmer umzuwandeln.

4

5

1 View from south with covered space
2 Living room with accents in Barragán pink and Corbusier coral red
3 Staircase from above
4 Staircase from below
5 View from west with dining room

1 Ansicht von Süden mit überdachtem Eingangsbereich
2 Wohnzimmer mit Akzenten in Barragán-Rosa und Corbusier-Korallenrot
3 Treppe von oben
4 Treppe von unten
5 Ansicht von Westen mit Esszimmer

1

2

1 Kitchen
2 Detail façade at the entrance
3 Site plan
4 Section
5 Southeast elevation
6 First floor plan
7 Northeast elevation
8 Ground floor plan
9 Southwest elevation

1 Küche
2 Fassadendetail am Eingang
3 Lageplan
4 Schnitt
5 Aufriss Südostseite
6 Grundriss OG
7 Aufriss Nordostseite
8 Grundriss EG
9 Aufriss Südwestseite

3

4

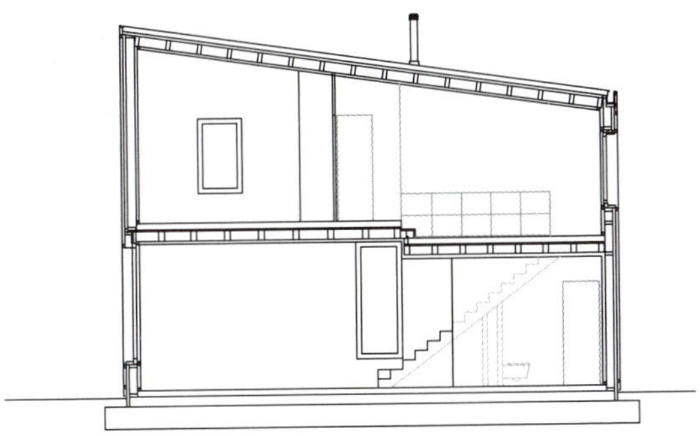

5

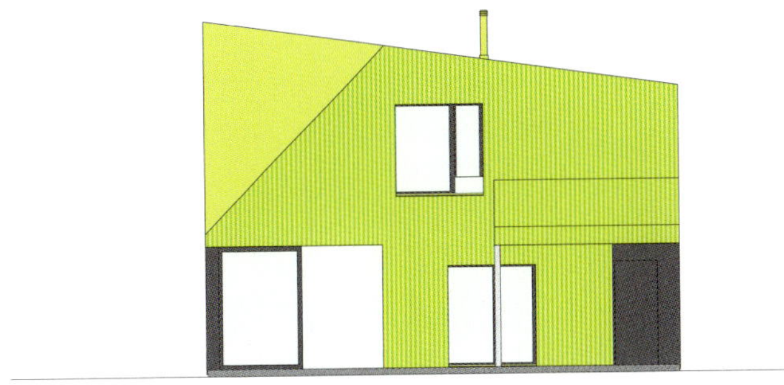

6

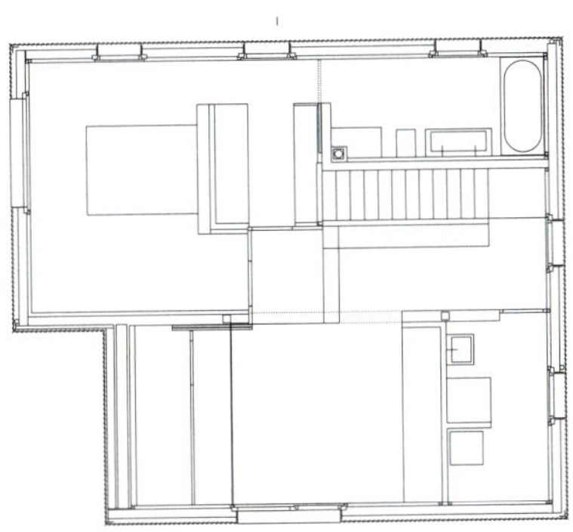

7

8

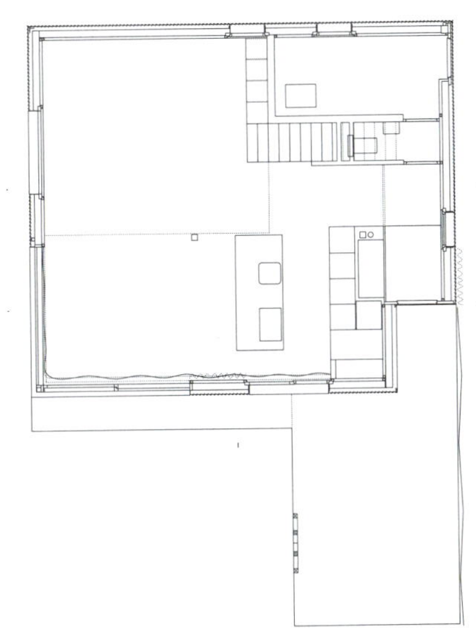

9

LEHMPUTZ-HAUS

1

The Clay Plaster House in Ludesch does not correspond in any way to the type of the classic Vorarlberg single-family house – because the cellar and the upper floor are missing. Even the obligatory hedge around the house will not be found here. All functions are organized compactly and barrier-free on one level. A patio extends the living space with a large garden room outside. In a later construction phase this will be supplemented by a pool. The wall construction consists of a monolithic brick with clay plaster. Rusty steel plates form the façades and are a robust weather protection. The rooms are practical and arranged with short distances. The room height of 2.9 meters contributes to the relaxed living atmosphere. Large window fronts offer a beautiful view of the surroundings.

Architects: HAMMERER Architekten
Completion: 2016
Location: Ludesch, Vorarlberg, Austria
Gross floor area: 160 m^2
Number of bedrooms: 3
Main materials / building construction: Poroton flat brick, clay plaster, Corten steel façade / reinforced concrete floor slab, mono brick walls, reinforced concrete ceiling
Ecological aspects: no polystyrene façade, breathable outer wall, clay plaster regulates room climate

2

3

Architekten: HAMMERER Architekten
Fertigstellung: 2016
Ort: Ludesch, Vorarlberg, Österreich
Bruttogeschossfläche: 160 m^2
Anzahl der Schlafzimmer: 3
Hauptmaterialien / Konstruktionsweise: Poroton Planziegel, Lehmputz, Cortenstahlfassade / Stahlbetonbodenplatte, Monoziegelwände, Stahlbetondecke
Ökologische Aspekte: keine Styroporfassade, atmungsaktive Außenwand, Lehmputz reguliert Raumklima

Dem Typus des klassischen Vorarlberger Einfamilienhauses entspricht das Lehmputzhaus in Ludesch in keinster Weise – denn es fehlen der Keller und das Obergeschoss. Auch die obligatorische Hecke ums Haus wird man hier vergeblich suchen. Alle Funktionen sind kompakt und barrierefrei auf einer Ebene organisiert. Ein Patio erweitert den Wohnraum mit einem großen Gartenzimmer im Freien. In einer späteren Bauphase wird dieser noch durch einen Pool ergänzt werden. Die Wandkonstruktion besteht aus monolithischen Ziegeln mit Lehmputz. Rostige Stahlplatten bilden die Fassaden und sind ein robuster Wetterschutz. Die Räume sind praktisch und mit kurzen Wegen angeordnet. Die Raumhöhe von 2,9 Metern trägt zum leichten Wohngefühl bei. Große Fensterfronten bieten einen schönen Ausblick in die Umgebung.

4

5

6

1 Exterior view at dusk
2 Side view
3 Inner courtyard
4 Terrace
5 Bathroom
6 Bedroom

1 Außenansicht bei Dämmerung
2 Seitenansicht
3 Innenhof
4 Terrasse
5 Badezimmer
6 Schlafzimmer

1

2

1 Kitchen
2 Vestibule
3 Ground floor plan
4 First draft

1 Küche
2 Vorraum
3 Grundriss EG
4 Erste Entwurfsskizze

3

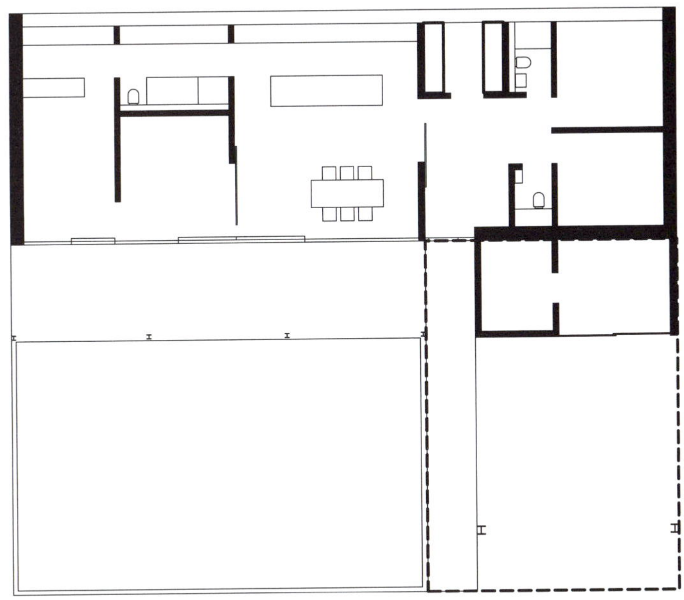

4

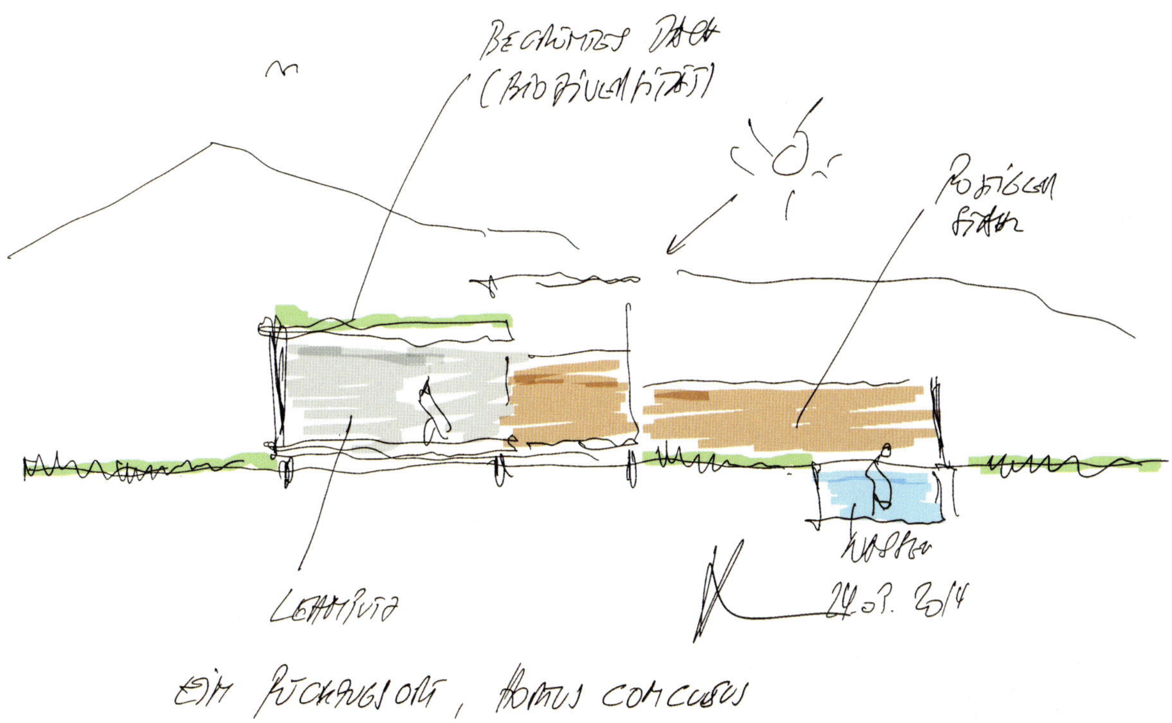
BEGRÜNTES DACH
(BIODIVERSITÄT)
LEHMPUTZ
WASSER
24.03.2014
EIN RÜCKZUGSORT, HORTUS CONCLUSUS

INDEX REGISTER

E

F

G

H

I

J

K

INDEX REGISTER

S

T

U

V

W

X

Y

Z

PICTURE CREDITS BILDNACHWEIS

Adolf Bereuter
→ 88–89, 91

Markus Beyeler
www.markusbeyeler.ch
→ 274–275, 277 (4)

Radek Brunecky
www.brunecky.com
→ 250–251

Sacha Conte
→ 121

Oskar Da Riz
→ 48, 49

Renaud Dupuis, Atelier Nord Sàrl
www.atelier-nord.ch
→ 66 (2), 69 (7)

Yorgos Efthymiadis
www.yorgosphoto.com
→ 144–146

EMIL Fotografie
→ 120

Evolution Design
→ 26 (3)

Ralph Feiner
www.feinerfotografie.ch
→ 94–96, 152–153, 155

Ditz Fejer
www.ditzfejer.at
→ 76–78

Felber-Spulak Fotografen
www.felber-spulak.com
→ 102, 103 (4), 104 (2)

Roger Frei
www.rogerfrei.com
→ 226–228

Eik Frenzel
www.dreierfrenzel.com
→ 198–200

Tamara Frisch
www.tamarafrisch.com
→ 222–223, 215, 230–232

Giancarlo Gardin
→ 72–74

GAUTSCHI LENZIN SCHENKER Architekten AG
→ 194–195, 197

Gregor Graf
www.gregorgraf.net
→ 270–271, 273

Martin Guggisberg
→ 206–207

Roland Halbe
www.rolandhalbe.eu
→ 290–292

Thomas Hämmerli, Daluz Gonzalez Architekten
→ 32, 33, 35

Bruno Helbling Fotografie
www.helblingfotografie.ch
→ 186–187, 189

Ben Huggler
www.benhuggler.ch
→ 190–191

Hertha Hurnaus
www.hurnaus.com
→ 44, 45, 46

Thomas Jantscher
www.jantscher.ch
→ 214–216

Valentin Jeck
www.jeck.ch
→ 80–81

Simon Jüttner / PK Odessa
→ 98–99, 101

Holger Kehne
www.plasmastudio.com
→ 92–93

Daniela Kienzler
www.danielakienzler.ch
→ 124–126

Bruno Klomfar
www.klomfar.at
→ 156–157, 159, 282–283, 285, 294–296

Philipp Kreidl
www.ateliers.at
→ 84–85, 87

Marion Lafogler
www.fotografielafogler.it
→ 14, 15, 17

Lichtbildkultur Martin Schlager
www.lichtbildkultur.at
→ 140–142, 262, 265

Joshua Loher, Balgach
→ 266–267

Hanno Mackowitz
→ 254–255

mahore architekten
→ 58, 59, 61

Walter Mair, Photography
www.waltermair.ch
→ 218–219, 221

Marcello Mariana, Andalo Valtellina
→ 40, 41 (3, 5, 6), 42

Hayato Mizutani
→ 41 (4)

moos giuliani herrmann architekten
→ 108 (1, 3), 109 (4, 6)

Thomas Moosmann
→ 238 (1)

Börje Müller
→ 162–164

Robert Niederl
→ 62, 63

Michael Nöbauer
→ 103 (3), 104 (1)

Michael Pezzei
www.mpezzei.it
→ 160–161

Nathalie Racheter
www.nr-photographie.ch
→ 66 (1), 67, 69 (8)

Petra Rainer
www.petra-rainer.at
→ 170–171, 173

Marcel Rickli
www.marcelrickli.com
→ 50–51

Sabrina Scheja
→ 108 (2), 109 (5)

Albrecht Imanuel Schnabel
www.albrecht-schnabel.com
→ 18–20

David Schreyer
→ 278–279

Charly Schwarz
→ 128–129, 131

Nicolas Sedlatchek
→ 166–167, 169

Manfred Seidl
→ 238 (2), 239, 241

Thomas Streitberg, Sabine Bungert
→ 174–175

Joël Tettamanti
www.tettamanti.ch
→ 112–114

Mag. Nicole Tintera
→ 246–247, 249

Juri Troy
→ 182–184

samuel trümpy photography
www.samueltruempy.ch
→ 202–203, 205

Aynur Turunc
→ 258–259, 261

Violetta Wakolbinger
www.viovio.at
→ 70–71 , 106–107

Jens Weber
→ 148–149, 151

Philippe Wiget, Daluz Gonzalez Architekten
→ 22, 23, 25

gustav willeit photographer
www.parterre3.com
→ 132–134, 286–287, 289

Andrin Winteler
→ 234–235, 237, 242–244

Harald Wisthaler
www.wisthaler.com
→ 36–38

Volker Wortmeyer
→ 210–211, 213

Stefan Wülser
→ 28–30

Peter Würmli
→ 26 (1, 2), 27, 136–138

Stefan Zenzmaier
ww.sbg.at
→ 263

Stanimir Zhelyazkov
→ 277 (5)

Jürg Zimmermann
www.zimmermannfotografie.ch
→ 54–56, 116–117

Alexandre Zveiger
→ 10–12

Markus Willmann
→ Front cover picture (House at Walensee by k_m architektur)

IMPRINT IMPRESSUM

The Deutsche Nationalbibliothek lists this publication in the Deutsche Nationalbibliografie; detailed bibliographic data are available on the Internet at http://dnb.dnb.de

ISBN 978-3-03768-265-4

www.braun-publishing.ch

1st edition 2021

Editor: Redaktionsbüro van Uffelen / Editorial office
Editorial staff and layout: Leon Aicklin, Michael Bungardt, Carlotta Schmid
Graphic concept: Die Brueder Publishing
Reproduction: Bild1Druck, Berlin

Die Deutsche Nationalbibliothek verzeichnet diese Publikation in der Deutschen Nationalbibliografie; detaillierte bibliografische Daten sind im Internet über http://dnb.dnb.de abrufbar.

ISBN 978-3-03768-265-4

www.braun-publishing.ch

1. Auflage 2021

Projektkoordination: Redaktionsbüro van Uffelen
Redaktion und Satz: Leon Aicklin, Michael Bungardt, Carlotta Schmid
Grafisches Konzept: Die Brueder Publishing
Reproduktion: Bild1Druck GmbH, Berlin